BRITISH COAL

The Rugby League Yearbo

1991–92

BRITISH COAL

The Rugby League Yearbook 1991–92

Edited by Tony Pocock

The Kingswood Press

First published in Great Britain 1991
by The Kingswood Press
an imprint of Methuen London
Michelin House, 81 Fulham Road, London SW3 6RB

A CIP catalogue record for this book
is available from the British Library
ISBN 0 413 66020 6

Photoset and printed in Great Britain
by Redwood Press Limited, Melksham, Wiltshire

Contents

Acknowledgements

With four exceptions, the photographs in this book, and on the cover, have been reproduced by kind permission of Andrew Varley. The exceptions are those showing the opening of the new BARLA headquarters (on p. 77), by permission of BARLA and Brian Worsnop; the departure of the BARLA Young Lions (on p. 82), by permission of the *Rugby Leaguer*; the St Helens v Turin match (on p. 137), by permission of the *St Helens Reporter*; and the action shot of Allan Bateman (on p. 98), by permission of Eddie Fuller, courtesy of the *Warrington Guardian*.

I am grateful to Philip Fearnley for supplying the extracts from a 1950s Yugoslav coaching manual with its endearing illustration of the play-the-ball (on p. 139) and the SARL advertisement (on p. 140). I must also thank Mike Rylance once again for his practical help and Ian Proctor for answering detailed questions at all hours of the day and night at great inconvenience to himself.

Above all, my thanks are due to the British Coal Corporation, especially Martin Cruttenden and Jeff Drinkwater, for their patience, understanding and continuing enthusiasm for the project; and to David Oxley for his constructive criticism, always generously given.

T.P.

Preface

David Oxley OBE
Chief Executive, the Rugby Football League

The 1990–91 season will surely be best remembered for the autumn's epic Test series between the Lions and the Kangaroos. Never before has the attention of the nation been so firmly focused on our game as during those exciting seven weeks in October and November. At last, the skill, athleticism, tactical brilliance, courage, fitness, commitment and sportsmanship of Rugby League players operating at the highest levels of the sport were widely recognised and deeply appreciated. True, the Kangaroos retained the Ashes with a superlative third Test display in difficult conditions at Elland Road, but Britain's triumph at Wembley and the drama of Old Trafford will live for ever in the memories of those who saw the two matches.

The question was, could the rest of the season live up to the drama and excitement of the Test series? To a large extent it did. Pride of place must go to the outstanding performance of a Wigan team which surely must rank with the very best in the game's long history. They set records not only in winning the Challenge Cup for a fourth successive season, but also in finishing top of the Championship table for the second successive year, despite having to complete their match programme by playing eight games in a frenetic last seventeen days.

Outstanding though they were, Wigan were not alone. Widnes, with Jonathan Davies proving what a brilliant talent he is, played some wonderful football; Warrington earned a worthy and most welcome victory in the Regal Trophy final; and Hull salvaged Yorkshire's pride with a gritty and thoroughly deserved triumph in the Premiership final.

On a truly positive note was the remarkable development of Rugby League football in the Soviet Union. A year ago Rugby League was just a talking point in the USSR. Today there are eight fully professional clubs operating on a regular basis; Rugby League is being introduced to thousands of youngsters in Moscow and in the Republics; there are marketing and merchandising operations in place both centrally and at club level; feeder leagues have been established in Asia and Central Russia; and we have our own headquarters in Moscow housing four full-time staff. If the present rate of progress can be maintained, there seems to be no reason why the Soviets should not make their full international debut sometime during 1991–92.

We continue to be deeply indebted to British Coal whose generous and caring sponsorship of this Yearbook, of Youth football, and particularly of international football we greatly appreciate and never take for granted.

Foreword

Martin Cruttenden

Director of Sales, British Coal Corporation

By any standards, the 1990–91 season was one of the most memorable in the long history of Rugby League. On the domestic front, the stranglehold of Wigan and Widnes on the game's major competitions was ended as Warrington and Hull battled heroically to claim the Regal Trophy and the Premiership respectively. After struggling in early season, Wigan responded like true champions by defying a mammoth fixture back-log to land the League and Cup double for the second year in succession, an achievement described by the Rugby League president, Harry Jepson, as 'the greatest Championship feat ever.'

Test-match Rugby League remains the flagship of the game, however, and the international scene produced even more excitement. The successful launch of the sport in the Soviet Union and the revival of the Welsh national side has opened up hopes of a genuine European championship in years to come, while Great Britain's convincing wins in the British Coal Tests against France strengthened our hopes of reaching the World Cup final. On the amateur scene, BARLA's Young Lions, now also sponsored by British Coal, recorded their first ever double against France, showing that at all levels the international future for British Rugby League remains bright.

Overshadowing all else in 1990–91, however, was the visit of the Australians, the 1990 Kangaroos. The successful British Coal tour of Papua New Guinea and New Zealand in the summer had raised our hopes of dethroning the world champions, but few really believed it would happen. No one who was present on that memorable afternoon at Wembley Stadium when Malcolm Reilly's Great Britain side, magnificently led by Ellery Hanley, took on and beat the might of Australia in the first British Coal Test will ever forget it. The message sent out by the series was loud and clear; Britain is back as a major force in international Rugby League.

Now we look ahead to another great domestic season – the first to feature the new three-division format – and beyond that lies the event the whole Rugby League world is eagerly awaiting – the 1992 British Coal tour to Papua New Guinea, Australia and New Zealand. We hope and believe that Malcolm Reilly's British Lions will return in triumph with the Ashes in British hands for the first time in more than twenty years.

Rugby League has never looked in better shape and we at British Coal – a great British company – are proud and pleased to be playing our full part in supporting a great British side, playing the greatest game of all.

Introduction

Tony Pocock
Editor

One of the pleasures of putting together this year's British Coal *Rugby League Yearbook* was that the contributors' enthusiasm for the game and for the season past stood out a mile: 1990–91 was memorable and we have the prospect of even more exciting things to come this year. Moreover, thanks to British Coal's continuing generosity, the *Yearbook* has now become a vehicle for general comment as well as being a record of the past year's international and domestic competitions.

The rather tentative steps taken in this direction last year have now become a pretty long stride. A central section called *Reflections*, wedged appropriately enough between the home and international sections, has been born, and I hope will maintain that important position as the years go by. Rugby League needs reflective comment of this sort, balancing the actuality of the match reporting which has formed the book's backbone until now.

Thus, the rebirth of a Wales side has drawn comment from Eddie Butler, Ray French and Huw Richards; Geoffrey Moorhouse compares the great Wigan side of today with those of the early 1950s; John Whalley's appraisal of the two contemporary Australian coaches, John Monie and Brian Smith, is timely; and Brian himself writes about the strengths and weaknesses of British Rugby League as he sees them from Australia. And there are telling comments, too, by Paul Wilson about the importance of London in Rugby League's scheme of things.

I am sure the game has never been as vibrant as it is today. But of course there are some weaknesses in the structure, and it is stimulating to have a few of them pointed out by some of the contributors with such care and understanding. As the game edges towards its centenary year there must be no holding back with helpful criticism whenever it is thought to be necessary.

1

The 1990–91 Season At Home

ONE

The Stones Bitter Championship and Premiership Trophies

Trevor Watson

THE STONES BITTER CHAMPIONSHIP

'Only a champion side like this could have done it,' were the words of the Wigan coach, John Monie, after his side's monumental achievement in retaining the Stones Bitter Championship. Monie, remarkably calm in the circumstances, was speaking after his side's comprehensive victory in their final fixture at Leeds that guaranteed them the Championship and left Widnes frustrated in second place.

Wigan had gone to Headingley for their fifth game in ten days, needing a point to clinch the title. They were well aware that defeat would leave Widnes, who were due to play twenty-four hours later, knowing exactly how many they had to score at home to the bottom dogs, Rochdale Hornets, to pip them. Leeds, who had dropped only 1 point from their previous six matches, seemed potentially dangerous opponents for Monie's men, but were never in the hunt as Wigan produced an exceptional performance to win 20–8.

Wigan looked the sharper side early on and a Leeds blunder gave Andy Goodway, playing at centre, a gift opening try, goaled by Frano Botica. Wigan then chipped steadily away with drop-goals to extend their lead. Their scrum-half, Bobby Goulding, feeling he had much to prove after being out of the side in recent matches, landed three and their inspirational skipper, Ellery Hanley, got another so that Wigan were 10–2 ahead soon after the interval.

After a mighty surge by Denis Betts, the hooker Martin Dermott plunged over from acting half-back, and celebrations began with Wigan 14–2 ahead. They were halted briefly when Garry Schofield sent John Bentley clear from a scrum forty-five yards out and Simon Irving added the goal to lift Leeds to 8–14. But Botica landed a penalty and Betts proved unstoppable near the line to collect the third try, and Wigan had done it.

Monie was probably right. No other side, already qualified for Wembley, could have survived that awesome late run of matches against St Helens, Castleford, Widnes and Bradford Northern before going to Headingley to play Leeds. There was talk of Andy Platt, Shaun Edwards, Martin Dermott and others playing only with the help of injections; of players being unable to sleep after the tension and excitement of night matches; but still they survived. Widnes weren't happy that a switch of date for their game at Central Park spoiled their preparations for that crucial fixture, but Wigan's winning run was a tremendous feat of a truly great Championship team and almost certainly is never likely to be repeated.

Opposite Wigan hooker Martin Dermott lost his Test spot to Lee Jackson, but was a key figure in his side's arduous Championship run-in and was outstanding in their 13–8 Challenge Cup final win over St Helens.

Ironically, Wigan had not started the season particularly well. A home draw against Sheffield launched a programme that produced only 11 points from nine matches. The former All Black, Frano Botica, was a new arrival as was the powerful prop, Kelvin Skerrett, from Bradford Northern as a replacement for Adrian Shelford, and both took time to settle.

There was competition on the wing, where David Myers replaced speedy Mark Preston and, of course, there was also the question of whether Goulding should replace Andy Gregory. Gregory had his own thoughts about that and his form throughout the season was superb. Edwards and Hanley, too, were in rare form so that the famous lethal midfield triangle was functioning as well as ever. Botica, regarded chiefly as a stand-off in Rugby Union, settled on the left wing and, although not highly rated as a kicker in the Union game, his goals proved an enormous asset.

A home defeat by Warrington on New Year's Day seemed to end any hopes of the title, only for it to spark a run of thirteen wins and a draw in the last fourteen fixtures to overhaul the other challengers. Monie summed things up further after the Leeds match when he said, 'Rugby League isn't meant to be an endurance type of thing and this is an achievement of which everybody can be proud.' No one was arguing with that.

Widnes were bitterly disappointed to be edged out but they had conceded a double to Wigan, including a 6–26 defeat at Central Park in that crucial final week, when they still seemed to be suffering a hangover from their Challenge Cup semi-final thrashing by St Helens. At times the Chemics were superb to watch with powerful forwards and thrilling backs led by Martin Offiah.

Once more they were hit by injury to Tony Myler, who missed many league games, and Alan Tait and Jonathan Davies also had lengthy spells on the sidelines. But Davies also produced some wonderful performances, and some of his late-season displays at stand-off were magnificent. He went on to beat Mick Burke's twelve-year-old club record of 316 points in a season and looked a complete all-round player. John Devereux showed pace and strength on the wing and Andy Currier collected a number of spectacular tries at centre.

Once again their coach, Doug Laughton, produced a sizeable rabbit out of his overseas hat, when the New Zealand prop, Esene Faimalo, was introduced. He showed great strength and pace and looked ready-made to take over the mantle of Kurt Sorensen, who built himself up for another bid at the title. Their hooker, Phil McKenzie, and back-row man, Richard Eyres, were solid and consistent, along with the gritty half-back, David Hulme, but injury meant that less was seen of the second-rower, Emosi Koloto, than had been hoped. Sadly, the season ended in some disarray for Widnes with Doug Laughton leaving the club for Leeds after the Premiership final, and Martin Offiah in formal dispute after putting in a transfer request which was refused.

Hull sprang a surprise by finishing third and at one time threatened to snatch the title, particularly when they demolished Widnes 32–6 and Wigan 24–4 at the Boulevard. But they proved vulnerable on their travels, losing eight of their thirteen away fixtures, and this was fatal. It may have been significant that the majority of those defeats came after the departure of their coach, Brian Smith, for Australia in January. His fellow Australian, Noel Cleal, took over as coach, injury causing him to retire as a player.

Widnes back-rower Les Holliday was sorely missed by his club when they lost out in the Championship, the Challenge Cup and the Premiership. Holliday was capped against France but was dogged by injury for much of the year.

Smith's influence undoubtedly helped their front three of Karl Harrison, Lee Jackson and Andy Dannatt to gain Test recognition with the first two producing sterling displays against Australia. The linchpin of the team was another Australian, the half-back Greg Mackey, whose organisation was top-class. He helped bring the best out of the livewire French scrum-half, Patrick Entat, and made his task of adjusting to British Rugby League that much easier. The winger, Paul Eastwood, was splendidly consistent and finished as the first division's leading scorer for the second successive season.

Castleford appeared to judge things nicely and a run of ten successive wins had them well poised for the first title in their history only for Easter to bring disaster with defeats at Bradford and at home to Hull, followed by the final week's set-back at Wigan. Their stand-off, Graham Steadman, was their danger-man with a number of sparkling tries, but their most consistent performer was the prop, Lee Crooks, whose distribution at times was exceptional.

The teenager Graham Southernwood had a fine start to the season at hooker, but then lost form and eventually his place to the experienced Kevin Beardmore, while John Joyner also proved that he is still one of the best craftsmen around. Shaun Irwin had some good moments, but it was again a season when at the end Castleford seemed not to have fulfilled all their expectations. Some supporters felt that, for the second successive season, the team struggled when the pressure was really on and their first Championship title a possibility.

Typically, Leeds caused a pre-season sensation when they signed the great All Black full-back, John Gallagher, who had just been voted the best Rugby Union player in the world. They followed that by signing a Kenyan Rugby Union international, Eddie Rombo, after he had played for them in the Wigan Sevens competition. They had also signed scrum-half Paul Harkin from Bradford Northern, but it soon became apparent that the side still lacked forward power. So they went into the transfer market again and emerged with props Shaun Wane, from Wigan, and Warrington's Steve Molloy.

Gallagher settled into the code with remarkable speed. He was a heavily marked man, but showed confidence under the high ball and his linking on attack was always a threat. However, he was injured in a controversial incident at St Helens in January amid claims that he had been spear-tackled, and on his return seemed to have lost confidence.

Rombo proved what many had expected, that he had much to learn, and he spent most of the season in the second team. Thus it was left to skipper Garry Schofield to give a lead from stand-off and he did it well, having a fine season. Carl Gibson did enough to earn a Test place as did the second-row man, Paul Dixon, with some storming running. Dixon's season faded amid injury and suspension, and the team as a whole seemed to lack the strength and pace to hold leading sides in crunch matches. There was one horrendous 0–38 home defeat by Widnes, who toyed with them, but a late run saw them finish fifth.

St Helens, the great eccentrics, finished sixth after a season which inevitably showed them at their dazzling best and their casual worst. Their defence was always suspect, but they had few equals on attack. Their wingers, Les Quirk and Alan Hunte, scored their share of tries, but the key figure was George Mann, at prop or second row, who made his strength tell with some mighty displays.

Bernard Dwyer earned full marks for effort and consistency and their big prop, Kevin Ward, was signed from Castleford. This was not altogether to the liking of their fans but, in fact, Kevin was a great inspiration and found a new lease of life in his usual robust fashion. Jonathan Griffiths developed at stand-off as the season went on and formed a useful partnership with Paul Bishop, who was signed in mid-season from Warrington.

Bradford Northern were another team left feeling that they should have done better, not by any means for the first time. They signed two New Zealanders, the scrum-half Brett Iti and the centre Darrall Shelford, along with Headingley's Rugby Union half-back, Neil Summers. Iti came on well in late season, while Shelford was always steady and consistent. Summers had to compete with Iti for a place and also appeared at stand-off and on the wing. Northern's lack of an established No. 6 was shown in late season, when the Australian Bob Grogan, on loan from Halifax, looked the part. Their second-

John Bentley was joined in the Leeds ranks by fellow Rugby Union converts John Gallagher and Eddie Rombo, but the Loiners' outlay was not matched by results in another inconsistent campaign.

row man, Paul Medley, had some spectacular moments, scoring sensational tries, but the pack did not always show full authority, despite a good season by the highly-promising prop, Craig Richards.

Featherstone Rovers did well to finish in the top eight; it would have been higher but for some strange lapses in defence. The Kiwi loose forward, Brendan Tuuta, was a quality signing and set a great example with his wholehearted approach and clever handling. There was a fine season too from the centre, Terry Manning, and the hooker, Trevor Clark, while Jeff Grayshon, at prop, sailed serenely past his 42nd birthday during the year, still thoroughly enjoying himself.

The team's heart was, of course, the scrum-half, Deryck Fox, with another busy and efficient term, rarely having a bad game. Ian Smales played well at times but injuries to Paul Newlove kept this valuable try-poacher out for some time and his finishing ability was missed.

The 1990–91 Season

Opposite
Half-back Mark Conway continued to star in a Wakefield Trinity side that promised much in 1990–91. They made a Yorkshire Cup final appearance, but eventually finished perilously close to relegation.

Warrington's league form was generally disappointing, a major reason being that injuries to their skipper, Mike Gregory, meant that he played very few matches; relegation was even a threat at one stage. Success in the Regal Trophy brought renewed confidence, however, with Gary Mercer making a highly successful switch from centre to the second row, and their well-organised defence made them difficult to beat until a dreadful final game at St Helens, when they conceded 62 points.

The Wire moved heavily into the Welsh market, signing the centre Allan Bateman, the scrum-half Kevin Ellis, and the second-row man Rowland Phillips. Ellis, in particular, made rapid progress with his strong running and skilled handling to gain Test recognition, while Bateman looked sharp with limited chances. The problem was lack of weight up front which made most games hard work, and their veteran winger, Des Drummond, was often wasted. David Lyon was a competent full-back and Duane Mann and Billy McGinty were the pick of the forwards, but too many visiting teams won at Wilderspool for the comfort of locals.

Wakefield Trinity had one outstanding moment when they beat Wigan, but were always looking over their shoulders at the relegation zone and were not safe until winning their final fixture at Rochdale. They signed the Kiwi, Adrian Shelford, and brought in the experienced Australian, Chris Mortimer, with mixed results. Shelford had some impressive games, but suffered in the latter part of the season from knee trouble.

Trinity's winger, David Jones, from Wigan St Patrick's, made himself popular with some spirited displays and the speedy centre, Andy Mason, showed his ability to score spectacular tries. Too often the backs did not see enough of the ball to make best use of their talents and they were a low-scoring outfit. Some shoddy late displays almost saw Trinity suffer relegation.

Trinity clearly need a bigger squad, as do Hull Kingston Rovers, who at one time were well placed but just one win from their last ten matches dropped them uncomfortably near the danger area. The Australian Bryan Niebling battled long and hard in difficult circumstances and there were some classic tries from winger Anthony Sullivan. But fans were not happy that their Australian centre, Greg Austin, was released in favour of the New Zealand prop, James Goulding, and the latter had a thin time, making little impact.

Adding to the uncertainty was the announcement of their coach, Roger Millward, in mid-term that he was breaking his twenty-five-year link with the club at the end of the season. Relegation was avoided by a point, amid numerous angry demonstrations from supporters, and the season ended with an alarming 16–62 defeat at Sheffield.

Oldham regarded themselves as unlucky to go down after some fine performances, but their away form was the weak link and they sacked their coach, Tony Barrow, in mid-season. John Fieldhouse took over as player-coach on a temporary basis, but he, too, was overlooked when a permanent appointment was made eventually in favour of the Australian Peter Tunks. Their scrum-half, Mike Ford, played exceptionally well in the circumstances and there were good efforts from such as the full-back, Duncan Platt, and the second-row man, Charlie McAllister. But another Cup semi-final appearance could not atone for relegation.

Mitre
MULTIPLEX
Officers

Relegated also were Sheffield Eagles after another spirited effort to stay in the top bracket, which included a draw at Wigan and a win at Widnes. The absence through injury of their scrum-half and organiser, Mark Aston, for the first half of the season was a blow the Eagles could not shake off. His return brought an improvement but too late. Their Test centre, Daryl Powell, switched to stand-off and formed a good partnership with Aston, but the form of their Australian loose forward, Ian Russell, from whom much had been expected, was disappointing. Their Kiwi centre, Sam Panapa, had some good games and scored some exciting tries, but again the lack of a big squad proved too great a handicap and the game's most spectacular stadium, at Don Valley, was consigned to the second division.

Newly-promoted Rochdale went straight back to the second division after winning only one game throughout the season, against Bradford. They had signed experience with such as Colin Whitfield, Neil Holding and Mike O'Neill, and had also recruited the centre, Darren Abram, who finished as top try-scorer. But so little went right and their coach, Allan Agar, left the club, as so often seems to happen with promoted outfits. Not until it was far too late was some hope seen for 1991–92, and that came from a young scrum-half, Steve Gartland.

The second-division title race was settled early on and Salford became runaway winners. Their coach, Kevin Tamati, in charge during the latter part of their relegation season, had worked hard during the summer, thoroughly preparing his side, and his efforts paid off. The eventual gap between them and Halifax was only 5 points, but there never seemed any danger of the Red Devils not winning the Championship; indeed, the main question was whether they would go through with a 100 per cent record. As it was, they suffered only one defeat, at Workington, and were held to a draw by Swinton, and many of their victories were overwhelming.

Their half-back, Steve Kerry, led the points-scoring. His goal-kicking was highly effective and he also developed into a sharp and clever craftsman behind a pack in which the New Zealander, Shane Hansen, created a big impression. There was good work, too, from Martin Birkett among the relative newcomers, and Adrian Hadley enjoyed his freedom on the wing to be well among the tries. The unfortunate factor was that some performances of real quality were not rewarded with particularly high attendances at the Willows.

It was unfortunate also that the quaint fixture arrangement of the division, with not all teams meeting each other, meant that Salford did not play a league match against their nearest rivals, Halifax. This was costly for both clubs so far as attendances were concerned. The Thrum Hall fans stuck solidly to Halifax, who invariably took a big following away with them; games against Salford would have been a huge attraction.

Halifax had their pre-season problems and just managed to survive a financial crisis. A take-over saved them and then Peter Roe emerged from the amateur ranks to do a fine job as coach. Austin's arrival from Hull KR gave the side genuine finishing power and he scored a considerable number of tries. There was a healthy tally also for Martin Wood, at centre and on the wing. Their threequarter, Warren Wilson, and back-row man, Alan Platt, added valuable experience to the willing efforts of such as Jason Ramshaw and the

Michael Ford played exceptionally well in an Oldham side who were unlucky to be relegated from a powerful first division, yet his frustration drove him to join Yorkshire Cup-winners Castleford in the close-season.

belligerent work of their prop and captain, Brendan Hill. Halifax raised a few doubts by losing three of their first ten games, but then winning became a routine and they suffered only one defeat in the next eighteen matches to storm into second place.

There was a keen tussle for third place, snatched on the last day of the season by Swinton, who just pipped Ryedale-York, despite the doubts of their coach, Jim Crellin, who believed the Lions were not equipped for the first division. The team and fans thought otherwise, and there were good contributions from Logan Edwards, Scott Ranson and Chris Johnson, and the arrival during the season of Tommy Frodsham and Chris Wilkinson brought experience and cover.

Ryedale-York had banked heavily on promotion, signing the Kiwi star, Tawere Nikau, to strengthen their pack and he did a fine job. Graham Sullivan was leading scorer and there was a late rush of tries from Nick Pinkney when he was switched from wing to stand-off. But too often the side failed against leading rivals, and this proved fatal at the end.

Leigh had all sorts of off-field problems, and contract difficulties cost them the services of John Woods and Tony Cottrell, two very experienced men. It certainly affected their promotion challenge, which faded badly despite good work by their full-back Paul Topping, David Ruane and Peter Ropati.

THE PREMIERSHIP TROPHIES

Once again there were black and white ribbons on the Stones Bitter Premiership Trophy, but this time they belonged to Hull. The Airlie Birds won the competition for the first time with a convincing 14–4 success over the holders, Widnes, in the final to prevent the Chemics taking the trophy for the fourth year in succession. There was a first success, too, for the champions Salford, who beat Halifax 27–20 in the second-division final, all before a record crowd of 42,043.

It came as no surprise that the champions, Wigan, should bow out of the competition at the first hurdle, even on home soil and to the eighth-placed club Featherstone Rovers. In the previous three years the Central Park side had departed the competition early after qualifying for Wembley. The heavy demands of the title run-in had also left their mark with numerous injuries; indeed, Wigan were without ten of their probable Challenge Cup final line-up when the quarter-finals began.

Even so, Wigan made Rovers work hard, staging a strong late rally only to be edged out 26–31. Deryck Fox, very much at the hub of things for Rovers, and their hooker, Trevor Clark, collected two of their six tries. There was also a first touchdown of the season for the second-row man, Chris Burton.

Wigan's Wembley opponents, St Helens, surprised Hull with the strength of their challenge at the Boulevard and had they taken their first-half chances they might well have won through. They led 12–6 early in the second half, but were hit by three tries in eleven minutes and that settled matters. The Hull

Greg Austin was sensationally axed from Hull KR's overseas quota at the start of the season, yet his arrival at Halifax gave the club genuine finishing power and his forty-seven tries propelled them to promotion and the second-division Premiership final.

tries came from Patrick Entat, Neil Turner, Russ Walker and Dean Busby, with Paul Eastwood landing six goals.

Widnes had not looked too effective in their late league matches, and there was the feeling that Bradford Northern might test them. However, even without Martin Offiah, they quickly snuffed out the Northern threat at Naughton Park and ran out convincing 46–10 winners. This was the match in which Jonathan Davies beat Mick Burke's points record for the Chemics as he collected two tries and landed five goals. Darren Wright and Andy Currier also scored two tries each.

The most dramatic game was at Wheldon Road, where Garry Schofield scored between the posts in the last seconds to give Leeds a 24–20 win over Castleford. Perhaps it was justice, for in the first half Schofield had a clear seventy-yard interception try ruled out for a knock-on and the TV replay proved the referee wrong for once. Schofield also landed two drop-goals as each side finished with four tries in a game in which Castleford pulled back from 10–18 down to lead 20–18 until Schofield struck.

There were a couple of surprises in the second division. Leigh won 11–6 at Ryedale–York, thanks to a try, three goals and a drop-goal from Paul Topping. Workington underlined their marked improvement during the season by scoring 17 points in the second half to win 19–12 at Swinton. Martin Wood collected four tries as Halifax beat Fulham 42–24, and Steve O'Neill touched down twice for Salford in a hard-earned 26–12 win over Carlisle.

The semi-finals in each division were contrasting affairs, one relatively easy win in each group and one tense contest. Again, Leeds were involved in the best match with the result decided in the last couple of minutes against Hull at the Boulevard. This time it went against the Headingley side after an absorbing contest. Leeds had gone ahead with a drop-goal by Garry Schofield and an excellent try, sparked by Paul Dixon and scored by Richard Gunn. Simon Irving had added the goal to make it 7–0. Leeds then tackled supremely well against wave after wave of Hull attacks, led by Jon Sharp, Karl Harrison and Andy Dannatt.

A penalty-goal either side of half-time by Paul Eastwood cut Hull's deficit to 3 points but it looked as if the Leeds defence would have the last word until a high kick by Greg Mackey was snatched by the substitute, Gary Nolan, for a try which sent the Boulevard wild. Paul Eastwood's goal was merely a bonus as Hull went through 10–7.

Widnes showed both sides of their character in a high-scoring game against Featherstone at Naughton Park. The Chemics shot into a 16–0 lead in fourteen minutes and it was 28–12 at the interval as John Devereux and Martin Offiah each scored two tries and Jonathan Davies added another. Ikram Butt and Paul Newlove touched down for Rovers, who were again hit by a scoring blitz early in the second half with Devereux completing his hat-trick and Steve McCurrie and Andy Currier adding others to ease Widnes to a 42–12 margin.

Widnes then went to sleep and Rovers provided a remarkable finish with tries by Terry Manning, Ian Smales and the splendid Andy Fisher to earn respectability at 42–28. So Widnes would be at Old Trafford again, meeting Hull for the second time in three years.

Excitement in the second division came from another fine effort by Workington, who forced Salford to a replay with a 9–9 draw at the Willows. Salford led with a try by Adrian Hadley, and Steve Kerry added two goals. But a try by Ian McLean and goals by Stephen Wear made it 8–8 at the interval. The second half was a tight affair. Salford nudged ahead with a drop-goal by Mark Lee, but Wear produced a similar effort late on to earn a replay.

A crowd of more than 6,000 at Thrum Hall saw Halifax withstand early Leigh pressure and the visitors had only a goal by Topping to show for a lively opening. The home side then took charge with a try by Peter Brown and a goal by Matthew Silva. In the second half their big pack dominated the play, and there were two tries each by Steve Smith and Greg Austin and another by Warren Wilson in a convincing 32–8 win. Topping with a try and another goal again collected all Leigh's points.

There was a crowd of more than 5,500 at Derwent Park for the Workington v Salford replay. The vast majority of them went home disappointed as Salford this time made no mistake, winning 28–6 with Martin Birkett scoring two tries and Kerry chipping in with a try and three goals to set up a final meeting between Salford and Halifax.

Old Trafford, Manchester, 12 May

The Second Division Premiership Trophy Final
Salford 27 Halifax 20

This was the final most people wanted to see because the sides, first and second in the table, had not met in the league. However, it was a patchy game with some good tries, bad mistakes and a flare-up at the end which damaged a few reputations.

There were few early signs of the attacking records of either side until a fine break from Steve Gibson sent Steve Kerry racing away for the opening try after fourteen minutes. It was the lift the game needed and strong Halifax pressure led to Roy Southernwood dummying his way clear for the equalising score. Salford looked the more dangerous, and had more of the play, before they nudged ahead again with drop-goals by Frank Cassidy and Kerry.

However, Halifax ended the half on a high when a fine break by Greg Austin gained the position for big Brendan Hill to plough his way over. Their substitute, Alan Platt, added the goal to make it 10–6 at the interval.

Kerry's speed and supporting play were always a threat and he staged a repeat of the first half when he followed another Gibson break to collect his second try. He also added the goal and then a penalty-goal to make it 14–10 to Salford. At this stage Halifax were struggling, but struck back through another quality break by Austin, who went up the right wing and sent an inside pass to Warren Wilson, who cut in to score between the posts. Platt's goal made it 16–14 to Halifax.

Then came the errors which decided the match. The first followed a grubber-kick by Salford's busy hooker, Mark Lee. Southernwood covered but failed to smother the ball, which rolled free to be gathered by Kerry, and quick passing sent Tex Evans away to score near the corner, Kerry adding a good goal.

Lee chipped over a third drop-goal to make it 21–16 to Salford and they settled matters after another Halifax error. Platt set himself for a long pass out to the left but the ball fell between Steve Smith and Mick Keebles. The Salford

Brendan Hill was a mighty figure for Halifax in the second-division Premiership final, but his efforts could not stop league champions Salford adding the Premiership trophy to their sideboard with a 27–20 win.

substitute, Mick Dean, playing on the wing, pounced and sent John Gilfillan racing gleefully to the posts for a gift score. Kerry added the goal to take his tally to 17 points and earn the man-of-the-match award.

Halifax tried to salvage things and Martin Wood, who had had one try disallowed for a forward pass, went over four minutes from time after good work by Peter Brown and Wilson. The game ended in a flare-up which continued after the whistle but it did not deter Salford's victory celebrations.

Salford: Gibson; Evans, Gilfillan, Birkett, Hadley; Cassidy, Kerry; Worrall, Lee, Hansen, Bradshaw, Blease, Burgess

Substitutes: Sherratt for Bradshaw after 40 minutes, Dean for Hadley after 52 minutes, Bradshaw for Worrall after 66 minutes

Scorers: tries – Kerry (2), Evans, Gilfillan; goals – Kerry (4); drop-goals – Cassidy, Kerry, Lee

Halifax: Smith; Wood, Wilson, Austin, Silva; Lyons, Southernwood; Hill, Ramshaw, Bell, Brown, Milner, Keebles

Substitutes: Platt for Silva after 24 minutes, Scott for Bell after 70 minutes

Scorers: tries – Southernwood, Hill, Wilson, Wood; goals – Platt (2)

Referee: B. Galtress (Bradford)

Old Trafford, Manchester, 12 May

The Stones Bitter Premiership Final
Hull 14 Widnes 4

Hull made it at last. After defeats in four previous finals, including one two years earlier by Widnes, the Airlie Birds got it right with a comprehensive performance which sent their huge following wild with delight. There was rarely any doubt. The mighty Hull pack was at its best, completely subduing the Widnes forwards, and giving time and space for their half-backs, Greg Mackey and Patrick Entat, to have a field day. Mackey took the man-of-the-match award for a performance of great authority and organisational skill, having a hand in two of his side's three tries and testing Widnes's nerve throughout with his shrewd use of the high kick.

Only for a brief spell, midway through the second half, did Widnes suggest that they would take charge. But they missed a crucial chance of taking the lead, and Hull recovered to continue their domination. It was soon evident that the power of the Hull front row – Karl Harrison, Lee Jackson and Andy

Greg Mackey and Lee Jackson celebrate Hull's outstanding 14–4 victory over Widnes in the first-division Premiership final.

Dannatt – would be used to the full to test Widnes, and the back three, inspired by Jon Sharp, were never far behind. It was no surprise when the first try came after thirteen minutes of almost non-stop pressure, Mackey's carefully timed pass enabling Richard Gay to dodge tackles and make the touchdown.

Steve McCurrie and Phil McKenzie almost got Alan Tait free in a rare Widnes attack, but Jackson, Mackey and Eastwood combined in a Hull counter-attack and more pressure came from Dannatt, Mackey and Entat. Hull stretched their lead after twenty-seven minutes when a curving run by Entat brought Eastwood powerfully inside and his well-judged pass sent Russ Walker diving over. It was 8–0 to Hull now and, despite a couple of Widnes flurries, it stayed that way until the interval.

The Chemics badly needed an early score on the resumption and it almost came from a solo dash by McCurrie, who was proving their best player. Davies was taken into touch just short of the line before Mackey, inevitably, led Hull away and Dannatt produced a thundering solo run. Both sides made substitutions, including Gary Nolan taking over at centre from Damien McGarry in what proved to be an important change. Widnes scored the try they sorely needed when Kurt Sorensen's break was continued by David Hulme, who gave Offiah the chance to race away and score his forty-ninth try of the season.

At last Widnes showed signs of confidence and Emosi Koloto was sent away with Darren Wright coasting on his left as they approached Gay. A try seemed certain but Koloto, having looked at Wright, inexplicably sent a high pass out the other way where John Devereux was marked and lost the ball in the tackle.

It was a massive let-off for Hull and then Offiah's speed saved Widnes when he got back to stop Gay after a fine run and pass from Sharp. Tait and David Hulme were held only a yard short before Hull worked clear and made it pay. Mackey again came across the line and found Nolan, who beat two men in little space and held off three others on the line to make the touchdown. Eastwood's fine goal was icing on the cake. Hull were safe and they and their fans knew it. The Widnes Premiership stranglehold was broken

Hull: Gay; Eastwood, McGarry, Webb, Turner; Mackey, Entat; Harrison, Jackson, Dannatt, Marlow, Walker, Sharp

Substitutes: Nolan for McGarry after 47 minutes, Busby for Marlow after 61 minutes, Marlow for Dannatt after 68 minutes, McGarry for Webb after 79 minutes

Scorers: tries – Gay, Walker, Nolan; goal – Eastwood

Widnes: Tait; Devereux, Currier, Davies, Offiah; Dowd, David Hulme; Sorensen, McKenzie, Grima, Paul Hulme, Koloto, McCurrie

Substitutes: Howard for Koloto after 28 minutes, Wright for McKenzie after 40 minutes, Koloto for Grima after 55 minutes

Scorer: try – Offiah

Referee: J. Holdsworth (Kippax)

Attendance: 42,043.

TWO

The Silk Cut Challenge Cup

Mike Rylance

After Wigan's record fourth successive Challenge Cup victory and their second Cup and Championship double in the two years in which he has been in charge, John Monie was saying some notable things. The theme of his remarks was the triumph of the Wigan spirit not just over St Helens, but over other kinds of adversity as well. This latest win, so much narrower than the previous three, had been achieved not with talent, he said, but with character, heart and guts. And all of that had been held together with 'needles and sticking plaster', a phrase which reappeared in almost every newspaper report of the match. Their man-of-the-match, he said, was the team doctor.

Monie has gritted his teeth against what many Australians would regard as the idiosyncrasies of the British game, yet the usually laconic coach was beginning to let some impatience show through. 'I just hope no other Rugby League team has to go through what we've been through,' he stated, 'because nobody will ever be able to do it again.' He was referring to his team's much publicised end-of-season schedule, which had forced them to play their last five Championship matches at the rate of one every other day. Their magnificent achievement in keeping their title in such demanding conditions had led to injuries which had thrown the Cup final build-up into disarray.

Like the thorough Australian coach that he is, Monie believes that good preparation is as important as the eighty minutes on the field, yet such a fundamental matter as team selection had had to be delayed until the eve of the final. He also confided that Joe Lydon, who was suffering from the same hamstring injury with which Ellery Hanley had actually played, had 'sacrificed himself' for the captain, 'our leader and inspiration', who, despite an unprecedented pre-match fitness test, was only '20 per cent fit'. Which is where Dr Zaman came in. Monie couldn't say how you spelt his name, but he was sure it should be engraved on the Lance Todd Trophy for having got the inspirational Hanley into a reasonable state to play.

The pressmen nodded. This was all good quotable stuff. And where else would they get it from? Not from Hanley, who, after his brief sortie into American Football hype, had declared a non-intervention zone around himself. The opposite dressing-room, too, was a no-go area, where Mike McClennan also wanted to be alone. Monie's final throwaway comment turned out to be one of the most revealing. 'I'm really proud of the players,' he said. 'It's their last day of work this year, they're a great side, they're very professional.' Now we know that Australians take their football seriously and it is commonplace to hear all kinds of coaches ask players to do a certain job, but was he suggesting that the game of Rugby League had become part of the daily grind for his players? Had Wembley become for the likes of Andy Gregory, seven times a winner there, just another workplace? Clearly not, even if Wigan were making visits there look merely routine. But Rugby League is at least part, if not the major part, of most Wigan players' routine. Whether or not the club eventually decides to become fully professional, as had been discussed on and off during the season, there is no denying that one of the main reasons they had been so successful yet again was that most of them had no other occupation that would prevent them from training and playing as required. The desirability of it all is another question, but you doubt whether they could have achieved what they did achieve if they had all been on shift work down the pit.

Of course, the strength of their squad – which meant that players of the calibre of Lydon and Kelvin Skerrett were barely missed – and the way in which Monie has managed it are also highly significant factors. Monie's job, when he first arrived to take over from Graham Lowe, looked a daunting prospect. But how much more intimidating will it look to his own eventual successor!

Frano Botica's first season in a Wigan shirt after switching from Rugby Union brought him Challenge Cup and Championship-winners' medals. His five goals in the semi-final against Oldham eased his side's way to a 30–16 win.

Wigan's ability to maintain and even improve on their own high standards was one of the features of the season, indeed of the present era. Discussing their Cup final victory in an article in *League Express*, Widnes's international scrum-half, David Hulme, made a relevant point when he wrote that Wigan 'will continue to dominate our game unless other British clubs adopt similar attitudes, routines and above all administrative leadership.'

By comparison, the competition which they have dominated for the past four years seems downright quaint. The launch of a competition can be almost as important, in media terms, as its finale. Yet the preliminary round is a modern manifestation of Rugby League's age-old failure to maximise its resources and potential. Brian Smith made the complaint that the game's most glamorous competition was to begin on a date no one was quite sure of. That was before his Hull side, then at the top of the first division, went out at the hands of Sheffield before most people had realised the competition had even started. It might have been good for Sheffield, but it was no good for Rugby League that the leading club, with all its crowd and media potential, should go out simply to satisfy a mathematical necessity and then only have a succession of blank Sundays to look forward to. The justification for what resembles some vague vetting procedure is usually expressed in terms of 'romance' and 'magic'. In the official Wembley programme there was actually a reference to the 'romance' of the preliminary round. Such sentiments cut no ice with Sheffield, who were drawn in the preliminary round of all three cup competitions during the season, losing two of the matches.

Huddersfield, who had not advanced beyond the first round in a decade, could not detect much romance in the air at Wilderspool, as they suffered their third preliminary round defeat in four seasons. With them went Carlisle, who lost by a 1-point margin to fellow-Cumbrians Workington, and the three amateur sides, Hensingham, Cutsyke and Leigh East. The Leigh amateurs at least had the distinction of putting up a better show against Bradford Northern than the town's professional club did in the next round.

Due to the weather, the first round proper stuttered into life over a period of ten days, with only three of the sixteen matches being played on the originally scheduled date. There was snow everywhere, but at Headingley it was cleared from the terraces for Leeds to beat a battling Dewsbury by 40–20 before a disappointing crowd of just over 4,000. Volunteers also shifted tons of snow from the Doncaster ground, where Widnes demonstrated the gulf between the two clubs and the two divisions with a 30–4 victory. Swinton's tie against St Helens was switched to Manchester City's soccer ground to take advantage of the undersoil heating. It was the Lions who warmed to their task better before eventually yielding 8–18 to their first-division opponents.

Despite expensive measures taken to protect the Wheldon Road ground, the match of the round, between Castleford and Wigan, had to be postponed until the following week. It promised to be a thrilling clash: Castleford were third in the league, having won eleven of their last thirteen games, while Wigan were just behind in fourth place and coming into form. But even at that stage Wigan made their intentions clear, with a sparkling performance in which they scored five tries to one. 'They were simply awesome,' admitted the Castleford coach, Darryl Van de Velde.

The only other all-first-division clash was at Sheffield, where Featherstone, who had recently beaten the Eagles in a league match, were unable to make up a 0–19 deficit and eventually went down by 12–19. Barrow also managed to reverse their league form of the previous week. Having suffered a 4–56 defeat at Elland Road, they got their own back on Hunslet with a narrow 13–8 win on their own ground. It was a good start for their new coach, Paul Kavanagh, who had taken over only in the middle of that week from Steve Norton.

The other Cumbrian clubs also enjoyed success: Whitehaven had to travel down to Nottingham for theirs and Workington made home advantage count against a bemused Hull KR. Despite the differing status of the two teams, Workington, revitalised under Ray Ashton's leadership and enjoying the backing of a sizeable crowd, were not to be outdone, with outstanding performances from their hard-working forwards, their young stand-off, Steve Wear, and their Australian centre, Ken Kerr. 'We bossed 'em up front,' said the Town captain, Colin Armstrong, using new words to express an old Workington tradition.

A new coach also produced the goods for Oldham. Their player-coach, John Fieldhouse, was no longer able to ask advice, as he had been doing, from his former international boss, Maurice Bamford, Bramley's general manager, but he didn't seem to need it as Oldham strolled to a 38–6 win at McLaren Field.

In three all-second-division encounters, Keighley beat Runcorn in the Cup and the Championship in the same week but there was no happy return to Thrum Hall for the ex-Halifax coach, Ross Strudwick, whose Fulham side lost by 6–46. Salford were too good for Batley, who had some consolation in the fact that their popular New Zealand second-rower, Sonny Whakarau, was named man-of-the-match.

Though Workington were the only second-division side to dispose of opponents from the top flight, three other clubs gave first-division sides a hard time. Warrington were helped by a Duane Mann interception try three minutes from time to settle their match against Ryedale-York; Trafford Borough made a disappointing Wakefield Trinity struggle at Belle Vue; and Rochdale just managed to fend off Chorley's pretensions.

Opposite
Kevin Ward's move from Castleford to St Helens gave him a new lease of life, and his barnstorming form in the second semi-final was crucial to his side's 19–2 success against Widnes.

Only five days later, in the second round, Hornets faced a much bigger test. Wigan, even with Shaun Edwards sent off before the hour, ran up 72 points against them, with Ellery Hanley helping himself to half-a-dozen tries and Frano Botica scoring a personal total of 28 points.

Widnes and Warrington maintained the west-of-Pennines grip on the competition and Oldham just had the edge on Workington, who before 5,500 spectators almost came back from being 0–12 down. St Helens were the first team through, playing on the Saturday in front of the television cameras, but they did not impress their demanding fans against a Wakefield side which failed to take its chances.

Sheffield might have been expected to take the Yorkshire challenge into the third round, which had always previously eluded them, but, having disposed of two first-division teams, they fell to the second-division leaders, Salford, who scored four tries to two, despite losing their skipper, Ian Blease, with a broken collar-bone. Their New Zealand second-rower, Shane Hansen, compensated for his absence with an astonishing fifty-five tackles, one try and a hand in another.

In fact, the white rose banner was carried by Halifax and Bradford. Halifax had been averaging 40 points a match at home in the second division and saw no reason to change their ways in the Cup against Whitehaven. The Bradford–Leeds encounter, a repetition of last year's preliminary-round tie, was a different matter altogether. Garry Schofield called it 'the most important game in my four years at Leeds. If we don't win,' he said, in the week leading up to the match, 'it looks like being another disastrous season for us.' Disastrous possibly, disappointing certainly, as Leeds fans began to wonder if they would ever see their team at Wembley again. A reshuffled side, with Schofield at scrum-half, David Heron at stand-off and Mike Kuiti in the centre, could find no purchase on the heavy Odsal surface against Bradford's big pack, in which the prop, Jon Hamer, was outstanding.

But after the third round there were no east-of-Pennines clubs left – for the third successive year. Halifax, a very different team and a very different club since they went to Wembley four years ago, gave their 1987 final opponents, St Helens, a fright but could not sustain their early pressure. Bradford had put Wigan out of the Regal Trophy but succumbed as they had in two of the previous three seasons as Wigan went inexorably on their Wembley way. Oldham were convincing winners against Salford, with whom they would change places in the league at the end of the season. Widnes's supremacy against the previous year's finalists, Warrington, was confirmed when they raced to a 26–2 lead, partly due to the Wire's generosity in gifting them 12 points in one five-minute spell. The Chemics looked ready to put recent disappointments in the Cup behind them.

When the semi-final draw was made, all seemed set for the dream final most neutrals were hoping for. Widnes, with their all-round pace and flair allied to muscle up front, were thought to be the one team capable of making a serious challenge to Wigan's long hold on the Cup. Wigan duly followed the script and played their part to perfection in the semi-final, but Widnes seemed yet again to suffer stage-fright, forgetting their lines and eventually losing their coach as well.

Burnden Park, Bolton, 23 March

The Challenge Cup Semi-final
Oldham 16 Wigan 30

Oldham had everything against them – the bookmakers' odds, their own record of never having reached Wembley despite five semi-final appearances, and a Wigan side which was undefeated in their last nine Championship and Cup matches and which had conceded a total of just 10 points in the three previous rounds, all against first-division clubs. Even the fact that Oldham were the last team to beat Wigan in the Challenge Cup, in the first round in 1987, had its downside: that was the year they were relegated and Wigan went on to win the Championship. They were to experience a sense of *déjà vu*, but without the cup-tie consolation.

After just over half an hour they virtually conceded yet another semi-final, when they handed Wigan two scores and ended any hope they themselves might have had of getting back into the game. Brett Clark and Des Foy, the only survivor from the 1987 triumph, were penalised for holding Steve Hampson down in the tackle and Frano Botica took Wigan's score to 20 without reply. Only minutes earlier Oldham's full-back, Duncan Platt, had spilled the ball into Andy Goodway's arms for a converted try. It was Andy Gregory, in commanding form as on so many occasions during the season, who had started to plot Oldham's downfall when first his grubber-kick led to Shaun Edwards's touchdown and then his short ball to Ellery Hanley brought the second.

Oldham made a number of breaks and played some enterprising, spirited football themselves, with their former Central Park men, Mike Ford and Richard Russell, outstanding, but they were unable to outpace Wigan's cover. It was not until the fifty-fourth minute that they made their mark and even then against the run of play. Stand-off Clark intercepted Gregory's pass to Hanley and ran twenty yards before letting winger John Henderson complete the remaining fifty to score his side's first points.

Tries by Wigan before and after that touchdown, from Kevin Iro and Botica, who took advantage respectively of some thin defence and a wild Oldham pass, left their opponents with an impossible task. It was made even harder when their second-rower, Paul Round, was dismissed for a spectacular, though none too serious, high tackle on Dean Bell.

Two late tries by Oldham showed only their persistence. The powerful second-rower, Charlie McAllister, took advantage of Russell's well-timed pass and there was some reward for Mike Ford, who finished a move in which Russell, Henderson and Ronnie Duane all figured strongly. Oldham's only other consolation was to equal the highest number of points scored by a losing side in a Challenge Cup semi-final. They had caught Wigan in what was for them a magnanimous mood.

Oldham: Duncan Platt; Irving, Foy, Anderson, Henderson; Clark, Ford; Donegan, Ruane, Fieldhouse, Round, McAllister, Russell

Substitutes: Duane for Anderson and Atkinson for Donegan at half-time, Donegan for Platt after 63 minutes

Scorers: tries – Henderson, McAllister, Ford; goals – Platt (2)

Wigan: Hampson; Lydon, Iro, Bell, Botica; Edwards, Gregory; Lucas, Dermott, Andy Platt, Betts, Clarke, Hanley

Substitutes: Goodway for Lucas after 26 minutes, Lucas for Clarke after 47 minutes, Myers for Lydon after 61 minutes

Scorers: tries – Edwards, Hanley, Goodway, Iro, Botica; goals – Botica (5)

Referee: J. Smith (Halifax)

Attendance: 19,057.

Central Park, Wigan, 30 March

The Challenge Cup Semi-final
St Helens 19 Widnes 2

Doug Laughton wasn't the only one who thought that this would be Widnes's year. Though realising that it is never wise to back against St Helens, impartial observers were expecting the Chemics to end their seven-year Wembley famine. They had the better form, were in top position in the league while St Helens were sixth, and an added incentive for them was that this was probably Kurt Sorensen's last chance to play at Wembley, where Jonathan Davies would surely become the darling of the television cameras and Martin Offiah would carry on where he had left off against the Australians in October. Although St Helens had upset Widnes's plans at this stage two years ago, few people, apart from Saints' own vociferous fans, expected lightning (which in 1989 took the form of Les Quirk) to strike twice.

The first forty minutes of this highly entertaining match offered few clues to the eventual outcome. Widnes did most of the attacking, though their forwards, who had been so destructive against Warrington in the previous round, could not quite get the better of their counterparts, who absorbed whatever was thrown at them. 'We dropped out from our goal-line on about five occasions,' said Mike McClennan, 'and we were under tremendous pressure. We never had field position in the first half to exert our authority.' St Helens's tackling was impressive, their defensive organisation capable of netting anything in a black and white shirt. In contrast, their attacking play suffered from too many handling errors and they also gave away needless penalties. But Widnes were not faultless either.

Instead of eventually giving way to the pressure, as many expected, Saints simply got stronger as the second half wore on. Kevin Ward led the way in an

outstanding pack, before the irrepressible George Mann came to the fore, driving forward, breaking the line and tackling with a huge appetite. It was he who set up the first try for their stand-off, Jonathan Griffiths, who held off the cover with great determination as he ran for the line.

With Paul Bishop's tactical kicking becoming more of a feature and the forwards beginning to sense that they held the upper hand, Saints never looked

Opposite Referee John Holdsworth signals a touchdown in the Challenge Cup semi-final as St Helens try-scorers Alan Hunte (left) and Jonathan Griffiths celebrate. Hunte scored again in the final, but Griffiths could not reproduce this glorious form at Wembley.

back. Alan Hunte gathered Bishop's high kick for another try before Griffiths finished off good work by Ward and Tea Ropati, as well as Widnes's hopes. The lively Paul Groves, brought on in the first half for the solid front-rower Jonathan Neill, added a drop-goal to keep the pressure on.

There was disbelief in the Widnes camp afterwards that their plans had gone badly wrong. They had been drawn into a forward game, which their own forwards had not seemed to relish. Their link with the backs was strained by Tony Myler's absence, with the result that few chances came the way of the threequarters. Widnes's season, which had promised so much, had fallen flat. St Helens, confounding everyone as usual, went off grinning to their third Challenge Cup final in five years.

St Helens: Veivers; Hunte, Ropati, Loughlin, Quirk; Griffiths, Bishop; Neill, Dwyer, Ward, Harrison, Mann, Cooper

Substitutes: Groves for Neill after 26 minutes, Bailey for Loughlin after 76 minutes, Neill for Ward after 79 minutes

Scorers: tries – Griffiths (2), Hunte; goals – Loughlin (3); drop-goal – Groves

Widnes: Spruce; Devereux, Currier, Davies, Offiah; David Hulme, Paul Hulme; Sorensen, McKenzie, Faimalo, Eyres, Koloto, Holliday

Substitutes: Grima for Holliday after 32 minutes, McCurrie for McKenzie after 58 minutes

Scorer: goal – Davies

Referee: J. Holdsworth (Kippax)

Attendance: 16,109.

Wembley Stadium, 27 April

The Challenge Cup Final
St Helens 8 Wigan 13

Twelve points down after twelve minutes, the St Helens fans, who ought to have been used to this sort of thing, were once again burying their heads in their hands. So much confidence, built up over the season and illustrated by the fact that their coach, Mike McClennan, had named an unchanged side not minutes but a whole week before kick-off, had suddenly been flushed away. Had their optimism after the semi-final been false, were they really no better than two years ago or was it all just bad luck?

There was certainly an element of misfortune in the way they conceded the first try. Phil Veivers's percussive clash with Shaun Edwards was one of those things, but it had been a searching kick he had had to field, three Wigan players were in pursuit of it and Kevin Iro and David Myers showed great presence of mind in creating the touchdown. Mistakes, however they are made, can prove costly when Wigan are the opposition. They don't want to know you when you're down and out.

Wigan's second try was pure class. Dean Bell saw half a gap, side-stepped through it and Denis Betts, looking full of running, carried on the move before releasing to Frano Botica, who dived in at the corner for a beautiful try. There

Opposite
Twelve minutes into the Challenge Cup final St Helens found themselves 0–12 down and facing a whitewash. The final result, a 13–8 victory to Wigan, reflected great credit on the improved showing of Saints such as New Zealand forward George Mann.

were moments of hesitation in the St Helens defence that could be faulted, but few teams could have done anything to stop that move. Botica converted from the touchline to record his second goal.

The first goal, a penalty, looked to have come from a harsh decision. As Wigan fed the scrum from the touchline side, the ball came out from the Wigan second row and the alert Saints second-rower, George Mann, dropped on it. He was penalised for breaking from the scrum, which would have been a differential penalty, but when captain Shane Cooper questioned the decision, as he may have wrongly thought himself entitled to do, referee Jim Smith marched ten yards and Wigan were given a shot at goal. That was one of three penalties St Helens conceded in the opening quarter of an hour, but when given a penalty themselves they failed to find touch.

There was no lack of purpose on Saints' part. Their fierce tackles showed they meant business. But Wigan were not going to fall into the same trap as Widnes had done in the semi-final and were already pinning them back through Edwards's and Gregory's tactical kicks.

Too many of Saints' problems were of their own making. They dropped the ball early in the tackle count, sometimes because they were taking it stock-still and not running from depth. By the end of the first half their handling errors were almost into double figures – the statistics showed that they had held the ball for only forty-one plays, against Wigan's ninety. 'We made silly mistakes,' said the Saints scrum-half, Paul Bishop, 'dropping the ball and giving Wigan field position.' To play like this at Wembley was reckless, as Bishop pointed out, but to play like this against Wigan at Wembley was folly.

'We knew they would play with a lot of courage,' said John Monie. 'But really they beat themselves in the first ten or fifteen minutes and we just played the percentages and it got us home.' He could have added that no one did better in controlling play than Ellery Hanley. Clearly unable to perform at his best, he nevertheless set a fine example in patrolling the edges of the rucks and in carrying the ball forward securely.

St Helens had chances, later on in the half, particularly when a finely-judged chip ahead by Shane Cooper could have led to points if Alan Hunte had collected the ball cleanly. And then, almost on half-time, came their closest opportunity, when Gary Connolly, who had followed up the hard-working Bernard Dwyer's long run from dummy-half, kicked ahead, but Botica, covering back but with Les Quirk in pursuit, snatched the ball from danger in the in-goal area.

A St Helens try at that point would have given them a huge boost, but they put that disappointment behind them and came out stronger in the second half, just as they had done against Widnes. As in the semi-final, Paul Groves had come on midway through the first half as a tactical substitution for Jonathan Neill, but what enlivened Saints' attacking organisation was the movement of Shane Cooper from loose forward to stand-off, as Jonathan Griffiths replaced the concussed Paul Loughlin at centre. When Dwyer suffered the same fate, as well as a torn ear, St Helens's Jeanette Smith proved to be not only the first female physio to work at a Challenge Cup final, but also one of the busiest.

An early second-half score was what St Helens needed, but it was Wigan

who crucially opened up a 13-point margin. After a previous attempt had failed, Andy Gregory, who came close to receiving a record third Lance Todd Trophy, dropped a goal in the forty-seventh minute – the first score in the previous thirty-five minutes' play. St Helens lost another opportunity to get back when Paul Bishop, looking to have as little success with his kicking as with Warrington the year before, could not avenge his own fouling by Steve Hampson, who was sin-binned.

Wigan's Andy Goodway is held by Paul Bishop in the Challenge Cup final, as Shane Cooper (left) looks on and Bernard Dwyer moves in to complete the tackle.

Then it was Saints' turn to punish a Wigan error, when Veivers, who had returned, seized a stray ball and kept it moving for Griffiths to evade all attempts to put him down and fling a pass out to Hunte, who crossed in the sixty-third minute. Bishop's conversion and a further penalty-goal put Saints back in with a real chance. But again it was a question of how long they could hold the ball before getting into position to do anything with it. Their handling had been so much better in the second half and consequently they had been able to put Wigan under as much pressure as they had experienced in all their previous three final wins put together. But old habits die hard and in the last five minutes they twice put the ball down on the first tackle.

Despite their failings in vital areas, this had been a much better St Helens performance than 1989, or even the opening quarter of this match, had suggested. The club had been under much pressure from fans in the course of the previous two seasons, and there had been considerable speculation that Mike McClennan would leave before his contract was up, or even before the season was out. But he could take some satisfaction from knowing that they had given Wigan their first real test in a Challenge Cup final since 1985.

As for Wigan, unlike that unforgettable final against Hull in 1985, there were no star performances this time. Denis Betts took the award as the best player, but this was no Brett Kenny-style show. Kevin Iro, in what was supposedly his last match for Wigan, gave a sound display but couldn't add to his remarkable six tries in previous finals. Shaun Edwards, the only player to figure in every one of Wigan's unbeaten run of twenty successive Challenge Cup matches, was his usual tactically aware self, in partnership with the ever-creative Andy Gregory. Props Ian Lucas and Andy Platt got through a mountain of work, the foundation for their team's success. Ellery Hanley became the first captain to take the Challenge Cup on three consecutive occasions, and possibly the least fit.

'Wigan are so professional' is the comment that has echoed around Rugby League terraces and losers' dressing-rooms for several seasons now. That's because to all intents and purposes they are literally that, but also because, more often than any other team, they get things right on the big occasion. John Monie conceded that they didn't play great football on April 27th, but their power and control saw them through. Those things have to be worked for. Most other teams, given the circumstances at the end of the season, might not have felt the need to prove themselves for a fourth time, and could have capitulated against such hungry opponents as St Helens. 'We feel we're the best team in the comp,' said John Monie after their Championship success, 'and we don't want it stolen from us.' On such simple philosophy this latest Challenge Cup success was also based.

St Helens: Veivers; Hunte, Ropati, Loughlin, Quirk; Griffiths, Bishop; Neill, Dwyer, Ward, Harrison, Mann, Cooper

Substitutes: Connolly for Veivers after 8 minutes, Groves for Neill after 26 minutes, Neill for Loughlin at half-time, Veivers for Neill after 57 minutes

Scorers: try – Hunte; goals – Bishop (2)

Wigan: Hampson; Myers, Iro, Bell, Botica; Edwards, Gregory; Lucas, Dermott, Platt, Betts, Clarke, Hanley

Substitutes: Goodway for Clarke after 22 minutes, Goulding for Dermott after 61 minutes, Clarke for Lucas after 69 minutes

Scorers: tries – Myers, Botica; goals – Botica (2); drop-goal – Gregory

Referee: J. Smith (Halifax)

Attendance: 75,532.

THREE

The Regal Trophy

John Huxley

During the latter half of the 1980s Warrington threatened to become one of the major powers in professional Rugby League. For one reason or another they failed to fulfil that potential, and Wilderspool seemed permanently beset by serious injury problems. It is difficult to recall another club being similarly affected and the situation continued into the 1990s. Although they never failed to unearth a stream of talented young players who promised much, the Cheshire club constantly fell short of expectation.

By the time the calendar's pages were stripped back to reveal November 1990 Warrington were besieged by yet more injuries and finding life in the Stones Bitter Championship tedious. Occupying fourth-from-bottom place in the table with four wins from eleven league outings they hardly looked the kind of threat that would disturb the market leaders, Hull, Widnes and Wigan.

While fate and lack of consistent success may have dogged Warrington, they did not lack courage or endeavour. Their progress to the Regal Trophy final was as bewildering as it was amazing. Considering their league position and the loss of their inspirational leader, loose forward and captain, Mike Gregory, injured inevitably, they did particularly well and overcame the favourites, Widnes, on their way to face another enigmatic side, Bradford Northern, in the final at Headingley.

The Wire had unearthed a rare talent from Welsh Rugby Union in their scrum-half, Kevin Ellis. He had come north from Bridgend in July 1990 after earning the man-of-the-match award in their Schweppes Welsh Cup final defeat by the steam-rollering Neath. Warrington's Australian coach, Brian Johnson, saw Ellis as a potential stand-off, and when Ellis was given his first-team chance in October he played in the No. 6 jersey. The departure of the scrum-half, Paul Bishop, to St Helens under something of a cloud and the return to form of their Australian stand-off, Chris O'Sullivan, ensured that the 23-year-old Ellis switched to the No. 7 spot.

The Welshman thrived in his new sporting environment. He took to Rugby League like the proverbial duck, or at least a duckling, to water. In spite of a collection of rough edges, Ellis clearly had all the right ideas together with a long-range spin pass which freed players on the flanks because of its speed of delivery and accurate trajectory. When Warrington reached the final Ellis was an established part of their game plan even though he was playing just his twelfth game of senior Rugby League.

Warrington had recruited heavily from the Welsh game. Besides Ellis they had also signed during the autumn the international centre, Allan Bateman, and the second-row forward, Rowland Phillips, from Neath. The crossover from Union, still a very difficult feat, is slightly easier for a threequarter, for in that position there are greater similarities between the two codes. Bateman, whose speed off the mark had impressed Rugby League, was thus assured of a place in the Warrington team in the final while Phillips, whose forward apprenticeship presented more problems, was a substitute.

Bradford Northern, like Warrington, had been striving to move from the promising into the top classification for several years and arrived at Headingley having collected a notable scalp and with several Rugby Union signings in their team. In the third round they had been responsible for eliminating Wigan, the first holders of the Regal Trophy, at Central Park. An impressive notch on their record but still not enough to convince observers that they should start as clear favourites over Warrington. They were, however, lying fifth in the Stones Bitter Championship and that, at least, gave them the greater number of predictions in their favour.

Warrington prop Neil Harmon puts in a thunderous drive towards the Bradford Northern posts in the Regal Trophy final at Headingley. Besieged by injuries and uneven form, Warrington's 12–2 victory was a great achievement.

Bradford had looked to both Wales and New Zealand Rugby Union to bolster their playing strength. The former Cardiff winger, Gerald Cordle, scored enough tries in his first professional season to earn an international call and respect from the professional game as a lethal finisher. Two more recruits from the other side of the world had also established themselves in the Bradford colours. The scrum-half, Brett Iti, had been categorised as a future All Black, a New Zealand Union international, but through the good offices of the former New Zealand international League coach, Tony Gordon, he decided that his future lay in Rugby League and, more particularly, in British Rugby League. The same route to West Yorkshire had also been taken by their centre, Darrall Shelford, a member of the famous New Zealand rugby dynasty. His willowy frame belied the power and determination he employed, especially close to the try-line.

Northern had also recruited from Yorkshire Rugby Union. At the same time as they had brought Iti and Shelford across the world they had acquired the half-back, Neil Summers, from Headingley Rugby Union club. The No. 7 jersey, which enjoyed the protection of a traditionally strong Northern pack, was vacant following the departure of Paul Harkin to Leeds during the close season and both Union half-back imports were able to fill the position. Each demonstrated a capacity to do the job but, for the final, Bradford's experienced player-coach, David Hobbs, elected to play Iti at scrum-half and Summers at stand-off.

In spite of the myriad of riches available to both teams, the final was not perceived as being from Rugby League's high table. Neither club currently enjoys the greatest following; and the effect of too many seasons on the periphery of real, lasting success restricted the attendance to 11,154.

While the gap between the first and second divisions remained clear, the amateurs, who had three entries in the competition in Egremont (Cumbria), Saddleworth Rangers (Oldham) and Dudley Hill (Bradford), emphasised that the top clubs outside the Rugby Football League had managed to improve their standards. Almost inevitably, it seemed, two of the amateur sides were drawn together in the preliminary round, Saddleworth and Egremont repeating the previous season's BNFL National Amateur Cup final, while Dudley Hill entertained second-division Dewsbury in what was always going to be a keenly fought contest.

Saddleworth took revenge for their BARLA Cup final defeat by beating the Cumbrians 35–18 to earn a first-round placing against their near neighbours, Rochdale Hornets, while Dewsbury won through narrowly 24–18 at Dudley. Thus the Dewsbury coach, Maurice Bamford, was spared an embarrassing defeat by the amateur club he used to coach.

The previous season's beaten finalists, Halifax, whose financial problems had nearly forced them out of existence during the close season, were still finding their feet under new management when Leeds thrashed them 58–6, and Bradford Northern had to steel themselves to dispose of a brave Sheffield Eagles side 12–8 at the Don Valley Stadium. The goal-kicking of their player-coach, David Hobbs, proved crucial. As both sides scored two tries, Hobbs hit the target twice while Eagles failed to make their kicks count.

With the preliminary round out of the way, the main contenders jostled for position. The Humberside challenge was summarily dealt with. Widnes eliminated the league leaders, Hull, 24–16 after a fascinating battle which was televised regionally, while Leeds reduced promoted Hull KR's contribution to just one round by winning 26–22 at Headingley. The holders Wigan eased through 24–6 at Whitehaven, taking their unbeaten run in the competition to thirteen games – their previous defeat had been by Leeds in the 1987–88 semi-finals – while St Helens survived a spirited first-half performance by Swinton to win 31–7.

The second-division leaders, Salford, relegated the previous season, found Oldham, fifth from bottom of the first division, too strong for them at Watersheddings, while Rochdale Hornets beat Saddleworth Rangers 30–10 in front of 2,434 spectators at Spotland. The West Yorkshire hopes, Castleford, beat

Kiwi centre Gary Mercer was switched to the second row in Warrington's Regal Trophy run. Here he shuns the attentions of Bradford's Marchant, Noble and Hamer to get his pass away.

Fulham 14–8 at Crystal Palace, while Wakefield Trinity cruised through 40–8 against lowly Hunslet.

The two finalists each met second-division opposition. Warrington weathered the enthusiasm of their neighbours, Runcorn Highfield, who were still gripped in a run of defeats that took them more than two years to break – it was their sixty-fifth game without a win – while Bradford Northern came within an ace of defeat by a much improved Workington Town side, inspired by player-coach Ray Ashton, winning 12–11 at Odsal Stadium. Doncaster and Trafford Borough produced a 10–10 draw but the Yorkshire club took the second-round placing by winning the replay 19–6. The second round had to be spread over several days with three ties – Rochdale Hornets v Doncaster, Bradford Northern v Bramley and Featherstone Rovers v St Helens – all falling victims to harsh winter weather.

The 1990–91 Season

The two favourites, Widnes and Wigan, enjoyed big wins. The Chemics inflicted a 22–6 defeat on Leeds, who had been unbeaten in their previous five games. The Yorkshiremen had their Test forward, Paul Dixon, sent off for an off-the-ball incident while a Kevin Iro hat-trick inspired Wigan to a 36–16 win over second-division Keighley, with hooker Martin Dermott also dismissed. However, the second-division clubs still had something to offer as Batley proved when they beat Oldham 20–16 at Mount Pleasant to reach the quarter-finals for the first time, with player-coach Keith Rayne scoring a career-first hat-trick of tries. Warrington came up against second-division Leigh and moved through after an 11–6 win. Castleford gained a quarter-final placing by winning 20–4 at Wakefield Trinity on a bitterly cold day.

In the postponed games, St Helens produced one of the best performances of the season to win 33–16 at Featherstone Rovers. Bradford marched on by sinking Bramley 28–0 and Rochdale Hornets earned their first quarter-final place since 1973 by winning 14–10 at Doncaster. Hornets could have been forgiven for thinking that they were out of luck when they were drawn at Castleford. They were bottom of the first division with just one league victory to their credit but, amazingly, they came through to win 19–14, rather spoiling an extra special occasion for Castleford's John Joyner who scored his 200th career try during the game.

Warrington stabilised their form long enough to beat St Helens 18–12, Bradford Northern brought Wigan's long run crashing to a halt by winning 12–6 at Central Park – it was their third successive win over Wigan – while Widnes thrashed Batley 56–6 with their winger, Martin Offiah, scoring four tries and centre Andy Currier three.

Victory was paramount in Bradford Northern's mind when they beat Rochdale 13–2 in the first semi-final, staged at Headingley. Their rugby was hardly attractive but David Hobbs was adamant that winning was more important than aesthetics as far as he was concerned. Northern had reached the final for the first time in eleven years but it was their third major final appearance under Hobbs's control.

In the second semi-final at Central Park, Warrington turned the form book inside-out by beating Widnes 8–4. It was the Chemics first defeat in nine games and they went down without their Welsh ace, Jonathan Davies, who had injured himself in training. It was the sixth time the Wire had reached the final of the competition, leaving them just one place behind Widnes's record of seven finals.

Headingley, Leeds, 12 January

The Regal Trophy Final
Warrington 12 Bradford Northern 2

Bradford Northern went to the final as favourites even though they were going to be without their Great Britain forward, Karl Fairbank, who was ruled out by suspension. However, Warrington's win over Widnes in the semi-final had given the Wire much needed encouragement, their erratic form having pushed them down to the relegation zone at one stage.

Injuries to their full-back, David Lyon, and the prop, Neil Harmon, had disrupted Warrington's preparation. Of the pair, Lyon caused the greater concern, having suffered serious eye damage in an away league win at Wigan the previous Sunday. Lyon had been rushed to hospital and the diagnosis was a torn eyeball. A stray finger in a tackle had caused the problem though there was no suggestion of malice. He had temporarily lost his sight in the eye and, for a while, there was concern for his long-term condition. Within hours, however, that worry subsided and it became more a question of whether or not he would be fit for the big game. Moreover, Lyon was being mentioned as a probable candidate for Malcolm Reilly's Great Britain squad to face France, and he was certainly anxious to play and to enhance his reputation. By the Thursday evening it was clear that Lyon was winning his race and though some of the scarring remained, he passed a fitness test as did Harmon who had a shoulder problem.

Warrington captain Des Drummond and full-back David Lyon, who shrugged off an eye injury to kick four crucial goals in the final, raise the Regal Trophy.

The incentive to win was there for both sides. Warrington had been severely embarrassed by their 14–36 Wembley defeat by Wigan the previous season, while Bradford Northern had been 6–28 victims when Widnes won the Stones Bitter Premiership at Old Trafford. Those memories had to be expunged. Both teams arrived at Headingley with a reputation for being able to defend their line under pressure and this set the whole tone of the match. Warrington, under their Australian coach Brian Johnson, had worked hard on their defensive patterns and Northern certainly believed their tackling would stand up to any scrutiny.

Goal-kickers were clearly going to be important. They were to be the long-range artillery in this war of attrition. Hobbs, a 30-year-old former international, coached his side from open-side prop. Besides carrying a formidable reputation as a front-row man, he also possesses an accurate boot and he found the range first with a fifth-minute penalty after the Warrington second-row forward, Billy McGinty, had strayed offside in his own half. Hobbs sent the ball flying between the posts and Warrington had been warned. They clearly heeded the omen because they were not penalised for being offside again during the rest of the game. Bradford, too, knew what to expect after Ellis had sent his Welsh compatriot Bateman romping away on a penetrating run which Bradford ended with some difficulty.

The score settled Northern's nerves, while Warrington found it more difficult to gather their momentum because their Australian stand-off, Chris O'Sullivan, who had joined them from the Australian premiers, Canberra Raiders, muffed the first two passes he made. However, if the Wire's nerves had been jangling they did not allow that to affect their tackling; Northern, using Iti, Summers and the loose forward, John Pendlebury, to switch the points of attack, could not find a path through the Cheshire club's defence.

Northern's battering continued virtually unabated, while Warrington seemed content to contain. After thirty minutes Warrington drew level, and if Lyon's eyesight was impaired he did not show it when he landed a penalty after Northern's discipline slipped. Three minutes later Northern allowed their composure to drop once more and Lyon put Warrington in front with his second penalty of the game. Bradford resumed their search for a vital chink of light in the Warrington defence and they appeared to have found it just before half-time when Pendlebury sent his second-row forward, Paul Medley, on an angled run which was halted ten metres short of the Warrington line.

Under severe pressure Warrington lost their cool, conceding a penalty, and Bradford continued to batter at their line. But the Wire succeeded in keeping them at bay for the minute that remained until half-time. The trend was reversed in the second half. Warrington, having survived the Northern push, started to seek the initiative for themselves. A move engineered by their New Zealand Test hooker, Duane Mann, sent the rangy Lyon up the touchline; the Warrington skipper, Des Drummond, took the ball on but he lost possession to save the Bradford defence any further worry.

Warrington held the advantage but every time they moved inside the Bradford 22-metre area they ran out of inspiration and the match remained locked in frustration. Bradford unleashed their high-stepping Welsh winger, Gerald Cordle, but Warrington, although their defence was stretched, kept him away from their line.

Time was beginning to tick away and once again Bradford's composure slipped. Warrington's New Zealand Test centre, Gary Mercer, who had been converted into a second-row forward, was unfairly pulled back and Lyon landed his third penalty. That looked like being sufficient to win the Trophy but a late flourish produced the decisive and only try in the dying minutes of the game. O'Sullivan created the gap and Warrington's substitute forward, Mark Thomas, normally the provider of such passes, steamed through to touch down. Lyon added the goal and Warrington had presented themselves with a 12–2 win.

The hard-working Warrington forward, Billy McGinty, was voted man-of-the-match which indicated that endeavour far outweighed artistry in a final that ensured that Warrington had something to show for a season that threatened to be a disaster

Warrington: Lyon; Drummond, Bateman, Thorniley, Forster; O'Sullivan, Ellis; Harmon, Mann, Chambers, Mercer, McGinty, Cullen

Substitutes: Thomas for Chambers after 41 minutes, Phillips for Harmon after 79 minutes

Scorers: try – Thomas; goals – Lyon (4)

Bradford Northern: Wilkinson; Cordle, Shelford, Simpson, Marchant; Summers, Iti; Hobbs, Noble, Hamer, Medley, Croft, Pendlebury

Substitutes: Hellewell for Marchant after 40 minutes; Richards not used

Scorer: goal – Hobbs

Referee: J. Smith (Halifax)

Attendance: 11,154.

FOUR

The CIS Charity Shield, the Greenalls Lancashire Cup, and the John Smith's Yorkshire Cup

Paul Wilson, Ian Proctor

THE CIS CHARITY SHIELD · PAUL WILSON

The idea of staging the 1990 CIS Charity Shield match in South Wales was to expose a fresh and potentially receptive audience to top level Rugby League; if not specifically to tempt Rugby Union consumers with the forbidden fruit, then to set out a costermonger's stall capable of withstanding close inspection.

An exercise in preaching to the converted was not envisaged, but that was before Jonathan Davies took a hand. Playing his first game in his home country since his switch of codes eighteen months earlier, the Widnes centre showed spectators at Swansea City's Vetch Field exactly what they had been missing, with a virtuoso hat-trick of tries in a 16-point contribution which won him the man-of-the-match award by a considerable distance.

South Wales's rugby followers would be among the last people in the world to need convincing of Davies's match-winning brilliance, but the former Welsh captain was not the only crossover from Union to impress in Widnes's 24–8 defeat of Wigan. In what was virtually a case of preaching by the converted, every point in the game was contributed by a recruit from the amateur code. John Devereux, Davies's fellow national, scored an important try for Widnes on the stroke of half-time, and Martin Offiah, once of Rosslyn Park, gained the first touchdown of a fourth successive chart-topping season. Davies kicked two goals for Widnes and saw two further attempts rebound from uprights, while all Wigan's points – a try and two goals – were supplied by their newcomer Frano Botica, a summer arrival from the New Zealand All Blacks.

But it was Davies, attitude and aptitude seemingly toughened by his success on the eventful Great Britain tour of New Zealand and Papua New Guinea, who predictably hogged the headlines. 'Everybody wants to do well in front of their own folk, and I couldn't have asked for a better return,' he said afterwards. 'That was the first hat-trick in my entire career, Union or League, but it was a super team effort. Keeping my place in this side is still going to be hard work, but I'm happy now that centre is my best position. It's where I want to play.'

As a showpiece, the Charity Shield was ill-served by the Swansea weather, though both sides won plaudits for their handling skills and their willingness to move the ball wide in spite of a day-long downpour. In the circumstances, a crowd of 11,178 was encouraging enough – with about as many curious locals present as dedicated followers on the 460-mile round trip from the north – though the value of the event, as public relations or as meaningful missionary work, can only be judged in the context of what comes next.

Jonathan Davies outstrips the Wigan defence to score one of his three tries in Swansea. The former Welsh Rugby Union ace finished with thirty tries for Widnes in 1990–91.

What comes next is a day trip to Gateshead. The year after, who knows? The concept of the Charity Shield as a moveable feast is an improvement on the Isle of Man years, when it was a very stationary picnic, but in essence the event is still a jaunt, a construction altogether too lightweight to bear weighty responsibilities like expansion and conversion. As long as this is realised there is no reason why it should not continue to be enjoyed by players, spectators and new audiences alike. Friends made one day may be lost the next, but no matter, no actual harm is done unless anyone confuses the Rugby League's annual outing for its expansion policy. As everyone knows, nothing of substance can be built in a day. The recipe for real progress is still the same as it ever was – requiring massive amounts of time, work and, above all, money.

Widnes's second row Emosi Koloto was one of seven former Rugby Union stars on show when the CIS Charity Shield match was played in the hotbed of the game in Swansea. The converts scored all the points between them as Widnes defeated Wigan 24–8.

Widnes: Tait; Devereux, Currier, Davies, Offiah; Myler, David Hulme; Ashurst, McKenzie, Grima, Paul Hulme, Koloto, Holliday

Substitutes: Sorensen for Paul Hulme after 20 minutes, Wright for Ashurst after 57 minutes, Ashurst for Holliday after 67 minutes

Scorers: tries – Davies (3), Devereux, Offiah; goals – Davies (2)

Wigan: Gilfillan; Myers, Byrne, Bell, Preston; Botica, Goulding; Skerrett, Bridge, Wane, Gildart, Platt, Betts

Substitutes: Forshaw for Gildart after 22 minutes, Gildart for Wane and Edwards for Botica after 40 minutes, Botica for Gilfillan after 62 minutes

Scorers: try – Botica; goals – Botica (2)

Referee: C. Morris (Huddersfield)

Attendance: 11,178

THE GREENALLS LANCASHIRE CUP · IAN PROCTOR

Eighty-five years after their introduction, the County Cup competitions are presently under greater scrutiny than ever before from the game's decision-makers. There are those who believe that the Lancashire and Yorkshire Cup competitions have overstayed their welcome and, by their very titles, invite criticism from those who claim that Rugby League is too parochial for its own good.

On the other hand, traditionalists argue that there is nothing wrong with a format which, throughout the game's history, has provided an early-season opportunity for coaches to assess their staff without dropping league points; which offers the clubs a chance to put a trophy on the sideboard; and which usually provides a feast of entertaining football for the paying spectators. Significantly, gates have greatly increased at County Cup-ties in recent years.

The Greenalls Lancashire Cup introduced a dreaded preliminary round in 1989, as Chorley gave birth to Trafford Borough. Appropriately, they had been paired together, but the 1990 draw brought an intriguing opening contest between relegated Salford and promoted Rochdale Hornets. It was a game which offered ample proof, if any were needed, that there was something drastically awry with the game's promotion and demotion system. The Reds, inspired by their two-try former Wales Rugby Union international, Adrian Hadley, and six-goal Steve Kerry, humiliated Allan Agar's team, 41–12, at Spotland. It was to be the start of a triumphant season for Kevin Tamati's men, and the beginning of a harrowing season for the Hornets.

The first round proper further emphasised the gulf in playing standards between the divisions. Thankfully, none of the results was on the scale of St Helens's 112-point slaughter of Carlisle in 1986, but the two pre-tournament favourites, Wigan and Widnes, handed out 70-point hidings to Barrow and

Whitehaven respectively, while Saints, with their Test prop, Kevin Ward, making a try-scoring debut, amassed 56 points against Trafford Borough, though Mike Peers's men stuck bravely to their task and replied with 24.

Those perennial strugglers, Runcorn Highfield, also conceded a half-century of points, at Fulham, where Greg Pearce equalled the Londoners' goal-kicking record, firing eleven in the 50–0 victory. Jonathan Davies was another record-breaker, for Widnes, emulating Andy Currier's points-in-a-match tally of 34, with four tries and nine goals in a magical display against Whitehaven at the Recreation Ground. There was, too, an inevitable hat-trick for Martin Offiah in Widnes's 70–6 away win.

Shaun Edwards, with four tries, led the way for Wigan, while the former All Black, Frano Botica, gave a hint of things to come with a try and eight goals in their 70–8 home defeat of Barrow, for whom Nigel Simpson recorded a consolation try. The holders, Warrington, welcomed their former Great Britain forward, Bob Eccles, back to Wilderspool in his capacity as player-coach of Chorley, then proceeded to win 36–4. Their Under-21 international, Neil Harmon, powered his way over for two tries and there was a fine goal-kicking display from David Lyon. Fittingly, Eccles scored Chorley's solitary try.

Salford, after their comprehensive defeat of Rochdale, had Andy Burgess in excellent form as they claimed the scalp of another promoted side, Oldham, by 27–24, in a highly entertaining encounter at the Willows. Carlisle emphatically won the Cumbrian derby against Workington, 38–18, with their under-rated centre, Kevin Pape, scoring two tries; and Alex Murphy's Leigh had little trouble in disposing of an outclassed Swinton, 26–6, at Hilton Park.

The crucial tie of the competition was the Widnes v Wigan quarter-final at Naughton Park, where the Chemics, fresh from a Jonathan Davies-inspired Charity Shield victory over the champions, repeated the victory, again thanks to the mercurial Welshman. In front of more than 13,000 fans, Widnes led at the interval, but looked likely to go out as they trailed going into the last three minutes. Then Davies scored a try at the corner to level matters and duly struck a soaring touchline conversion to earn his colleagues a win bonus and keep Widnes on course for an overdue first County Cup-final in eight years.

Salford produced the shock of the tournament, inflicting a 21–7 defeat on a disappointing St Helens side at the Willows. Four tries to one emphasised their right to a semi-final place and Kevin Tamati had the satisfaction of putting one over on his fellow-New Zealander, Mike McClennan. Carlisle, after their impressive start to the season under yet another New Zealander, Cameron Bell, bravely tested Warrington for an hour in their Gillford Park encounter. But, after sharing the spoils at half-time, Martin Crompton,with two tries, and an inspired Paul Bishop steered the Wires a step closer to a second successive final. Leigh comfortably saw off the Fulham challenge, with Ian Jeffrey scoring a hat-trick of tries in a 40–8 victory and the prodigal, John Woods, skipper of Leigh's last Lancashire Cup-winning side a decade earlier, contributed two more.

The semi-final draw ensured an inter-divisional final, Widnes being paired at home with Warrington, who had denied them at this stage twelve months previously, while Salford were rewarded for success over the Saints with yet another home tie against Leigh.

Warrington defended resolutely for a long time at Naughton Park, two 'Rocky' Turner penalty-goals giving them a slender interval lead, but the floodgates opened in the second half. The new Widnes skipper, Tony Myler, the sole survivor from their previous Lancashire Cup-final appearance in 1983, opened the try-scoring and inspired his men to a 20–4 victory. Darren Wright and Alan Tait embellished the victory with further tries.

At the Willows, Salford booked their second County Cup-final appearance in three years with a comfortable 16–7 defeat of Leigh. Rugby Union converts, David Fell (from Orrell), the scorer of both tries, and Steve Kerry (from Preston Grasshoppers), with four goals, led the way, while Mike Round scored a vain try and Paul Topping kicked a goal and a first-half drop-goal for Leigh.

Central Park, Wigan, 29 September

The Lancashire Cup Final
Widnes 24 Salford 18

Doug Laughton's decision to gamble on the fitness of his ace winger, Martin Offiah, paid rich dividends, as his unique finishing qualities earned Widnes their first Lancashire Cup triumph for eleven years. But, for long periods, gallant Salford had threatened to cause a major upset.

The ex-Widnes favourite, Kevin Tamati, had his young team fired up for the start of this decider, a repeat of the 1974 and 1975 finals, and, after conceding an early penalty to Jonathan Davies, the second-division side took the lead following an uncharacteristic blunder from the full-back, Alan Tait. The Scot completely missed a kick-through by busy Andy Burgess and Peter Williams was on hand to complete the formality of touching down.

Steve Kerry missed with a difficult conversion and was also off-target with a penalty chance. When Widnes opened out in flamboyant style to take a 12–4 lead, the writing appeared to be on the wall for Salford. They were their own worst enemies during this unsettled period. David Fell's ambitious pass was gratefully intercepted by Andy Currier, who raced sixty yards for the try, and, five minutes later, Arthur Bradshaw was banished to the sin-bin following a dangerously high tackle on Sorensen. Almost immediately, Currier did further damage, unloading from a tackle and sending Tony Myler jinking to the posts.

Tamati threw his fellow-countryman, Shane Hansen, into the fray, replacing the hard-working prop, Chris Whiteley, and Salford were transformed. Kerry reduced the arrears with a penalty-goal before Salford squared matters a minute from the break. The Cumbrian, Martin Birkett, produced a scintillating forty-yard break, and hooker Mark Lee sent Ian Blease over, for Kerry to level matters.

On the resumption the pendulum swung back in favour of the underdogs as Sorensen was sin-binned for a tackle which left Lee prostrate, and Offiah had a try disallowed. Then Salford, not Widnes, broke the deadlock with a piece of brilliant individualism from Peter Williams. His short grubber-kick on the half-way line was perfection itself and the former Great Britain centre regathered the ball at pace, fed Adrian Hadley, and there to take the Welshman's inside pass was the man-of-the-match, David Fell, who scooted away for a glorious try. Kerry made it 18–12.

The turning point came seventeen minutes from time, when Kerry missed with a kickable penalty attempt from forty yards. Salford seemed deflated by

Salford's scrum-half Steve Kerry was the top points-scorer in 1990–91, largely by virtue of his 177 goals. Yet his three missed kicks were the difference between the sides in the Lancashire Cup final, which Widnes won 24–18.

the miss, and, from that point, Widnes stepped up the pace to salvage their expected victory. Twelve minutes from time, Sorensen sent the substitute, David Smith, crashing over for an equalising score, and, with six minutes remaining, and only the first Lancashire Cup final replay in twenty-three years looming, Phil McKenzie created the position for Offiah to show his incomparable finishing qualities from close range. Consolation for Salford came with the nomination of their stand-off, David Fell, as man-of-the-match.

Salford: Gibson; Evans, Birkett, Williams, Hadley; Fell, Kerry; Sherratt, Lee, Whiteley, Burgess, Blease, Bradshaw

Substitutes: Hansen for Whiteley after 30 minutes, Cassidy for Kerry after 70 minutes

Scorers: tries – Williams, Blease, Fell; goals – Kerry (3)

Widnes: Tait; Wright, Currier, Davies, Offiah; Myler, David Hulme; Sorensen, McKenzie, Ashurst, Eyres, Koloto, Holliday

Substitutes: Smith for Ashurst after 31 minutes; Devereux not used

Scorers: tries – Currier, Myler, Smith, Offiah; goals – Davies (4)

Referee: A. Burke (Manchester)

Attendance: 7,458.

THE JOHN SHITH'S YORKSHIRE CUP · IAN PROCTOR

The preliminary round, played in mid-August, contained two matches of contrasting quality. One, at Nottingham, brought a cricket score in cricket weather for newly promoted Hull Kingston Rovers; but there was a real fright for the holders, Bradford Northern, in their home meeting with Sheffield Eagles.

The Robins ran in no less than eighteen tries and amassed a club record score in the 100–6 victory over Mel Wibberley's men. Their Australian centre, Greg Austin, scored six of those tries and winger Anthony Sullivan five, while Colin Armstrong equalled the club goal-kicking record, landing fourteen in a game which can have done little for the game's credibility in the East Midlands.

At Odsal, Bradford and Sheffield produced a titanic struggle, with the tantalising prospect of a lucrative visit to Leeds being the prize for the winners. Beaten at the second-round stage by Northern in 1989, Sheffield were unfortunate to have a Mark Gamson 'try' disallowed in a first half which they dominated territorially. The sin-binning of their volatile forward, Sonny Nickle, also proved costly, and tries from David Cooper, Gerald Cordle and Ian Wilkinson ensured a 20–12 Northern win.

The only all-first-division ties of the first round produced the anticipated top-drawer football, but also two unexpected away victories for Bradford at Headingley, and for Castleford against Hull. More than 14,000 fans saw John

Gallagher's debut for Leeds and while the former All Black was involved in a stunning move which brought a quality try for Phil Ford, it was the ex-Leeds pair, Paul Medley and Mark Wilson, who had the last laugh. Medley stormed through for two tries in a man-of-the-match display and Wilson got the better of his duel with Paul Harkin, the man he had previously understudied, as Northern, for a second successive year, took the spoils in a first-round tie against their arch-rivals.

At the Boulevard, another player tormenting his former club was Lee Crooks, who pulled all the right strings in Castleford's 10–6 defeat of Hull. There was a debut try for Hull's Aboriginal threequarter, Brad Webb, but it came too late to alter the outcome, after the visitors had established a match-winning 10-point cushion.

Halifax, following a summer of grave uncertainty about their future, gave their incoming coach, Peter Roe, a fine start as Colin Atkinson scored three tries in the 40–4 defeat of disappointing Doncaster. Dewsbury, with a 26–14 home defeat of Keighley, and Batley, coming from behind to gain a home win over Huddersfield, also made progress in other all-second-division contests.

Bramley never looked capable of pulling rank over Featherstone at Post Office Road, where Rovers' internationals, Chris Bibb and Paul Newlove, were impressive in a 36–4 home victory. Hunslet caused one or two flutters at Belle Vue, though, Tim Lumb and Michael Jackson inspiring their side to a shock 18–14 interval lead against Wakefield. The front-rower, Stephen Potts, sporting a Mohican-style haircut, and Mark Conway led the Trinity fightback which ended in a 28–18 victory. Hull KR found their visit to Ryedale Stadium much more demanding than their preliminary visit to the Harvey Haddon Stadium, but emerged 10–0 victors, despite a masterly scrum-half performance from the veteran York player-coach, Gary Stephens.

Bradford's clash with Castleford was the outstanding tie of the quarter-finals, and Northern, unable to use Odsal, were forced into a switch to Bradford City's Valley Parade. It was a move which hardly benefited the 'home' side and they became victims of the finest goal-kicking exhibition of Lee Crooks's free-scoring career. The former Great Britain forward hit the mark nine times in a dazzling Castleford exhibition and the size of their 42–12 victory margin must have been beyond the wildest expectations of their demanding Australian coach, Darryl Van de Velde. Not surprisingly, Castleford were immediately installed as favourites to regain the trophy they had last won in 1986.

Hull KR, with Austin and Sullivan again to the fore, produced an incredible second-half rally to erase a 3–18 deficit and win 31–22 at Post Office Road in a game in which ten sparkling tries were evenly shared. It was to be a foretaste of Featherstone's entire season as a profligate defence regularly undid the work of one of the most potent attacking forces in the game.

Dewsbury triumphed in the 'Heavy Woollen' derby against Batley, 18–8, at Crown Flatt, with the ex-Batley Boys product, Paul Shuttleworth, outstanding. Maurice Bamford's men booked their first semi-final place for eleven years, while Wakefield Trinity had too much forward power for Halifax at Belle Vue, where the second-rowers, Andy Kelly and Gary Price, proved irresistible in their hard-earned 26–17 home victory.

Paired at home with second-division opposition for a third successive round, David Topliss's men were handed a golden opportunity to book their first Yorkshire Cup final appearance for sixteen seasons, and they did not squander it. Their big-kicking, ex-Under-21 international, Kevin Harcombe, took his Yorkshire Cup goals tally to thirteen in three games, and Trinity plainly possessed too much class for gallant Dewsbury. Their 25–2 victory margin was the by-product of four quality tries.

At Wheldon Road, Castleford never looked in danger against the second-division champions, Hull KR, and two tries in a five-minute spell just after the interval proved the turning point. Castleford's record signing, Graham Steadman, was outstanding and their teenager, Graham Southernwood, scored a memorable try as they booked their seventh Yorkshire Cup final appearance in a decade. But the Elland Road venue was hardly a favoured one, the Glassblowers having lost a series of major matches there, including three Yorkshire Cup finals, during the 1980s.

Elland Road, Leeds, 23 September

The Yorkshire Cup Final

Castleford 11 Wakefield Trinity 8

David Plange, appearing in his first match of the season, emerged as the hero of Castleford's fourth Yorkshire Cup final triumph in a tense meeting with neighbours Wakefield. It was his controversial sixty-third-minute try which separated two well-matched teams at the finish, after the winger's earlier try-saving tackle on Trinity's Andy Mason had saved a certain 4 points and kept depleted Castleford in the hunt.

Plange had been in dispute with the club at the start of the season but settled his differences in time to make a fifth Yorkshire Cup final appearance. It was just as well for a Castleford side lacking evergreen John Joyner, a hero of their three previous triumphs in 1977, 1981 and 1986, and the influential Australian half-back, Gary French. Gary Atkins, a recent signing from Ryedale-York, deputised at scrum-half.

Wakefield were seeking their first major trophy since lifting the Championship back in 1968. They settled quicker than Castleford, took the lead after five minutes and held it for almost an hour. There could be no faulting the effort of a side which contained the man-of-the-match in Tracey Lazenby, but, as David Topliss admitted afterwards, they lacked the finesse to finish off a side which was on the ropes for a long spell.

Trinity should have been on the scoreboard in the opening minute, when Kevin Harcombe failed with a thirty-five-yard penalty attempt after Mark Conway had been flattened by Dean Sampson, but four minutes later they opened the try-scoring with a glorious move involving Lazenby and the centre, Andy Mason. From a scrum heel, the former Colts international set off on an arcing run and produced a perfect inside pass which invited Mason to complete a straight run to the line. Harcombe added a touchline conversion and Trinity were in the driving seat.

Almost immediately Castleford hit back. Quality handling in the opposition quarter ended with Neil Roebuck's short pass sending Atkins over for his first try for the club. Crooks missed with the goal attempt, and Trinity extended their lead to 8–4 in the seventeenth minute, when Harcombe made Castleford

Castleford's Jeff Hardy and Wakefield Trinity's Billy Conway pursue a loose ball during the Yorkshire Cup final, as grounded Kiwi prop Adrian Shelford looks on. Castleford defeated a gallant Wakefield side by 11–8.

pay for being caught offside. Castleford dominated the spell before half-time, forcing Trinity into two goal-line drop-outs but being unable to breach a defence in which Nigel Bell and John Thompson, and the New Zealander, Adrian Shelford, making his debut for Trinity, worked overtime.

The turning point came three minutes into the second half, as Wakefield went for the killer try. Plange, somehow, got back to make a miraculous cover tackle on Mason, after Lazenby had repeated his first-half run to create the opening for his centre. Trinity never really threatened again and Crooks reduced the deficit to 6–8 with a penalty-goal after Mark Conway was adjudged to have held down Irwin in a tackle.

Seventeen minutes from time, Plange broke the deadlock. St John Ellis and Steve Larder did well on the right, and a long pass from Graham Southernwood uncovered Plange but the try still needed scoring and the former Doncaster man arrowed himself bravely for the corner. Trinity's David Jones desperately threw himself at Plange and there was some doubt about whether there had been a double-movement before the actual touchdown. But Mr Smith had no hesitation in awarding the try, and it became a different game as Wakefield were forced to chase a result.

Despite piling on the pressure in the dying minutes, Trinity never really seemed likely to regain the lead, and the final score came with the last kick of the game, Roebuck firing a simple drop-goal to secure a 3-point victory. For Lee Crooks it was his fifth winners medal from as many finals and he joined the elite band of players to captain three different clubs to success, having previously skippered Hull in 1984 and Leeds in 1988.

Castleford: Larder; Ellis, Irwin, Anderson, Plange; Steadman, Atkins; Crooks, Southernwood, Sampson, Battye, Hardy, Roebuck

Substitutes: England for Atkins after 48 minutes, Ketteridge for Battye after 76 minutes

Scorers: tries – Atkins, Plange; goal – Crooks; drop-goal – Roebuck.

Wakefield Trinity: Harcombe; Jones, Mason, Eden, Wilson; Lazenby, Mark Conway; Shelford, Billy Conway, Thompson, Kelly, Price, Bell

Substitutes: Slater for Billy Conway after 37 minutes, Perry for Kelly after 54 minutes

Scorers: try – Mason; goals – Harcombe (2)

Referee: J. Smith (Halifax)

Attendance: 11,800.

FIVE

The Slalom Lager Alliance League

Ian Proctor

In the Alliance League's Yorkshire Senior Cup final, at a bleak and blustery Odsal in November, few of the 1,126 diehards present fancied the chances of Bradford Northern, from the second division of the Alliance, unsettling a Hull side from the first division and at that point still unbeaten. But, with their 1990 Lions tourist, Roger Simpson, scoring an outstanding first-minute try from seventy-five yards, the only one of a game in which defences dominated, Bradford emerged 6–4 victors.

Then, compelled to travel to the Boulevard for the semi-final of the Alliance Challenge Cup, Northern's youngsters surpassed even Simpson's expectations by securing a 10–8 winning margin and becoming the first side ever to defeat Hull's Alliance team on their own soil. Bradford's former local Rugby Union centre, David Cooper, was the hero, scoring both tries. Northern eclipsed five first-division clubs – Wigan, St Helens, Salford, Hull, and, in the final, Castleford – to take the Challenge Cup, and the £1,000 winners cheque, for the first time in the competition's seven-year history.

The final was again watched by a healthy 3,000-plus crowd and they saw Northern completely overrun Mick Morgan's experienced Castleford side. Superior in every department, winning comprehensively by 25–4, Bradford's side contained the outstanding individual of the match in the promising young back-row forward, Paul Rhodes. His strong-running display duly earned him the man-of-the-match award, but there were equally impressive performances from the rotund prop, Paul Grayshon, son of Jeff, the goal-kicking stand-off Alex Green, the busy scrum-half Mark Wilson, and Great Britain's Under-21 international full-back, Darren Moxon. In the vanquished Castleford ranks, the teenage loose forward, Andy Hay, confirmed the Wheldon Road belief that he is a player with an immense future.

Hull retained their first-division title almost at a canter. Winning their first fourteen league matches, avoiding defeat until going down to John Holmes's Leeds at Headingley in January, where Leeds's Kenyan winger, Eddie Rombo, scored a memorable try, they opened up an unassailable 10-point gap at the top of the table. There was never any doubt that their promising young coaches, Steve Crooks and Stan Pickering, and another well-disciplined young side would reap their due reward.

The Boulevarders have shown the way at Alliance level for a number of years and there was great satisfaction at the club when Steve McNamara, man-of-the match in last season's Cup final, was named in the Great Britain Under-21 sides which opposed France in January and February. A sobering moment, too, for those who remain sceptical about the value of Alliance football, came when Hull deservedly won their Premiership final against Widnes at Old Trafford in

May. More than half-a-dozen of that side started their professional careers in the Alliance team.

Promotion and relegation issues were less clear-cut than the championship in each division. Leigh and Salford finished in the bottom two positions in the first division, after Warrington Wizards had staged a marvellous comeback to avoid a seemingly inevitable drop into the second. Workington Town's admirable revival was not confined to their first team and, after a remarkable show of consistency in the latter stages of the season, their Alliance side will be Cumbria's sole representatives in next season's first division.

Sheffield Eagles' skipper, Neil Kellett, deserves a creditable mention, too, for his achievement in averaging almost a try a game during the course of a vastly improved Alliance season for the South Yorkshiremen. In only their second season at this level, the Eagles maintained a constant outside challenge for promotion. With a young team full of potential, which performed admirably for their coach, Eric Fitzsimons, who has now sadly departed for Oldham, they seem likely to be major promotion contenders in 1991–92.

By their own high standards, Wigan, fifth in the first division, and Widnes, fourth from bottom, enjoyed modest seasons. But they contested the Lancashire County Shield final at Central Park in November. It proved to be a game in which Wigan's teenage British Lions tourist Bobby Goulding starred. Frustrated at his lack of first-team opportunities, following an outstanding contribution to the success of the 1990 Lions tour, he toyed with his hometown team and claimed the man-of-the-match award after his side's 22–10 victory.

The Alliance League chairman, Roy Waudby, in his end-of-season speech, paid wholesome tribute to those individuals and clubs who had had the belief and desire to resurrect reserve-team football in the dark days of 1984. He also expressed the hope that the three professional clubs without Alliance sides – Runcorn Highfield, Nottingham City and Chorley – would eventually see the light. There were words of warning, too, from this deep-thinking official, and Mr Waudby was scathing in replying to a comment in one of the game's publications, which criticised Alliance teams for allegedly playing under-age players.

The Alliance League's player-of-the-year award went to Salford's Shaun Brown, a player who battled in vain to prevent his side from being relegated from the first division. Following in the footsteps of Hunslet's Tim Lumb, who took the individual title in identical circumstances in 1990, Brown, denied a first-team spot only by the league's leading points-scorer, Steve Kerry, was a model of consistency for the Red Devils. His aim now will be again to emulate Lumb, who was named in the Great Britain Under-21 international squad in January.

WEBSTER'S
YORKSHIRE BITTER

Bradford Northern celebrate their 25–4 victory over an experienced Castleford side in the Alliance Challenge Cup final, adding the trophy to the Alliance League's Yorkshire Senior Cup which they won earlier in the season.

Final Slalom Lager Alliance League Tables, 1990–91

Division 1

	P	W	D	L	Points F	Points A	Pts
Hull	26	24	–	2	729	336	48
Hull KR	26	18	–	8	616	424	36
Castleford	26	16	–	10	690	527	32
Oldham	26	14	–	12	488	514	28
Wigan	26	13	1	12	596	553	27
Leeds	26	13	–	13	680	569	26
Halifax	26	12	2	12	546	604	26
St Helens	26	12	1	13	660	601	25
Warrington	26	12	–	14	621	600	24
Featherstone R	26	10	2	14	559	591	22
Widnes	26	11	–	15	628	681	22
Wakefield T	26	10	–	16	466	590	20
Salford	26	8	–	18	488	663	16
Leigh	26	6	–	20	374	878	12

Division 2

	P	W	D	L	Points F	Points A	Pts
Bradford N	24	20	–	4	900	354	40
Workington T	24	18	1	5	517	411	37
Rochdale H	24	17	1	6	521	355	35
Carlisle	24	15	3	6	632	311	33
Hunslet	24	16	1	7	572	445	33
Dewsbury	24	14	2	8	490	389	30
Sheffield E	24	14	–	10	636	489	28
Batley	24	13	1	10	481	399	27
Swinton	24	12	2	10	534	463	26
Doncaster	24	11	1	12	405	377	23
Ryedale-York	24	9	–	15	460	453	18
Huddersfield	24	9	–	15	507	555	18
Barrow	24	9	–	15	361	562	18
Fulham	24	9	–	15	352	568	18
Keighley	24	7	1	16	448	636	15
Bramley	24	7	–	17	332	734	14
Trafford B	24	6	–	18	395	596	12
Whitehaven	24	3	1	20	257	703	7

SIX

Five Players of the Season

Trevor Watson

My main difficulty in again selecting five players of the season was deciding whom to leave out. It would certainly have been possible this time to have chosen five quite different players and still have gained personal satisfaction and perhaps an entirely different group of supporters for my choice.

The lack of overseas names gives some feeling of satisfaction and suggests that 'Made in Britain' is once again a label of which all of us can be proud, particularly with the Lions next tour to Australia just around the corner.

I make no apology for the reappearance of some of the names. In my view, they were simply the best during an intriguing season.

GARRY SCHOFIELD (LEEDS)

Garry won one of the game's top awards at the year's end when he was named man-of-the-year for his efforts. But another massive tribute to Schofield came over the Easter period when Wakefield Trinity's coach, David Topliss, observed: 'If we had Schofield, we would be in the top five and Leeds would be struggling against relegation.'

Topliss, as a former quality stand-off himself, recognised the efforts of Schofield at No. 6 in doing almost every conceivable job to keep Leeds ticking over in what was a very hit-and-miss season for them. He was leader, organiser, tactical kicker, tackler, occasional goal-kicker and top try-scorer for Leeds. He did well enough to keep out several leading candidates and gain the stand-off position for Great Britain; and his slick chip and regather helped to bring about one of the tries of the season in the first Test at Wembley.

Schofield also collected a hat-trick of tries in the second Test against France and his role in that game was recognised by the man-of-the-match award, despite the fact that Martin Offiah had scored five tries.

Schofield has become a much stronger player and it is possible to see him eventually settling at loose forward and perhaps gaining representative honours there too.

Left
Garry Schofield

Above
Jon Sharp

JON SHARP (HULL)

Perhaps this is a surprise choice because Sharp's name is unlikely to figure among the leading try-scorers. But it should always be one of the first on the Hull team-sheet for he is that precious asset, the 100 per cent worker.

Sharp is not an elegant player but his bustling, wholehearted style of play has made him an important member of a team that created its share of upsets, not least in the Premiership final. In that match he had the knack of being on hand time and again to drive the ball in. His strength enabled him to break many tackles and to run that important forty yards to clear his lines and set up an attack. Throughout the match he helped Hull to keep ticking over when things were threatening to go wrong. He may not gain many representative honours, but if he stays free of injury he will play many more matches for his club.

Defensively, too, Sharp did his stint, beavering away in his unobtrusive manner, rarely spotted by the crowds, but so effective on behalf of his team. His efforts at least were recognised at the Boulevard, where he was named player-of-the-year, and there were no complaints at such a choice.

ELLERY HANLEY (WIGAN)

If nothing else, the 1990–91 season underlined Wigan and Great Britain's enormous debt to Hanley as player and captain. He led from the front, again proving a tremendous driving force, using that superb mixture of balance and strength to make openings where none appeared to exist. There was no better example of this quality than in the first Test at Wembley when his driving run, kick and follow-up created the position for Britain's opening try. Little wonder that in the remaining Tests he was marked so closely.

At Wembley for Wigan in the Challenge Cup final his value as captain stood out. Clearly far from fit, the fact that Ellery was there inspired a weary team when the pressure was on. He was unable to produce sustained bursts, but did enough to make his presence felt, with his organising powers and his habit of always making a crucial tackle. This was evident in the second half when he stopped St Helens's second-rower, George Mann, when there was a sizeable overlap.

Hanley never shirked the tricky tasks, driving the ball in and making the awkward tackle, and had the knack of seeming always to be in position to drop on the loose ball. And an abiding memory remains of his familiar curving run towards the right wing, invariably making the opposition tremble.

Left
Ellery Hanley

Above
Denis Betts

DENIS BETTS (WIGAN)

It was fitting that the non-stop efforts of Betts throughout the season should be recognised in Wigan's last match, when he was awarded the Lance Todd Trophy for the outstanding performance in the Challenge Cup final at Wembley. Typically, he felt it should have gone elsewhere, to his colleague Andy Platt.

One of the new breed of full-time players, Betts appeared in every match for Wigan and also produced all-out performances for Great Britain in the fiercely competitive Ashes series. And he was still young enough to be elected young-player-of-the-year.

Though a relative lightweight by today's standards, Betts made his presence felt by the strength and pace of his running. Ever ready to take on the hard graft, he proved an exceptionally difficult man to stop and frequently made ground in the well-defended area down the middle. He also had the knack of forcing his way over the line through close-tackling defenders, and three of the twelve tries he scored for Wigan came this way in those vital last three matches of the season.

There was much relief at club and international level when Betts showed his good sense in turning down a substantial offer to play in Australia during the summer in order to conserve his considerable energies for home duties during the 1991–92 season.

JONATHAN DAVIES (WIDNES)

Jonathan Davies has scarcely been out of the limelight since he turned professional, but this was the season in which he made his mark to his own and everyone else's satisfaction.

Davies proved himself to be a magnificent all-round player, appearing in several positions, and enjoying outstanding games at full-back, centre and stand-off. He certainly made some devastating appearances at stand-off, but his coach, Doug Laughton, preferred him at centre and caused much consternation by playing him there in the Challenge Cup semi-final when Widnes were beaten, against all the odds, by St Helens.

Whatever his position Davies did well enough in them all to rewrite the record books at Widnes in great style. He finished the season with a tally of 342 points from thirty tries, 110 goals and two drop-goals and this despite an enforced lay-off of around nine weeks after injuring himself practising goal-kicking!

However, Davies perhaps took most personal satisfaction from the vote of his fellow professionals who elected him the first division's player-of-the-year. No accolade can be higher and it was a great tribute to the determination, persistence and all-round ability of the Welshman.

SEVEN

The Amateur Game

Ron Girvin, Huw Richards

THE DOMESTIC COMPETITIONS · RON GIRVIN

Amateur Rugby League was given the royal seal of approval when Queen Elizabeth II opened BARLA's new headquarters in Huddersfield on November 30, 1990 – just a drop-kick away from the George Hotel where the game was founded in 1895. The Queen spent three hours at headquarters, looking at numerous displays and also taking lunch with officials. 'It was the greatest day in BARLA's history,' said the president, David Knight. 'After all, you cannot have a higher honour than a visit from the Queen.'

That was the highlight of another year in which BARLA continued to expand. The Association's national organiser, Maurice Oldroyd, was named the amateur game's first chief executive just a couple of months after receiving an award from the Rugby League Writers Association for his outstanding contribution to the game. Geoff Owen became the first Great Britain youth team supremo, and he marked his appointment by seeing the Great Britain Under-19s chalk up a double over France – an ideal foundation for the summer tour of New Zealand.

There was a record entry of 225 teams for the BNFL National Cup – the world's biggest RL tournament – and Saddleworth became the first club to win both that and the National Youth Cup in the same season. Then the Sports Council ploughed no less than £640,000 into a four-year plan for the amateur game, and Opencast British Coal invested £100,000 in the National League.

On the field, it was a series of first successes in most competitions. York clinched the British Coal National Youth League Grand Final Trophy with a 36–20 win over Oldham at Watersheddings in a pulsating match. Oldham had not included a professional in their ranks all season, but York had five who had made several first-team appearances with Ryedale-York. Indeed, three of them went with Ryedale-York on their pioneering trip to the Soviet Union with Fulham in May. In the final, Oldham swept into an 8–0 lead with tries from Barry McDermott and Jon Perks but before half-time York hit back to lead. Tony Barratt and Kevin Martin both scored tries, with Mick Ramsden adding a goal.

At the start of the second half, the Yorkshire side really got a grip on the game with three quick tries from David Fellowes (2) and Richard Holt, plus a Ramsden goal. That could have broken Oldham hearts but not a bit of it. Back

Opposite
Jonathan Davies

they came with tries from Daryl Rogers and Jake Green, and two Perks goals, to cut the deficit to just 4 points. However, fitness finally told when Barratt and Holt added tries for York, which Ramsden goaled. The York scrum-half, Richard Holt, was named man-of-the-match.

Oldham: Daryl Rogers; Wilde, Barnes, Perks, Snape; Julian Rogers, Green; McDermott, Eaves, Smith, Platt, Hill, Jewitt

Substitutes: Buckley, Harlin

York: Young; Fagan, Barratt, Judge, Fowler; Render, Holt; Gatus, Pickles, Daniels, Ramsden, Fellowes, Shaw

Substitutes: Martin, Hardwick

Referee: N. Oddie (Halifax)

Wigan were champions of the premier division, with York heading the first division (east) and Leigh the first division (west).

The Yorkshire domination of the Opencast National League, which the county had won since the formation of the League five years ago, came to an end. With two extra teams in the first division, the League faced a backlog which took the competition to the end of May. Leigh Miners had finished their programme three weeks earlier, knowing that any one of five teams could overtake them. But they sat back and watched them fall by the wayside . . . all except their neighbours Leigh East. They defeated the champions, Egremont, on the last Saturday of the season to take the crown by a point. Easts had been promoted as runners-up only the previous season.

Sadly, the once great Pilkingtons club, who finished bottom of the table, announced that they would be returning to the Burtonwood NW Counties League for the 1991–92 season. West Hull, twice champions, were also relegated just as the second champions, Milford, had been the previous year.

Barrow Island won the second-division title, and Askam were promoted with them. Yorkshire, in fact, were left with nothing as the Cumbrian side, Millom, snatched a dramatic 14–13 win over Dudley Hill in the National League Challenge Cup final at Barrow. A try from acting half-back by their scrum-half, Clive Mossop, three minutes from time, snatched victory from Dudley Hill, who had dominated the second half. Peter Knowles gave Millom an early 4–1 lead with two penalties against a Darren Walker drop-goal, but in the sixteenth minute Vic Potapi crashed over for a Dudley Hill try which Dave Savage goaled. Savage sent Lee Humphries in for a second try, but five minutes from the break Millom cut the gap to 10–11 as their centre, Roy Robinson, sent his brother Glyn in by the posts, and Knowles had an easy kick. Knowles added a penalty in the second half before missing a simple shot in front of the posts. And that's how it stayed until player-coach Graham Lupton's superbly marshalled side snatched the spoils with that Mossop try.

In November 1990 Queen Elizabeth II paid BARLA the supreme honour of opening their new headquarters in Huddersfield.

The County Cup competitions produced a few surprises. Leigh East were the only Opencast National League club to lift one of them when they stopped Thatto Heath winning the Burtonwood Lancashire Cup for a third successive season. Heath looked to be on their way to a hat-trick when they led 13–4 thanks to tries from Chris Honey and a brilliant seventy-yard solo effort from Steve Dudley, plus a couple of Mark Cook goals and a drop-goal. David Kay had scored Easts' try but in the five minutes before half-time the Leigh side began to show some class. In the second period it was one-way traffic as Easts ran out 29–13 winners. With their scrum-half and skipper Steve Grimshaw calling the tune, David Kay, the Kiwi Darren Kohlhase (2), Mark Dainty and Tim Fletcher scored tries, with Kay also kicking two goals and Grimshaw a drop-goal.

The undefeated Castleford side, Cutsyke, were the surprise winners of the Bartlett Yorkshire Cup, beating the National League champions, Dudley Hill, 14–10. It was the club's first major trophy and they took a grip on the game in the opening eight minutes when Peter Steels and Ian Watson went in for tries which Richard Pell converted. Kevin Whiteley pulled a try back for Dudley Hill but then got himself sent off and Pell extended Cutsyke's lead to 13–4 at half-time with a drop-goal. Dudley Hill's gallant twelve battled well against the odds and had the man-of-the-match in Craig Robinson. Lee Humphries crossed for a try, to which Dave Savage added the goal, but Cutsyke had the final say with a Trevor Dunn drop-goal.

Hensingham toppled Millom, National League title-holders, by 7–0 in the Tetley Cumbria Cup. The Cumbria League leaders showed tremendous defensive qualities with man-of-the-match Kevin Saunders and hooker Richard Todd outstanding. Brian Tunstall went over from acting half-back right on half-time for the game's only try and added the goal. Then, ten minutes from time, their stand-off, Dave Cartmel, dropped a goal.

The Silk Cut Challenge Cup preliminary round draw gave Leigh East a plum home tie with Bradford Northern; Cutsyke a trip to the unbeaten second-division leaders, Salford; and Hensingham a home game with Dewsbury. No one expected any of those three to topple the professionals, but equally no one expected to see Leigh East give Bradford Northern the fright of their lives either. Easts went down 12–24 at Hilton Park, but matched the Yorkshire side for pace and skill. There was even a suspicion of infringements in the first two Bradford tries. Darren Kohlhase scored both Easts' tries and their scrum-half and skipper, Steve Grimshaw, romped away with the man-of-the-match award. Bradford Northern's skipper, David Hobbs, himself a Lance Todd Trophy winner with Featherstone Rovers at Wembley in 1983, commented: 'I wish my side had shown the sort of commitment which Leigh East did.'

Although they went down by 4–44 at Salford, Cutsyke were by no means disgraced. They made the Red Devils work hard for an hour or so and got the biggest cheer of the afternoon when John Steele went over.

Hensingham drew first blood with a Brian Tunstall penalty against Dewsbury but went under 7–24. Martin Whitehead scored their try and Tunstall dropped a goal.

It was the second time in three months that Dewsbury had had to face amateur opposition. In the preliminary round of the Regal Trophy they had visited the Opencast National League champions, Dudley Hill, and scraped home 24–18 winners. Now against Hensingham, Dewsbury achieved a more convincing margin. Among the scorers, there was a try for Dave Savage and five goals for Hill.

In the same preliminary round, Saddleworth gained revenge for their National Cup defeat of the previous season, with a 35–18 win over Egremont, which gave them a first-round derby against Rochdale Hornets at Spotland. Like the other amateur clubs in the Challenge Cup, Saddleworth did the amateur game proud before losing 10–30. Paul Coates and Cunliffe crossed for Saddleworth, with Sean Whitehead kicking a goal.

May 19 will go down as the day BARLA history was made at Knowsley Road, St Helens, in the BNFL National Cup finals. Saddleworth came back from 0–12 down to beat Wigan St Jude's 29–20 in the National Youth Cup final, and the open-age lads followed them with a 29–14 triumph over Hull Dockers.

St Jude's, who had lost three times to Saddleworth during the season, got the perfect start with scrum-half Neil Dutson diving over for a try in the first minute which Lee Gallagher goaled. Gallagher got the second try in the twentieth minute and added a superb goal which had everyone thinking a shock really was on the cards. However, in the last three minutes of the half, Saddleworth made ground with tries from Daniel Wilkins and Damien Walker; and then Alvin Carnekie kicked a goal to make it 12–10 at the break.

After a Chris Garforth drop-goal for Saddleworth, who were showing signs of getting their act together, Dutson set up the position for Paul Norton to cross for St Jude's to make it 16–11. Just before that Saddleworth had missed two great chances, but the signs were there that they were beginning to contain the big Wigan pack, as well as putting together some dangerous raids. It was fitting that the second-row, Martin Maders, should be the man finally to put Saddleworth ahead with a storming try, which Carnekie goaled, just twelve minutes from time. With Saddleworth's half-backs, Chris Garforth and Shaun Porter, now dictating everything, plus the running of Maders and Walker, St Jude's conceded two more tries in quick succession from Chris Bailey and Porter with Carnekie kicking his fourth goal. St Jude's were defiant to the last, and Steve McCormick crossed right on the whistle.

Saddleworth: Garrett; Guilfoyle, Carnekie, Harris, Bailey; Garforth, Porter; Wallace, Wilkins, Walker, Brown, Maders, Herring

Substitutes: Wilks, Tesz

Wigan St Jude's: John Derbyshire; Norton, Hill, Gallagher, Ian Derbyshire; Jones, Dutson; Makin, Fairhurst, Dunne, McCormick, Davies, Molyneux

Substitutes: Heaton, West

Referee: R. Duckworth (Wakefield)

Even a 9-point margin seemed a little flattering to Saddleworth, but that was not the case in the senior final. Although Hull Dockers led 14–11 at the interval it was one-way traffic in the second period as Saddleworth put more steel into their lively play to win 27–14. The man-of-the-match award went to their stand-off, Gary Hitchens, who sparked several attacks as well as doing some trojan work in defence. Their second-row, Steve Mawdsley and John Fleming, ran strongly as did the centres, Terry Hester and Peter Gallagher.

Dockers never really had anyone to dictate play in the same way as Saddleworth's skipper, Shaun Whitehead, although their stand-off, Stuart Farr, and loose forward, Dave Roe, did their best to keep the interval lead. Their centres, Dave Jones and Ian Walker, scored Dockers' tries, with Roe kicking three goals. Hitchens, Peter Gallagher, Duncan Maders, John Fleming and Tony Hurst scored tries for Saddleworth, with Whitehead kicking three goals and a drop-goal.

Hull Dockers: Stead; Sawden, Walker, Jones, Goodwin; Farr, Smirk; Holland, Brookfield, Faulkner, Suddaby, Livingstone, Roe

Substitutes: Wadforth, Young

Saddleworth: Gary Cunliffe; Hurst, Hester, Gallagher, Coates; Hitchens, Chadwick; Dobbs, Phil Cunliffe, Maders, Fleming, Mawdsley, Whitehead

Substitutes: Dalton, Gill

Referee: D. Redfearn (Huddersfield)

Lancashire lifted the open-age County Championship for the first time in five years, under the coaching of John Foran, three times a Wembley finalist with Widnes in the 1970s. It was a success which earned John the Great Britain coaching role and places for eleven Lancashire players in the international squad. In the opening game, Lancashire recovered from having their full-back, Dave Webster, sent off in the opening quarter to defeat Yorkshire 24–14 at Hilton Park. Skipper Chris Honey, who had to switch to full-back when Webster left, gave an inspirational lead, scoring two of Lancashire's five tries. But the best was a brilliant sixty-yard solo by Steve Dudley, who left a trail of players in his wake.

What a magnificent performance the final turned out to be for the Red Rose as they toppled Cumbria 24–6 with their stand-off, Steve Warburton, taking the man-of-the-match award by miles. His swift breaks caused all sorts of problems for Cumbria, and there were also top class displays from the centre Glen Prince (Langworthy), Phil Penkywicz (Leigh East) and Steve Kemp (Langworthy).

Prince's success continued when he took the man-of-the-match award as Great Britain lost 14–30 against France, fielding six full internationals, in St Estève. The strong running Langworthy centre had been a late call-up to the Lancashire squad – but how well he took his chance for Britain. With Foran as coach for the first time, Great Britain turned in a splendid performance considering that they played with only twelve men for the last thirty-two minutes following a controversial dismissal of their full-back, Dave Webster. Steve Kemp and Steve Mawdsley scored tries for Britain who were led by Thatto Heath's Chris Honey, his country's youngest ever captain.

But 1990–91 was very much a season for youth – in fact, 1991 had been designated a Year of Youth. Geoff Owen, in his new role, had a mighty task ahead – planning for the two internationals against France, a summer tour to New Zealand, and a visit to Britain by the crack Australian Combined High Schools side in the autumn.

It could not have started better. Great Britain went to Bordeaux and clinched a superb 24–6 win, thanks by and large to the dominance of their forwards. Not surprisingly, Widnes Tigers' prop, Terry O'Connor, took the man-of-the-match award. Tries came from David Bradbury (Leigh Miners),

Richard Chamberlain (Greatfield), Gary Christie (Widnes Tigers), Paul Hourigan (Leigh Miners) and Gary Burns (Widnes Tigers), with Hourigan and Paul Anderson (Redhill) kicking goals.

In the return Test at Whitehaven, Great Britain won 20–2, again with O'Connor and Paul Anderson leading the forwards who dominated the proceedings. Five tries came from Darren Williams (2), Gary Christie (2) and O'Connor. The forwards' efforts helped their stand-off, Gary Burns, to lift the man-of-the-match award, chosen by the Great Britain coach, Mal Reilly. 'It was a good all-round effort which has given everyone encouragement for the tour of New Zealand,' said Owen.

The selectors chose a squad of twenty-six players for the tour: Paul Anderson (Redhill), David Bradbury (Leigh Miners), Gary Burns (Widnes Tigers), Leslie Carney (Hensingham), Sean Casey (Pilkingtons), Richard Chamberlain (Greatfield), Gary Christie (Widnes Tigers), Lee Deakin (Heworth), Mark Dusher (Branshclme), Jeremy Dyson (Thornhill), Anthony Fenlon (Widnes Tigers), Darren Fleary (Moldgreen), Richard Goddard (Stanley), Alex Golbourne (Northern Dairies), Colin Hodgkinson (Leigh Miners), Steve Holgate (Hensingham), Paul Hourigan (Leigh Miners) (captain), Simon Knox (Hensingham), Ian McCrae (Greatfield), Barry McDermott (Waterhead), Terry O'Connor (Widnes Tigers), Abraham Phillips (Moldgreen), Craig Robinson (Dudley Hill), Nicholas Rushton (Barrow Island), Gareth Stephens (Middleton), Darren Williams (Woolston). Later, Stephens pulled out of the squad to sign as a professional with Leeds and Craig White of Widnes Tigers took his place.

THE NEW TERRITORIES · HUW RICHARDS

BARLA's declared aim of a worthwhile Rugby League presence in every sizeable community by 1995 always looked ambitious. The 1990–91 season was the point at which it became clear that it was not so much ambitious as impossible.

Three years into his appointment the code's national development officer, Tom O'Donovan, could say, 'The sheer enormity of the task has become clear . . . trying to expand more in seven years than in the previous ninety-three'.

The learning process over the last twelve months has been painful. In mid-1990 there was a development officer in London and talk of further appointments to come in the west and east Midlands. London, designated as the priority area for expansion, suffered a bitter blow before the start of the season when Ken Johnson resigned his post as the capital's development officer after a single year. A full season later the job remains vacant. Ken's schools' work has gone to waste, although oases such as St Mary's, Hendon and the Rotherhithe project battle on. The curtain-raiser before the Wembley Test against Australia proved a hollow triumph for the game in London. The appearance of a London team was the sole gesture made in the direction of development – and the organisation of this fixture provoked further rows.

The BARLA Young Lions side, sponsored by British Coal, set off for their summer tour of New Zealand with two convincing wins over France under their belts. Here they meet Garry Schofield at the Greyhound hotel, Leigh, prior to departure.

The resources of the Rugby League Foundation, the fountainhead of development, remain inadequate for its appointed task. It has considerable, extremely valuable, commitments to schools, to Student Rugby League and to existing development officers. But after three years there are no Foundation-funded development officers outside the traditional heartlands, with the arguable exception of Sheffield, and at the time of writing little prospect of new appointments.

This is not to say that there are no bright spots. Hard-working, well-organised enthusiasts, possessing ambition tempered by patience and a sense of strategic direction, are always likely to make some steady progress. Sheffield, the north-east and Hemel Hempstead provide examples.

Hemel's aim is to play their senior team in the Rugby League Alliance while keeping two sides in the London ARL and placing their Under-19s in the British Coal competition under the district label 'Chilterns'. They see this as the next logical step towards the aim of full membership of the Rugby Football League by 1995. Their secretary, Bob Brown, argues, 'BARLA's National League is not a feeder league and its teams have no profile in this area. The Alliance could be a feeder into the RFL, and names like Hunslet, Huddersfield and Batley are recognisable as League names to our potential public'. Both the RFL and BARLA have now accepted this development.

Hemel have taken the game into schools – six secondary and eleven primary schools in the area now play Rugby League – and have built up local recruits.

Last season they had only two Australians, both in their third season. Early on they devoted time and energy to creating a clubhouse – a social and community focus for the club. This generated income for the appointment of their own development officer, Chris Tate, at the start of the 1990–91 season. Preparing for the Alliance they started a new lottery, appointed to their staff the ex-Fulham coach, Paul Johnson, a member of the first-ever Hemel team, and planned ground improvements.

A letter to *Open Rugby* magazine in February defined the game's non-existent development policy, not without justice, as 'waiting for businessmen to form clubs wherever they want'. Hemel's patient build-up and long-term planning show that there is an alternative.

The breakdown of relations between the London ARL and the national body – over development, Wembley, and BARLA's over-enthusiastic organisation of the Southern Counties Cup without consulting London entrants – contributed to a miserable year for LARL officials. The LARL committee was reduced to only three members for most of the season. The closure of Hornsey Lambs, two years ago the most promising London club, epitomises the decline of non-Antipodean Rugby League in the capital. Of LARL's serious contenders only Fulham Travellers had a mainly Londoner squad.

The Anzacs continued to dominate. South London, mainly Kiwi, took their first championship for three years and completed the double with their fifth cup triumph in six years, defeating their mostly Aussie arch-rivals, London Colonials, 14–8 in a fiercely competitive final.

A tough draw, plus belated realisation by some northern clubs that they have to give of their best against London opposition these days, meant that few LARL clubs progressed in the BARLA National Cup. But London Colonials became the first southern club to reach the fifth round with wins over Eccles, Punch Bowl (York), Knottingley Rockware and Panthers (Castleford) before going out to the Yorkshire Cup holders, Cutsyke, in the final seconds of extra time in the replay.

Hemel, Peckham – who won the London Bowl, beating Metropolitan Police 20–10 in the final – and Travellers provided the strongest challenges to Anzac hegemony. Much of LARL's good news was to be found in the second division. The longtime whipping boys, Bexleyheath, won more games than they lost, started to form a second team and, after years as a one-man band, improved organisation to the extent that they challenged Essex Scimitars as the LARL's best-run club. Once-powerful Ealing revived to take the second-division championship, while the Metropolitan Police, hit by work demands, showed considerable resilience in their Bowl final against a much more powerful and experienced team.

Second-division Tendring (Essex) failed to start the season, while in the first division Milton Keynes and St Mary's managed only one appearance between them after January. Peterborough were contemplating a LARL application before meeting South London in the BARLA National Cup and not enjoying the experience.

With talk of a new Eastern Counties League, drawing in several LARL clubs plus Peterborough, Nene Valley and one or two others, the LARL's future was uncertain at the time of writing. A reduced league would have to operate as a single division, with too wide a variation in playing standards.

Such concerns are familiar to the Midlands and South-West Amateur Rugby League Association (MASWARLA) as they try to organise their affairs across one-third of the country. The format of regional competition pre-Christmas followed by the formation of first and second divisions across the whole area in the new year was retained for a further year. Bath and Stoke won the regional competitions; Aberavon, who won the pre-season Chester Sevens, dominated after Christmas, taking the first-division title and completing the double with a 22–16 Cup victory over Bath. Stoke won the second-division title, with Birmingham beating Crewe 46–26 in the Plate final.

The south-west and the Welsh continued to set playing standards. Bath took the Southern Counties Cup, boycotted by London, and did well to hold the Cumbrian champions, Hensingham, to 18–42 in the Challenge Cup play-off. They lost by a similar margin to Leigh Miners A in the BARLA National Cup, where the only team to progress were Aberavon, winners at Keighley Albion.

However, the closure of the Dursley, Cheltenham and Plymouth clubs suggested that both organisation and travelling remained problems, though happily Plymouth were immediately replaced by a three-team Devon RL. Meanwhile there is hope of new clubs in Oxford and possibly in Didcot. Areley were lost in the Midlands, but Stoke, drawing on the Cumbrian nucleus of the old Biddulph club, made impressive progress.

Keith Cockroft's valiant efforts in west Midlands schools were expected to bear fruit with a summer mini-rugby tournament, while the association's secretary, John Simkin, had no doubt about the best news of the year – the recruitment of several new referees and the setting up of a MASWARLA Society run by Georgina Pickett.

Nevertheless, after high hopes a year ago that a development officer would be appointed for the area, there is disappointment that prospects have now receded. That feeling is shared to the east where David Stephenson, secretary-chairman of the East Midlands (formerly Mansfield and Notts) ARLA says: 'I accept that they're short of cash, but when you look at the money spent on things like tours I can't help thinking that the odd £1,000 might be found for coaching and referees courses here'.

Changes of name aside, EMARLA was a model of stability – the exchange with the West Yorkshire League of the outgoing Hexthorpe Barons for the returning Garibaldi was the only change in their nine-team competition. Garibaldi won the Cup for the fifth year running, beating Hexthorpe, and took the league as Nottingham faltered in late season. Derby are expected to join the competition this season.

Most activity in London, the south-west and Wales and in the Midlands lies in open-age rugby. The north-east, too, has its own open-age success story in the Gateshead club, playing at the 1991 Charity Shield venue, who carried all before them in the York and District League. A Durham University club also appeared for the first time, but the real emphasis in the north-east is on youth and schools rugby. Indeed, Durham ARLFC gave up open-age rugby in the late 1980s, the organiser, Steve Rich, reasoning that, 'There's no future in open-age by itself. We must get young players coming through'. Last season the club fielded Under-9, 11, 13 and 15 teams.

Rich believes that standards at Under-13 level match those in Sheffield, and expects Under-15s and Under-17s to reach that level soon. Two two-day coaching sessions attracted a total of ninety-three youngsters – a demand that impressed John Joyner, the coach with James Leuluai of the first session.

Durham's progress is the fruit of painstaking effort by Steve's small group of enthusiasts: 'It isn't enough to get kids to sign up. You need to go and see their parents and get them on your side. It's a long process, an almost molecular type of growth. But there's no other way and no short cuts in a development area', he says, adding that even a part-time development officer could make an immense impact.

The award of the Charity Shield to Gateshead was a considerable boost, with Steve and his co-workers determined to ensure that last season's neglect of the development potential of showpiece games at Swansea and Wembley is not repeated. Rich may then regard a Union-minded Durham-area headmaster with considerable gratitude: 'He's been trying to stop his kids playing League and that really helps. It gives us the appeal of "forbidden fruit".'

Union backers have tried to tempt schools away from League in Sheffield as well, offering them money, in a strange inversion of the amateur ethic, to change codes. League's development officer for the area, Tim Butcher, notes that there was little rugby of either sort in the city's schools a few years ago and says, 'Kids should play what they want'. He is confident that most will want to play League, now established in twenty-one secondary and forty-one primary schools in Sheffield plus others in Rotherham and Barnsley.

International recognition as players for the full-time coaches, Daryl Powell and Mark Aston of Sheffield Eagles, added further to the game's growing credibility with Sheffield youngsters. Advanced courses for the Under-14 age-groups and above were well attended, and Tim can even point to three aspirant teenage referees!

Sheffield Eagles, unlike other professional clubs, have played an integral part in the development of the game and can expect a playing return on their efforts before very long. A number of development scheme products have turned out for their A team and the 18-year-old centre, Jason Davidson, became the first to sign a professional contract with Eagles just after the end of the 1990–91 season.

One worry is the need for new funding as Sports Council backing runs out: 'We're consolidating at the moment and haven't the resources for expansion', admits Tim. But the game in Sheffield, thanks to superior planning and long-term strategy, has proved capable of surmounting a succession of set-backs and obstacles over the last seven years and it would be surprising if this problem were any different.

Andy Green made the transition from amateur to professional Rugby League when he left Woolston, the BARLA National League side, for Trafford Borough in August 1989. He has made a mark on the professional game during the last two seasons and has thus followed in the footsteps of his father, Jimmy, the former Blackpool Borough stalwart.

EIGHT

Student Rugby League

Neil Tunnicliffe

In the early days of the Student Rugby League, certainly before the 1989 Student World Cup at York, the benefits of developing Rugby League in the universities and colleges of Britain were considered to be one-dimensional. The hope was that, if a large number of students could be introduced to the game while passing through tertiary education, at least some of them would turn into captains of industry, high financiers and politicians who, in thirty years time, might possibly return some favours to Rugby League. As we begin the countdown to the next World Cup, on the Gold Coast in Australia in August 1992, the developments of the 1990–91 student season suggest that this is fairly unlikely to happen.

The season was one in which all the student competitions without exception were won by teams outside the accepted heartlands of Rugby League. Cardiff Institute flew the flag for Wales by winning both the NatWest SRL Cup and the British Colleges Cup; Newcastle Polytechnic topped the UK Corrugated merit table and won the British Polytechnics Cup; the UAU Cup went to Leicester University for the first time; and the UK Corrugated Premiership final was won by West London Institute, who saw off Oxford University in the final. The shifting power base of the Student Rugby League was underlined by the inability of Leeds Polytechnic, who wiped the board in 1989–90, to win anything.

Similarly, in the international competition, Wales ended the season as the undisputed champions of Europe, despite suffering an early set-back against an inspired Ireland side before the Charity Shield match at Swansea in August. They travelled to France to pull off a 10–10 draw before returning to beat England 25–11 and Scotland 42–4. This success served to add substance to the claims that Clive Griffiths's powerful pack of forwards would be a sound base on which the resurrection of the full Welsh national side could be built. England, despite fielding five players contracted to professional clubs, failed to capitalise on their thrilling 25–14 win over France, and in the end were little more than efficient in beating a well-ordered Scottish side 24–2. Scotland travelled to Dublin for the other match of their season, an 18–18 draw with Ireland.

What this suggests is that the Student Rugby League more than any other body has been successful in selling the game throughout the country to precisely those people who are likely to embrace it, young people with an abnormal amount of leisure time afforded to them by their position in tertiary education. Yet to achieve that success, the SRL's associate directors, Bev Risman and Mal Reid, have realised that there are a lot of other sports competing for that leisure time, and that theirs must be presented in an attractive, efficient and structured manner to achieve priority. They have realised that this costs money, and so have forged their own sponsorship deals with NatWest Bank, UK Corrugated and Dibb, Lupton, Broomhead and Prior. They have been able to introduce new clubs to an effective organisation and offer them positive assistance from the beginning, to the extent that there are now thirty-three student clubs in Great Britain, with another three or four anticipated for 1991–92. This is the stuff of development: getting people to play the game so that they will continue playing after they leave their university or college, perhaps returning later as administrator or sponsor.

England Students captain Mark Calverley looks for the gap during the international against Wales at Wilderspool, which Wales won 25–11. Calverley is one of a number of student players who have attracted considerable attention from the professional game.

Yet the student game develops in isolation. It's true to say that there's Rugby League in Wales but, apart from Aberavon, it's Student Rugby League; and since the student calendar is now so hectic, sides have so many commitments that they do not have the time to play against local teams and so develop any sense of strength in the game in their own area. (The sole exception to this is Exeter University, who have been defeated by geography and play a full part in the Devon County Rugby League.) Thus it is Student Rugby League that develops, not Rugby League *per se*; once term ends or a player leaves his university or college, there is no guarantee that he will continue to be a Rugby League player, as the game outside the student realm is a different one.

The difficult part has been done: the student has been made into a Rugby League player, with such good effect that professional clubs are knocking doors down to get to players from, especially, the England and Wales student sides. Yet what should be the easy part, getting Rugby League to adapt to students, remains a problem. This manifests itself in a number of ways, be it resistance to the initiative to develop a spring/summer season in Scotland to allow Rugby Union players to fulfil their club commitments and then play Rugby League; reluctance to release contracted players from professional club duties to play representative student football; disinterest in the valid and functional American Students venture, if only because fashion has now switched from west to east.

Student Rugby League should be part of a pyramid of co-operation embracing the whole structure of the game. For example, there should be a London network linking the scores of graduates, coming to the capital to work, with amateur clubs in the area via whom they could be fed into the Fulham club; indeed, if Oxford University and West London IHE are to remain at the top of the student tree, some sensible arrangement of that sort must be worked out. Similarly, if there were to be a way of keeping tabs on graduates after they have moved on (as the Rugby League Graduates Association is attempting to do), so that they could be pin-pointed as players, coaches or administrators for new clubs or placed in contact with established clubs, then the work done so far would not be wasted.

The UK Corrugated Premiership final, in which West London IHE defeated Oxford University, demonstrated the shifting power base of the Student Rugby League, in a year in which not one of the major trophies went to a side from a traditional Rugby League area.

Yet there is more to it even than that. One of the England Students players graduated during the summer of 1991 and took up a teaching position in London. Having looked around the local scene for an amateur club with which to play, he was discouraged by the Sunday-morning pub-brawl mentality that existed, and by the air of confusion that pervaded the administration. Encouraged to look to Fulham, he was subsequently discouraged by the experience of two former colleagues who had followed the same path, but twelve months on had not yet received their signing-on fees. A Rugby Union player of ability and note, his transition to Rugby League was thankfully not reversed by these options; he returned instead to his old student club, where the regulations of the Student Rugby League allow him to play for a further twelve months. Had it not been for the lure of the Gold Coast at the end of that twelve months, he might well not have bothered.

Oxford University, coached by the much travelled Tim Wilby, proved to be a major force in the Student Rugby League in 1990–91 and posted an emphatic 24–4 victory over Cambridge University in the Varsity match at Headingley.

Rugby League, both amateur and professional, has a responsibility to people like that, a responsibility which extends beyond congratulating them on their on-field prowess and on the progress they have made in the student environment. The Student World Cup in 1992 will be the biggest Rugby League tournament ever held in the history of the game, bigger even than its predecessor in York; there will be four British teams there, France, the Soviet Union, the USA, New Zealand, Australia, and perhaps also Holland, South Africa, Papua New Guinea, and the South Sea Islands. There will be players there who have played Rugby League since they were 7-years-old and who are either contracted to or pursued by big professional clubs; but there will also be players there who have just discovered the game, who have enough natural rugby ability to be a success at it and who will want to know more about what they can achieve once all the hullabaloo dies down. By then the game must have decided how it wishes to treat its students: whether it really wants to embrace them as an integral part of itself; or whether it prefers to treat Student Rugby League as an interesting intellectual sideshow, perhaps even a glorious irrelevance.

Appendix 1

The Greenalls Lancashire Cup

Preliminary Round

Rochdale H	12
Salford	41

1st round

Salford	27
Oldham	24
St Helens	56
Trafford B	24
Leigh	26
Swinton	6
Fulham	50
Runcorn H	0
Whitehaven	6
Widnes	70
Wigan	70
Barrow	8
Carlisle	38
Workington T	18
Warrington	36
Chorley	8

2nd round

Salford	21
St Helens	7
Leigh	40
Fulham	8
Widnes	24
Wigan	22
Carlisle	7
Warrington	28

Semi-finals

Salford	16
Leigh	7
Widnes	20
Warrington	4

Final

Salford	18
Widnes	24

Appendix 2

The Regal Trophy

Preliminary Round

Sheffield E	8
Bradford N	12
Dudley Hill	18
Dewsbury	24
Carlisle	10
Wakefield T	28
Doncaster	14
Ryedale-York	12
Saddleworth	35
Egremont	18
Leeds	58
Halifax	6

1st round

Whitehaven	6
Wigan	24
Huddersfield	13
Keighley	15
Bradford N	12
Workington T	11
Bramley	30
Dewsbury	16
Wakefield T	40
Hunslet	8
Fulham	8
Castleford	14
Trafford B	10
Doncaster	*10
Rochdale H	30
Saddleworth	10
Widnes	26
Hull	16
Leeds	26
Hull KR	22
Nottingham C	4
Batley	35
Oldham	26
Salford	6
Warrington	33
Runcorn H	7
Leigh	66
Chorley	5
Barrow	16
FeatherstoneR	54
Swinton	7
St Helens	31

*(*Replay*: 19–7 to Doncaster)

2nd round

Wigan	36
Keighley	16
Bradford N	28
Bramley	0
Wakefield T	4
Castleford	20
Doncaster	10
Rochdale H	14
Widnes	22
Leeds	6
Batley	20
Oldham	16
Warrington	11
Leigh	6
Featherstone R	16
St Helens	33

3rd round

Wigan	6
Bradford N	12
Castleford	14
Rochdale H	19
Widnes	56
Batley	6
Warrington	18
St Helens	12

Semi-finals

Bradford N	13
Rochdale H	2
Widnes	4
Warrington	8

Final

Bradford N	2
Warrington	12

Appendix 3

The John Smith's Yorkshire Cup

Preliminary Round

Bradford N	20
Sheffield E	12
Nottingham C	6
Hull KR	100

1st round

Leeds	16
Bradford N	24
Hull	6
Castleford	10
Featherstone R	36
Bramley	4
Ryedale-York	0
Hull KR	10
Wakefield T	28
Hunslet	18
Doncaster	4
Halifax	40
Dewsbury	26
Keighley	14
Batley	17
Huddersfield	10

2nd round

Bradford N	12
Castleford	42
Featherstone R	22
Hull KR	31
Wakefield T	26
Halifax	17
Dewsbury	18
Batley	8

Semi-finals

Castleford	29
Hull KR	6
Wakefield T	25
Dewsbury	2

Final

Castleford	11
Wakefield T	8

Appendix 4

The Silk Cut Challenge Cup

Preliminary Round

Warrington	22
Huddersfield	4
Carlisle	8
Workington T	9
Sheffield E	19
Hull	6
Salford	44
Cutsyke	4
Leigh East	12
Bradford N	24
Hensingham	7
Dewsbury	24

1st round

Halifax	46
Fulham	6
Nottingham C	10
Whitehaven	26
Swinton	8
St Helens	18
Wakefield T	18
Trafford B	7
Keighley	36
Runcorn H	4
Ryedale-York	1
Warrington	8
Barrow	13
Hunslet	8
Doncaster	4
Widnes	30
Workington T	18
Hull KR	12
Bramley	6
Oldham	38
Sheffield E	19
Featherstone R	12
Salford	36
Batley	14
Rochdale H	14
Chorley	10
Castleford	4
Wigan	28
Bradford N	50
Leigh	4
Leeds	40
Dewsbury	20

2nd round

Halifax	46
Whitehaven	12
St Helens	16
Wakefield T	2
Keighley	10
Warrington	42
Barrow	4
Widnes	28
Workington T	15
Oldham	20
Sheffield E	16
Salford	19
Rochdale H	4
Wigan	72
Bradford N	5
Leeds	0

3rd round

Halifax	16
St Helens	24
Warrington	14
Widnes	26
Oldham	40
Salford	3
Wigan	32
Bradford N	2

Semi-finals

St Helens	19
Widnes	2
Oldham	16
Wigan	30

Final

St Helens	8
Wigan	13

Appendix 5

The Stones Bitter Championship Final League Tables

Division 1

	P	W	D	L	Points F	Points A	Pts
Wigan	26	20	2	4	652	313	42
Widnes	26	20	–	6	635	340	40
Hull	26	17	–	9	513	367	34
Castleford	26	17	–	9	578	442	34
Leeds	26	14	2	10	602	448	30
St Helens	26	14	1	11	628	533	29
Bradford Northern	26	13	1	12	434	492	27
Featherstone Rovers	26	12	1	13	533	592	25
Warrington	26	10	2	14	404	436	22
Wakefield Trinity	26	10	2	14	356	409	22
Hull Kingston Rovers	26	9	3	14	452	615	21
Oldham	26	10	–	16	481	562	20
Sheffield Eagles	26	7	2	17	459	583	16
Rochdale Hornets	26	1	–	25	317	912	2

Division 2

	P	W	D	L	Points F	Points A	Pts
Salford	28	26	1	1	856	219	53
Halifax	28	24	–	4	941	311	48
Swinton	28	21	2	5	523	370	44
Ryedale-York	28	20	2	6	559	294	42
Leigh	28	18	1	9	698	372	37
Workington Town	28	18	1	9	497	323	37
Fulham	28	17	2	9	450	338	36
Carlisle	28	16	2	10	613	425	34
Doncaster	28	16	–	12	507	434	32
Hunslet	28	13	2	13	519	438	28
Huddersfield	28	13	1	14	493	477	27
Whitehaven	28	13	–	15	412	592	26
Keighley	28	12	–	16	456	588	24
Dewsbury	28	10	1	17	410	455	21
Trafford Borough	28	10	–	18	508	618	20
Batley	28	10	–	18	337	466	20
Barrow	28	8	2	18	415	705	18
Chorley	28	7	1	20	388	721	15
Bramley	28	7	1	20	379	726	15
Runcorn Highfield	28	3	1	24	351	779	7
Nottingham City	28	2	–	26	284	945	4

Appendix 6

The Stones Bitter Premiership

Division 1

1st round		Semi-finals		Final	
Castleford	20	Leeds	7	Hull	14
Leeds	24				
Hull	28	Hull	10		
St Helens	12				
Widnes	46	Widnes	42	Widnes	4
Bradford N	10				
Wigan	26	Featherstone R	28		
Featherstone R	31				

Division 2

1st round		Semi-finals		Final	
Halifax	42	Halifax	32	Halifax	20
Fulham	24				
Ryedale-York	6	Leigh	8		
Leigh	11				
Salford	26	Salford	9	Salford	27
Carlisle	12				
Swinton	12	Workington T	9		
Workington T	19	(Replay: 26–6 to Salford)			

Appendix 7

Leading Scorers

Tries

Offiah (Widnes)	49
Austin (Halifax)	47
Wood (Halifax)	31
Davies (Widnes)	30
Hadley (Salford	30
Hanley (Wigan)	29
Quirk (St Helens)	26
Hunte (St Helens)	26
Schofield (Leeds)	25
Steadman (Castleford)	23
Currier (Widnes)	23
Devereux (Widnes)	23

Goals

Kerry (Salford)	177
Botica (Wigan)	126
Eastwood (Hull)	119
Davies (Widnes)	112
Irving (Leeds)	99
Sullivan (Ryedale-York)	94
Loughlin (St Helens)	94
Platt (Halifax)	91
Vickers (Carlisle)	88
Lumb (Hunslet)	85

Points	Trs	Gls	Dr.-gls	Pts
Kerry (Salford]	19	170	7	423
Davies (Widnes)	30	110	2	342
Botica (Wigan)	18	126	0	324
Eastwood (Hull)	14	119	0	294
Irving (Leeds)	11	99	0	242

2

Reflections

Former Neath and Llanelli fly-half Jonathan Davies created a huge media storm when he signed for Widnes in 1989. Two and a half years later he stands on the threshold of Rugby League greatness.

The final whistle blows on the first Test against Australia at Wembley, and Paul Dixon (No. 10) and Kevin Ward (No. 15) leap in celebration of Great Britain's first home victory over the old enemy for twelve years.

Back-rower Bob Lindner was perhaps the most consistent performer for the Kangaroo tourists, both in Tests and in the club matches. Here he drives into the tackles of Roy Powell (No. 12) and Lee Jackson (No. 9) in the first Test at Wembley.

Gary Belcher took over the mantle of Garry Jack as Australia's leading full-back during the Kangaroo tour, yet it was his dropping of Ellery Hanley's high kick that gave Martin Offiah a crucial try at Wembley.

Martin Offiah was carefully policed by the Australians to the extent that he received few positive running chances during the Tests, although his opportunism was well demonstrated at Wembley and he again finished the season as the country's top try-scorer.

Wigan's Denis Betts established himself as Great Britain's premier second-rower during the 1990–91 season, appearing in all five Tests and carrying off the Lance Todd Trophy in the Challenge Cup final and the young-player-of-the-year award.

Once again Ellery Hanley was an inspirational captain of Great Britain, giving perhaps the performance of his life in the first Test against Australia at Wembley and leading his country to a record 60–4 victory over France at Headingley.

Featherstone Rovers centre Paul Newlove recovered from the problems that dogged the latter part of the 1989–90 season for him, and regained his place in the Great Britain Under-21 side that defeated the France Espoirs 48–2 in Limoux.

French scrum-half Patrick Entat enjoyed a remarkable season in the colours of Hull and was a key figure in their 14–4 Premiership final triumph over Widnes. With Australian Greg Mackey he formed one of the most potent half-back combinations in the domestic game.

Despite his disappointment at not being a first-choice Test selection, Widnes's Jonathan Davies was outstanding in the domestic game, breaking his club's points-scoring record and being voted player-of-the-year by his fellow professionals. In a triumphant return to south Wales, he was instrumental in Widnes's 24–8 Charity Shield victory over Wigan at Swansea.

Lee Crooks of Castleford lifts the Yorkshire Cup after his side's nail-biting 11–8 win over neighbours Wakefield Trinity at Elland Road. It was Crooks's fifth winners' medal from as many finals, and the third different club he had skippered to success.

Tony Myler's season was again riven by injury, but he managed to lead Widnes to their first Lancashire Cup win for eleven years. The Chemics defeated second-division Salford 24–18 in a match settled only by an Offiah try six minutes from time.

Wigan won the Challenge Cup for a record fourth successive time, so completing their second Cup and Championship double in two years. Despite being only 20 per cent fit because of a hamstring injury, Ellery Hanley led his team to a 13–8 victory over brave St Helens.

Welsh half-back Jonathan Griffiths played a prominent role in St Helens's Cup run, his two tries in the semi-final putting an effective end to Widnes's Cup hopes. Here he takes on opposite number Shaun Edwards in the final.

Wigan's Stones Bitter Championship triumph was achieved in extraordinary circumstances as they played five matches in ten days at the end of the season, clinching the title with an emphatic 20–8 win over Leeds at Headingley. Skipper Hanley was only one of the walking wounded whose endurance seemed superhuman.

Salford were runaway winners of the second-divison title, dropping only 3 points throughout the season, but their biggest achievement was their 27–20 victory over closest rivals Halifax in the second-division Premiership final. Captain Ian Blease holds aloft the trophy.

NINE

Aspects of Wales

Huw Richards, Ray French, Eddie Butler

The announcement that after a gap of nine years (or seven years if you count the friendly against England at Ebbw Vale in 1984) Wales were once again to field a national Rugby League team to play Papua New Guinea during the latter's tour of England and Wales in the autumn prompted the following pieces from Huw Richards, Ray French and Eddie Butler.

A BIT OF A DREAM REALLY · HUW RICHARDS

Ever since Rugby League, still in relative infancy, became possessed of what the science fiction writer, John Wyndham, termed the 'outward urge', Wales has had an unmatched allure for supporters of expansion. London possesses the advantages of population, influence and power. But those seeking new regions for Rugby League to conquer have seen in Wales a reflection of the game's heartlands – sociological similarities, a mass following for rugby and an apparently limitless supply of talent.

That supply of talent has been the most important refresher of streams to the heartlands – 154 internationals plus a host of uncapped Welshmen, including three of the eight inaugural Hall of Fame members. The price of their professional contracts was leaving home for the north of England – generally for warm, close-knit industrial communities similar to those they were leaving. But it still wasn't easy for many, while others were undoubtedly deterred by the prospect of leaving. It is worth remembering that one of the most emotionally-charged words in the Welsh language is *hiraeth*, or longing for home.

The dream of giving Welsh players the option of professional rugby without leaving home, and of ensuring that their talents would be used to entertain the inhabitants of Cardiff, Pontypool or Merthyr Tydfil rather than those of Widnes or Halifax is a recurring one. Nine Welsh teams have entered the Rugby League – including six active simultaneously in 1908–09. Pontypridd tried from 1926 to 1928, Cardiff from 1951 to 1952, then again through the Dragons between 1981 and 1985, concluding with a black comedy of a season at Bridgend. Between them they have lasted twenty-one seasons, with Ebbw Vale's five years from 1907 to 1912 the longest single tenure.

Today the few oases of student and open-age Rugby League are highly successful in playing terms. Swansea University are consistently competitive and South Glamorgan Institute (now Cardiff IHE) proved themselves considerably more than that last season as they ran out winners of the British Colleges and Student Rugby League Challenge Cups. Aberavon won both major MASWARLA trophies plus the Chester Sevens, and Wrexham and North Wales Coasters have taken the game for the first time into North Wales with its close links with Lancashire.

Former Neath centre Allan Bateman (left) was one of three Welsh Rugby Union imports signed by Warrington in 1990, of whom scrum-half Kevin Ellis graduated rapidly to the Great Britain national side, while forward Rowland Phillips endured a more painful transition.

But the south is the prime target and clubs there remain isolated strongholds, with no prospect of any new open-age clubs. The Aberavon stalwart, Danny Sheehy, points out that there is no shortage of players, but that finding administrators is next to impossible: 'We have got no shortage of players and I'm sure we could find enough players in Neath or Bridgend and other towns. But who's going to run the teams? People like myself and Phil Melling are fully taken up running our own clubs. We can help other people, but we can't actually do the organising needed for new clubs'.

Sheehy hopes that a planned programme of League open-days, featuring top players, may sow a few seeds: 'But it needs a follow-up as well. A development officer would make an enormous difference', he says, echoing heartfelt views heard on League's other frontiers. The game barely exists in the schools, with little prospect of breaking the Union stranglehold: there is no rugby vacuum such as appears to have assisted progress in Sheffield's schools. Last season's Charity Shield game at Swansea was an isolated one-off with any development effort or intentions well camouflaged.

But one reason why League has struggled in Wales is that, in contrast to the indifference of Union's upper-crust, southern-based rulers in England, Welsh Union has always seen League as a genuine threat – and frequently the actual thief of their best players. The Union luminary, Rowe Harding, told the 1950 WRU AGM that the new Welsh RL was, 'Only an infant, but it wants strangling'. Affection had hardly been increased a year earlier when the

71-year-old Bridgend club were outbid for their ground, the Brewery Field, by a new Rugby League club and did not return until 1957.

There is undoubted public interest. Cardiff Dragons' debut was attended by a crowd of more than 9,000. The Welsh public is sophisticated, critical and well used to a diet of high quality Union – of which, international indications to the contrary notwithstanding, there is a copious supply. Offered the choice between familiar Union played well and comparatively unfamiliar League played only reasonably at best, they naturally opt for the tried and trusted.

Even more than in London, a League team in Wales would need real success. And that would hardly come without buying a strong side including a leavening of local heroes. Cardiff Dragons could not do it in the early 1980s, and costs at top level have rocketed since then. And Welsh internationals don't come cheap, for a good reason. Investigations into payments by Welsh Union clubs last season came up with less than staggering amounts – hardly enough to satisfy a second-division player in a bad season. But the indirect benefits of stardom in Welsh Union, even in a time of playing and economic recession, can be considerable.

So don't hold your breath waiting for the next Welsh members of the Rugby Football League. But anyone who fancies trying might consider that the luckless nine have been predominantly East Wales – none further west than Bridgend. Yet the short-lived grassroots League movement between 1949 and 1955 had a majority of western clubs, with Ystradgynlais arguably the most successful. Aberavon carry the flag today. So Swansea, major city of West Wales, consistently receptive to international League and with three major stadia – St Helens, Vetch Field and Morfa – all council-owned, might be a better bet than a third-time lucky bid in Cardiff.

PAST AND PRESENT HEROES · RAY FRENCH

Welshmen have found a place in the hearts of Rugby League folk since the James brothers, Evan and David, stunned the Swansea faithful and secretly stole away from the valleys in 1892 to join Broughton Rangers. 'The curly headed marmosets', as the brilliant half-back pair were called, were among the first to trade their rugby talents for the 'filthy lucre' barred to them by the Union authorities. For a fee of £2.00 per match, the two brothers' antics so entertained the crowds that the rugby-playing sons of Wales laid the foundations of a tradition that, almost 100 years later, burns as brightly as ever.

The near 12,000 crowd that packed into the tiny Naughton Park ground at Widnes, the fifty-strong press corps, and the numerous TV and radio commentators who watched the debut of the former Wales Union skipper, Jonathan Davies, on 15 January 1989, against Salford produced the biggest nationwide publicity for any event in Rugby League's history. This was proof, if ever it was needed, of the continuing impact of Wales's rugby heroes on League, despite the fact that, apart from brief flirtations with League at Pontypridd, Cardiff, Ebbw Vale, Bridgend and others, the principality has never been able to sustain the 13-a-side code at professional level for any considerable period of time. And yet the lack of any League background has rarely restricted natural talent from blossoming once the switch to the rival code has been made. It is, and always has been, precisely that natural talent – exciting running and footballing flair – which has attracted interest and helped to build such an enduring rapport between Welsh players and the fans.

That trio of all-time greats, Jim Sullivan, Johnny Ring and Gus Risman, in the 1920s and 1930s, set the standards and the style by which successive Welshmen were to be judged. Sullivan, who at 17-years-of-age was paid the amazing sum of £750 by Wigan to leave Cardiff, became a prolific points-scorer by virtue of his trusty right boot, while the former Aberavon wing flyer, Johnny Ring, topped Rugby League's try-scoring chart for four successive seasons from 1922 to 1926. The softly spoken Gus Risman was to prove the ideal captain and leader of men with Salford and later, in the immediate post-war period, with Workington Town. All three League giants would be proud of their successors.

The Welsh Rugby Union fly-half factory, as revered in the ballads of the folk singer Max Boyce, has served League well, even though many of its finest practitioners have switched positions when turning professional. From Bradford Northern's Willie Davies through Leeds's Lewis Jones and Salford's David Watkins, to the current Welsh wizard, Jonathan Davies, no finer quartet of gifted runners and points-gatherers has ever graced the sport. Willie Davies, the gifted Gowerton schoolboy who, in 1935 along with his school pal Haydn Tanner, helped Swansea defeat the All Blacks, proved the tiny inspiration behind Bradford Northern's success in the 1940s. Three appearances with Northern at Wembley in 1947, 1948 and 1949 and the award of the Lance Todd Trophy for his polished performance in the win over Leeds in 1947 are ample evidence of this gifted runner's contribution to League. And his immediate disciple at Leeds, the 'golden boy' Lewis Jones, continued the traditions of flair and creative football.

Often barracked by crowds away from his beloved Headingley, Jones in 1952, at the time a world-record signing from Llanelli for £6,000, belied his somewhat frail and fragile appearance with an incredible array of skills. His passing and eye for the gap proved uncanny, while his unique hitch-kick of a side-step left opponents, including myself, sprawling on the floor and severely embarrassed. He ghosted past defences with consummate ease, played touch football with heavyweight forwards, and rewarded Leeds for their heavy financial layout with a world record of 496 points from thirty-six tries and 194 goals in the 1956–57 season.

Opposite
Former Cardiff winger Adrian Hadley enjoyed his most productive season in the professional ranks in 1990–91, scoring thirty tries and proving a real handful for second-division defences.

Points records and Welsh stand-offs have always gone hand in hand as the mercurial No. 6 from Newport, David Watkins, was to prove on joining Salford for yet another record fee of £16,000 in the late 1960s. Never the strongest of players, David tells this story against himself: after missing a tackle on his debut for Salford, a wag in the crowd ordered him to 'hit him with your wallet'. But, as a tricky runner in broken play, whether from his preferred League position of full-back or at stand-off, and as a deadly accurate goal-kicker, he reigned supreme with Salford. Wonderful Watkins, with his unique skills and a world record of 221 goals in a season, proved the catalyst for a mighty Salford side and helped chairman Brian Snape attract others of the

calibre of Keith Fielding, Mike Coulman, Steve Nash and Colin Dixon to join him at the Willows. Today, Jonathan Davies has performed a similar role at Naughton Park, Widnes.

One try in the 1990–91 Regal Trophy against Hull, when the Welsh maestro feinted to kick before racing around, dummying and side-stepping a clutch of bemused defenders, excited millions on BBC TV's *Grandstand* programme and epitomised Davies's many skills. Like his namesake, Willie, he is blessed with rugby vision, has an eye for a gap and the try-scoring ability of Lewis Jones. He could also be the one goal-kicker in the 1990s to challenge David Watkins's record. Within two seasons Davies's tiny frame has become a target for all opponents but few come to grips with this present-day will o' the wisp. To be voted by his fellow players the player-of-the-year at the end of the 1990–91 season was the ultimate praise for a player who readily admits to be still learning the game.

Other recent acquisitions, Adrian Hadley of Salford and the former British Lion and current Widnes wing, John Devereux, are ample evidence that not all of Wales's rugby exports are tiny, nimble-footed half-backs. These two 14-stone wingers are part of that strain of powerful Welsh flyers of whom Cardiff's Johnny Freeman and Clive Sullivan are good examples from the past and for whom 'Bouncin' Billy Boston is the ultimate role model.

On many a wintry morning, when rising from bed, I experience a pain around the shoulders, a twinge or two in the lower back, and I think of Billy Boston, Wigan's phenomenal 15-stone wing of the 1950s and 1960s. Many a time the pride of Cardiff bounced off my shoulders as I vainly tried to grasp his waist or clasp my arms around his powerful thighs. Often he strode over me on one of his thundering runs down the Central Park touchline, and frequently flattened me to the ground with one of his bone-crunching tackles from the wing. As 'Billy B', as he was known for seventeen years at Wigan, swept through tackles, the crowd roared and the terraces were filled with 'oohs' and 'aahs' as some poor unfortunate found himself in his way en route for one of his 571 tries. Truly a great Welshman, a crowd-puller supreme, and rightly honoured in his native Cardiff with the freedom of the city.

Few can deny the part played by the Welsh in Rugby League's history, and there is little doubt that, with the recent influx of former Union internationals from the principality, they will play an even bigger part in its immediate future with the rebirth of a Wales national team. Warrington's acquisition from Bridgend of Kevin Ellis, a lively and pugnacious scrum-half, and from Neath Allan Bateman, a cultured, pacy centre; the arrival of the strong-running Jonathan Griffiths at St Helens from Llanelli; and the signing of Pontypool's full-back, Matthew Silva, by Halifax have helped to swell the ranks of Welshmen now vying for international League honours. The switch of codes by the former Union international forwards, Mark Jones (to Hull), David Young (now with Salford), Rowland Phillips (to Warrington) and Paul Moriarty (to Widnes) – what a powerful forward he will be if only he can recover from his horrific knee injury – means that at last a pack of powerful forwards can be pencilled in to confront the tough, nuggety Kumuls of Papua New Guinea at Vetch Field, Swansea in the autumn.

Union converts from the pack have, in recent seasons, struggled to adapt to their new code, such is the speed and handling ability required of the present-day League forward. The learning process and apprenticeship for a forward is invariably much longer than that for a back. But, if any of the present crop of former Welsh international Union forwards can emulate the deeds of their predecessors, Trevor Foster, Don Vines, John Mantle, Kel Coslett, John Warlow and company, then those exceptionally talented Welsh backs need have no fears in future battles at international level. As one who packed down in the scrum alongside many fiery Welsh forwards I can recommend no finer companion when the heat of battle is at its most intense.

At St Helens in the 1950s and 1960s so many Welsh forwards made their way to Knowsley Road that a certificate in spoken Welsh was an advantage to any St Helens player born locally like myself. George Parsons, Ray Cale and the hooker, Reg Blakemore, set the trend when the Saints coach, the legendary Welshman Jim Sullivan, led the team to a golden era. And in the 1960s there were no greater entertainers than Don Vines, who later in his career made a huge success of wrestling, and the prop, Stan Owen, whose permanent smile, when playing, lured many an opponent to his doom. Stan, a rough, rugged, balding open-side prop raced all over the field with a huge grin adorning his face, but woe betide any novice who mistook the smile for friendship. His smile grew even larger when, having dumped an opponent unceremoniously to the ground, he stood over him awaiting the play-the-ball. As the dazed, shaken player staggered to his feet Stan's grin took on a demonic aspect.

Reared on the hard local Union derbies in Wales, Welsh forwards invariably stand their ground and rarely call for help when in trouble. John Warlow, the former Llanelli second row, and my partner in the 1966 Challenge Cup final, certainly stood his ground before the huge Dewsbury pack in a tough, torrid semi-final. But he never bargained for his highly excitable landlady rushing on to the pitch wielding an umbrella and laying into the Dewsbury pack with powerful strokes. Before an audience of millions on BBC TV's *Grandstand*, John's landlady, Minnie Cotton, leapt over the surround at Station Road, Swinton and proceeded to attack a Dewsbury forward who had had the audacity to hit her lodger. Rarely have I seen a Welshman so embarrassed – or a Dewsbury forward so humbled.

One forward who could embarrass the opposition was the former Newport Union star, John Mantle, whose speed would have few superiors today. Indeed, I would be prepared to wager with those who claim that the modern game is so much faster than that of previous decades that there is no forward today blessed with the speed of this dashing Saints second row. When put through a gap he left defenders trailing as he raced away for the inevitable try. The winger, Roy Mathias, the big, bustling, flame-haired flyer, was another who, on switching to the pack at the latter end of his career, set up many a try for St Helens in the 1970s with that extra yard of pace that took would-be tacklers by surprise.

With Rugby Union embedded so deep in Welsh folklore, it will always be difficult to sow the seeds of a first-class professional club in Wales. But, as the Welsh Students success in 1990–91 has shown, and as Aberavon at amateur level regularly illustrate, the Welsh can and do play Rugby League as the equal of anyone. And there is no doubt that the public, who in ever increasing numbers flock to Naughton Park, Knowsley Road, and the Willows from the towns and villages of Wales, will support a successful Welsh club side. Wales are poised to extend Rugby League's international horizons; its team can, and surely will, enhance the image of Rugby League throughout Britain, and its players will be rewarded by international recognition once again.

Any rugby player, whether Union or League, has ambitions to represent his country and dreams of playing before his own kind in his own land. Rugby League is now restoring that privilege to some of Wales's finest players and will provide an incentive for many, still in Union, to add their names to Rugby League's roll of honour.

NO MORE FORWARDS PLEASE · EDDIE BUTLER

Somewhere between 1979 and 1985 the attitude of the Welsh towards Rugby League changed. It had nothing to do with the last attempt to camp the sport in the Taffs' back-yard, first in Cardiff, then in Bridgend. The French will produce off-spinners before Wales becomes a flourishing outpost of the northern empire.

But somewhere between Clive Griffiths and Terry Holmes, leaving Llanelli and Cardiff respectively, the Welsh began to view League in a different light. In the old days a few of the less enlightened gentlemen of the Union committee-rooms insisted on banning from the clubhouses of Newport, Cardiff and Swansea all those who had signed and departed. But, in general, Wales has always been sympathetic to the players who could not refuse what was on offer. And for every cold shoulder there have always been ten warm embraces. A reunion between Ray Prosser, who stayed, and Malcolm Price, who went, whenever Pontypool played against Sale, Waterloo or Fylde, was living proof that one day the cold war would end.

So, despite the stories of petty-mindedness and hypocrisy in the Union camp, the period in question – the early 1980s – did not see League grow either more loved or more hated. But, prior to Clive Griffiths, one thing was always clear. If you signed, you knew exactly what you were doing. Good luck to you and all that. But don't worry. We can always find somebody to replace you.

This was an era when Wales spoke from strength, proud of its own standing in the rugby world, confident in the attractiveness of its product. As long as there was Edwards, Bennett, Barry John, JPR or Gerald, Rugby League was welcome to the rest. When Terry Holmes, captain of Wales, signed for Bradford Northern five years into the next age, the country winced. Holmes may have been plagued by injury, but he stood out as a rare beacon of class. What's more – and he was far too much of a gentleman to express such feelings in public – the scrum-half was just another in a very long line of players putting faith in the committee men responsible for the future of the Union game in Wales.

Apart from the ill-fated experiment with the Cardiff Blue Dragons, League left Union well alone between 1979 and 1985. In that time, Wales went from the heights of crowning a decade of glory with yet another Triple Crown, to the

Former Llanelli scrum-half Jonathan Griffiths won only two caps for Wales in Rugby Union, but he made sufficient progress with St Helens in 1990–91 to suggest that, if the Welsh Rugby League team were to prove a success, he would soon leave that number far behind in his new career.

mid-band of mediocrity, en route to the despair of today in the 1990s. The men who had sat back and applauded Edwards, John and others from the committee-box, without making any investment in the future, now had to sit through the aftermath. Throughout the early 1980s Welsh rugby simply stood still. Meanwhile, Rugby League was doing quite nicely without the Welsh, thank you very much. Progress didn't come without the odd spot of heartache, like the Australians of 1982 exposing a flaw or two. But the speed of reaction among the decision-makers was so much greater. Changes were actually introduced without civilisation, as the men of the north knew it, coming to an end.

By 1985, League, with its Kiwi and Kangaroo imports and Wembley occasions, was being viewed by Union from a position of weakness. Terry Holmes was the first of a new generation to head north, and he was also one of the last of an old school. Now to make a couple of bob in the twilight years before the body packed up for good! Unfortunately for one of the most honest rugby players of all the time, the ailing limbs spoke louder than the bank balance – in game 1 in fact – and the Holmes legend was never writ as large in Yorkshire as it had been in the scrum-half's native Cardiff. After him, though, would come a more ambitious set of younger men who regarded League as a career-move upwards. Any success in Union – Wales's third place in the World Cup of 1987 and the Triple Crown in 1988 – was merely a lever to help the agent when the hard bargaining started with St Helens, Widnes or whomever.

Since Paul Thorburn began his international career in Union in 1985, twenty-one Welsh players of note have followed the trail of Terry Holmes. They have not all been united by instant success in their new code, but all have shared common disenchantment with the game they left behind. The game in Wales is just starting to pull itself together again, restructuring itself from the bottom upwards and even trying to make the fiddles of old shamateurism the saintly images of the 1990s. But it may be too late.

In the meantime, the sleeping giants of Union, England, have finally woken up. They may be lumbering around at the moment, yawning through their rolling mauls, but a strong England should now and for ever more hold sway over a strong Wales, if only because they have really superior numbers of players to choose from. Which explains why Wales now view League differently. Even before Holmes went north the public had an inkling of what was going to happen. In an age of increasing pressure and demands on the players, people such as Jonathan Davies made no secret of the fact that they could be tempted. The longer he stayed in Wales, playing in sides that lost at home against the Romanians, the fewer noughts there would eventually be on his price tag.

Holmes started the trickle which became a rush with the loss of Davies. It wasn't just other Welsh players who followed. Busloads of supporters now travel up the M6 every Sunday, partly in acknowledgement of the advances League has made in terms of providing entertainment, but mostly so that Welshmen may gaze mistily at the players with chevrons on their chests and dream of what might have been had they all stayed at home. If only Jonathan had stuck it out just a little longer.

As Wales slip further and further behind England, so those who have crossed the divide are mourned more and more. First among those for whom tears are shed is Davies, able to employ the same gifts of pace, balance and cheek to skip between the two games without apparent difficulty. He is a symbol of how League and Union remain cousins, and as a star in his second rugby career he is probably doing the cause of Welsh Rugby Union a great deal of damage.

For me, however, Davies is not the player Wales miss most. The problems back home are not related to the fly-half berth. Instead, they lie entirely up amongst the big boys. And here, no loss has been felt more deeply than that of Stuart Evans. At the time of his departure from Neath, Evans – despite a tendency to break bones in his feet on the eve of internationals – stood on the brink of greatness. A specialist scrummager, he was the cornerstone of the last Welsh unit to frighten the life out of the English. And he could also do a fair bit of the running around required of the modern Union player.

Evans has not found it nearly so easy to adapt to League. Mobile for a prop in Union, Evans's frame still looks excessive for League. Nor has David Young, who nearly perfectly filled the hole left by Evans, settled in effortlessly. In fact, only Paul Moriarty of the present forward signings has shown that the big men can adapt as easily as the backs. All the thanks Moriarty got was a shattered knee-cap. At the same time as Jonathan Davies, Jonathan Griffiths, Kevin Ellis, Gerald Cordle, even the *enfant terrible* David Bishop, have given proof that rugby is rugby is rugby, the forwards have struggled for pace, run too upright, gone to ground too quickly, seeking in vain the comfort of the long lost ruck. Young, Evans and Mark Jones are living proof that the traditions of League are not as easily absorbed after all, and that it requires years to understand the essence of life in the 13-a-side code.

For truly the two codes are light years apart, as different as any winter sports can be, given that the shape of the ball remains the same. And if that is the case, then Rugby Union has as much to fear from League as it does from Australian Rules or Gaelic or Grid-iron. We're talking about different sports with different cultures and separate specialisations. If, however, League is simply a better-paid stage for Jonathan Davies to parade the same skills he demonstrated at Stradey Park, Llanelli, then the barriers between the two games are likely to remain in place for a long time to come. Rugby Union is still bound to the same protectionist policies that it upheld in an age of amateur purity and snooty superiority. And it matters not a jot that, if Jonathan Davies had been born in Glasgow, he would probably have used the same skills to play for Rangers.

Rugby League was, is and always will be the monster on Union's doorstep. And so say all the committee men who never got caught having a sneaky trial for Barrow and who still make David Watkins wait in the rain for as long as possible before letting him through. Except that in Wales very few people think like that any more. So, what's the harm in declaring an amnesty?

Nice try, Stuart Evans, but we don't think the nutritionist has yet been invented who can trim your girth. But, it just so happens, Brian Thomas of Neath has been on the phone and wants a tight-head to play against Pontypridd on Saturday. He says there'll be a couple of selectors there too.

Thank you very much, David Bishop. We thought money might be able to control you, but the sooner you take yourself and your sunglasses and your personalised T-shirts and your infernal talents back to Pontypool, the better off we'll all be.

OK, Jonathan Griffiths. So perhaps we should have given you a few more caps. But you've made your point. Come on home and let's call it quits.

Would the players who have stayed and battled on through Wales's roughest patch ever be resentful? Of what? Most are far too busy on the phone to their agent to worry about ancient desertion and abuse of amateurism.

And nothing would do the overall cause of Welsh rugby and the players' marketability greater service than to have a scrummage that was no longer scattered; half-backs with a League appetite for tackling; an influx of players fitter than ever before. New Zealand may remain out of reach, but it would be nice to get back to the days of slapping an Englishman around.

The benefits to League are obvious. No more high-profile stabs in the dark. No need to up the signing-on fee to cover the heartache of, 'Goodbye, mam. I'll write as often as I can.' A hard-hearted trial period with no strings attached would surely appeal to the club's financial director whose coach likes the look of Mark Ring, but isn't 100 per cent sure about all this ball-behind-the-back lark. A friend of that bloody Bishop, too, isn't he? The M6 would echo to the sighs of relief among returning forwards, grateful to have had the opportunity of playing against Ellery Hanley, but thank God it's only the All Blacks next Saturday.

Pie in the sky. Such interaction is to reckon without the objections of the people who still hold sway in Rugby Union in the British Isles: Twickenham – the RFU. The English like nothing better than to see a stream of Welshmen running for the money. Dashed unfortunate that rugger ever caught on in those grubby valleys in the first place. Serves them right. Greedy oiks. Now, what was that about young Carling's contract for the after-dinner stuff?

So, despite a groundswell of opinion in Wales in favour of bringing down a few pillars in the temple, it appears that nothing is going to change. Wales will reform itself at schools and youth levels and give its premier athletes a fine apprenticeship before the scouts start calling.

But, if we do have to live with the system, then at least let's cause each other as few problems as possible. First, buy backs, no forwards. We've got plenty of the first and precious few of the second. And they don't find it easy. And they miss home. Second, if anyone hasn't got a full quota of overseas players, there are a few All Blacks who might be tempted. Even a few young Englishmen running around in poncy tracksuits wondering if they'll ever get a chance to join Dad's Army.

Well, why not. Don't see why the Welsh should be the only ones to suffer.

Opposite
John Fieldhouse was given the almost impossible task of keeping Oldham in the first division when he was appointed player-coach halfway through the 1990–91 season. Although he took the team to a Challenge Cup semi-final, his failure led to his being replaced by Peter Tunks.

DINGTONS

TEN

The Greatest Wigan Side?

Geoffrey Moorhouse

The question therefore arises . . . has John Monie coached the best Wigan team of all time? I'm not really qualified to answer it because I haven't been around that long, and some of the great sides of the past I know only from what I've read. One of the two biggest sporting disappointments of my life is that I missed seeing Jim Sullivan's last game by just three months, which excludes me from one of the finest eras in the history of the club. The other grief is that I saw only eleven of the 2,428 runs Don Bradman made during his fabulous tour over here in 1948; courtesy of young Malcolm Hilton, who had the great man twice for very little in the match against Lancashire. But Wigan's performance in the 1990–91 season was such that it makes speculation inescapable.

It's clear that, from the moment Sullivan signed for Wigan in June 1921, a very fine team began to take shape at Central Park, with players like Johnny Ring, Tommy Howley and Danny Hurcombe in the backs, and in the forwards two long-striding giants in Van Heerden and Van Rooyen from South Africa, and the Maori Len Mason from the Antipodes. In the following decade Wigan were twice champions, something they hadn't been since the First World War. They also won the Challenge Cup twice, which they had never previously achieved, including victory against Dewsbury in the first final to be played at Wembley. But it will be noticed that every name I have mentioned so far was that of an import to the town, from Wales or even further afield, and with the exception of Mason all were converts from the Union code. It was to be a little while before the great Wigan tradition of producing a superabundance of local Rugby League stars began.

My great good fortune was to start watching our game as a schoolboy when the club began to reap the benefits of its homegrown talent. What was even more impressive than the dominance Wigan exerted over the game for several seasons after the war was the fact that it was with very few exceptions the handiwork of Wigan lads. Of the players who turned out regularly for the club under Joe Egan's captaincy between September 1945 and April 1950, two were New Zealanders, two were Welshmen, and three were Yorkshiremen; and that was about it as far as outsiders were concerned – half a dozen of them spread across five seasons, which by the standards that had prevailed earlier and have done these past few years is a very remarkable record indeed. Since the autumn of 1986, a comparable period, Wigan have called upon at least six New Zealanders, four Australians, three South Africans, four Yorkshiremen and a Welshman – and that is only to have gone looking for aliens on the other side of the Pennines and beyond. Not all the Lancashire players in the cherry and white shirts have been local men.

All this says, of course, is that forty years ago, Wigan's successes were more truly Wigan's than they are today. I regret the general trend in Rugby League to import large proportions of a team from out of town, let alone from overseas, for one of the glories of our game has been its social stability, which I happen to think has had much to do with the local loyalty – and, even more important, local accountability – of the players. But the trend is there and will probably never be reversed now, for all sorts of reasons. All that's really relevant in contemporary terms, when arguing about the best side a club has ever put out, is its rate of success when compared with that of all its competitors.

It's a bit pointless to speculate on the relative skills of footballers who played the game so many years apart, because the game has changed in so many ways since the immediate post-war years, especially with regard to forwards and what's expected of them. There is absolutely no question that Joe Egan was head and shoulders above any Wigan player who has worn the No. 9 shirt in the 1980s and since, but that can scarcely be taken as a reflection on the hooking ability of Martin Dermott or Nicky Kiss or anyone else who has occupied the position in the last decade. They have never been encouraged to do what Egan did; and, even more to the point, they've never known anything like the same adherence to the relevant laws of the game by the referees.

One of the things that made Wigan's football so very special in the late 1940s was that the loose play of their forwards was atypical of the general mode at the time. Billy Blan, Les White and Bill Hudson ranged around the field at high speed, much as Denis Betts, Andy Goodway and the great Hanley himself are capable of doing nowadays. They were not unique in this capacity to shift their weight like threequarters – Ike Owens of Leeds, Trevor Foster of Bradford, David Valentine of Huddersfield, and Billy Ivison of Workington are four of their contemporaries who also come to mind – but the norm in the second row especially was sturdier and rather slower activity, as practised by Harold Palin, Bob Ryan, Alec Dockar, Bryn Goldswain and Co. Most of the classier forwards stood out from their contemporaries because of their toughness and their handling skills, not their mobility. Wigan's pack was dominant because every man jack had all these attributes. Kelvin Skerrett in his final games for Wigan in the spring was at last beginning to show the sort of form that Ken Gee exhibited week after week for year after year. And the great bald prop had the wit to avoid suspension during the last crucial games of a season, too!

Outside the scrum, Egan's threequarter line more or less matched Hanley's, though I think Kevin Iro at his best has been significantly harder to stop than were either Ted Ward or Ernie Ashcroft; and I believe Botica may yet finish up as one of the half-dozen greatest backs ever to wear a Wigan shirt. At full-back Martin Ryan was a wonder in his day simply because players in his position did not attack as daringly or as ceaselessly as he did; whereas what Steve Hampson does match in and match out is no more remarkable than the performance of several rivals – except when it comes to fielding the high ball, where he is, on form, the very best I have ever seen. It's at half-back that I think the most fascinating choices have to be made between the two sides. Tommy Bradshaw was a very fine scrum-half indeed, not least because of his uncanny defensive interplay with Ryan; but Andy Gregory is incomparable when he is not so weary with overwork that his brain addles and he overdoes the grubber-kick or

Opposite
Frano Botica, the goal-kicking All Black utility back, was the final piece in John Monie's Wigan jigsaw, and his 324 points in 1990–91 brought him not only domestic honours in England, but also New Zealand Test caps in the summer of 1991.

some other usually devastating ploy. Like Hanley, and second only to his captain, he can mean the difference between defeat and victory to the team. I yield to no one in my admiration of Shaun Edwards's natural ability, either, which is of a brilliance to take the breath away at times. If I put Cecil Mountford ahead of him it is because of only two things. Mountford, too, was brilliant and his excellence was more consistent than Edwards's, which has its dying falls as well as its soaring revelations of what is possible in this game. I'm sure Ces must have had a bad game now and then, but I can't remember ever seeing one. Nor was he as susceptible as Edwards to injury: he was the most durable footballer I have ever known.

Such comparisons, as I say, are of very limited value because playing conditions have changed in certain respects in the period between those two sides (and also because memory cannot *always* be trusted at such long range). It is probably safer to rely on the statistical evidence of how well teams performed against their contemporaries. A difficulty in this case is that the Wigan club was competing for different prizes in the two periods under review, as well as for some that have stood the test of time. The Lancashire League trophy has not now been on offer for more than twenty years, whereas Hanley's team can aim for the Regal Trophy, which was not available to Egan's men. The old Championship play-off and the Premiership may be said to cancel each other out. In spite of the caveat, however, there are some interesting comparisons between the playing records of the two sides, which may be set down as follows:

Season 1945–46 to season 1949–50
Champion team: 4 times (runner-up once)
Championship final victory: 3
Challenge Cup: 1
Lancashire Cup: 4
Lancashire League: 3

Season 1986–87 to season 1990–91
Championship: 3 times (runner-up once)
Premiership: 1
Challenge Cup: 4
John Player/Regal Trophy: 2
Lancashire Cup: 3

As good a way as any of measuring the supremacy of these two Wigan sides in their respective eras is by noting the points scored for and against in the years when they headed the Championship table, which produce these figures: 1945–46, 783–219; 1946–47, 567–196; 1947–48, 776–258; 1949–50, 853–320. 1986–87, 941–193; 1989–90, 699–349; 1990–91, 653–313.

Two other pieces of evidence may be adduced. One of those Championship play-off finals noted above from the Egan period was the famous occasion when Wigan thrashed a much-fancied Huddersfield side at Maine Road 20–2, without eight first-team players who were on their way to Australia with Ernest Ward's Lions. That remains a record for the number of tourists from one English club, though Wigan came close to breaking it themselves when the

team that Mike Gregory eventually led so well was originally picked for the tour of Papua and New Zealand in 1990. On the other hand, Hanley's team can point to that phenomenal run of four consecutive victories at Wembley and, for the last two seasons, the Cup and Championship double, which Egan's side didn't manage. But there really isn't much in it between the two XIIIs.

I myself think that since the war there have been three seasons which may each be reckoned *annus mirabilis in excelsis*. The first was in 1946–47, when Wigan might have become the fourth side in the history of the game to win the traditional 'four cups', a feat that only Hunslet, Huddersfield and Swinton ever achieved and which can never now be equalled (though it could, theoretically, be surpassed). Egan and his men won everything that season except the Challenge Cup, which slipped away from them one appallingly muddy afternoon at Central Park when Leeds won 5–0 in the third round, after Bert Cook had kicked a stupendous penalty from just inside his own half. The second truly outstanding season, even for Wigan, was in 1986–87, when the side Graham Lowe coached also won everything in sight except the Challenge Cup, after being beaten 8–10 in the first round at Oldham; but then compensated for that failure before 1987 was out by defeating Manly in the World Club Challenge, a match I still think was the most exciting try-less encounter I've ever seen.

And then there's the season just past, 1990–91, which I include in my trio not so much because it took the Challenge Cup back to Central Park for the fourth year on the trot, and the Championship for the second, but because of the manner in which the Championship was won, which made it of little consequence that Wigan failed to secure either the Lancashire Cup or the Regal Trophy last year. The four games that the fixture pile-up caused them to play in the last week of the regular season might all have been lost, and Castleford, Widnes, Bradford and Leeds in turn must have fancied their chances against an increasingly bruised and exhausted team, even with three of the fixtures involving Wigan's formidable sixteenth member of the squad, the Central Park crowd. Only a side of truly heroic character and fortitude – not to mention outstanding football ability – could possibly have played that sequence without losing at all. Indeed, I rate the game with Bradford Northern as one of the two most remarkable fight-backs I've seen in recent years. When Wigan were trailing 2–18, neither I nor any of my neighbours in the Douglas Stand would have given anything at all for their chances of survival; they were finished and we knew it. But *they* didn't know it, and the 18–18 draw at the hooter was as glorious as any victory the Wigan club has ever won. It was in the same category as Oldham's resurrection against Hull KR in the second-division Premiership final at Old Trafford a couple of seasons ago. Now let John Monie's team go forth to trounce Penrith or whoever else may face them in a few weeks' time, and the all-time crown shall be theirs!

I see I haven't mentioned Ellery Hanley as much as many of his admirers might expect. Of him I can only say that he is the living proof that athletic genius is just as possible as the variety exhibited occasionally by a musician, a playwright, a philosopher, a scientist. He may be nominated alongside a few other rarities – Babe Ruth, Don Bradman, Pelé, and not many more – of someone whose skill transcends that of all contemporaries, with a temperament on the field of play that is well-nigh perfect for what's asked of it. No one who has worn a Wigan shirt in my time has been able to dominate a match so completely and so often as Hanley has done for several seasons now; has had the ability single-handed to snatch victory from almost certain defeat, to rally his team for yet another and crucial effort when normal men have had enough and cannot raise a puff of extra steam. Possibly Jim Sullivan, among the Wigan giants of the past, had these capacities, too. But that, alas, I'm in no position to judge.

ELEVEN

Gauging the Difference: Rugby League and Rugby Union

Huw Richards

Isambard Kingdom Brunel, to British engineering what Alexander James Murphy was to half-back play, never saw a rugby game of either code. This is hardly surprising, since when he died in 1859 William Webb Ellis was still a blameless clergyman, the alleged exploits of 1823 yet to be fabricated.

But the fate of one of Brunel's most remarkable inventions is a warning to League fans prepared to entertain the idea of amalgamating the League and Union codes. In the 1830s he became chief engineer on the new Great Western Railway. Instead of accepting the normal 4ft 8½in gauge, he displayed the perfectionism of genius, devoting endless time and calculations to finding the ideal width – and came up with 7ft.

Tests proved that Brunel's broad gauge gave a smoother, more comfortable, faster and safer ride. Yet in little more than fifty years the broad gauge lines had been torn up and the GWR was working the same way as everybody else. Brunel was right, but engineering logic proved as nothing against massive interests and investment backing the standard gauge. Like those 19th-century railways, the rugby codes have followed separate tracks since the great schism of 1895 over the issue of broken-time payment. But as Union pursues an unsteady path in the direction of professionalism, the original reasons for the separation of the codes are becoming considerably less relevant.

If Union went open, would there be any further valid reason for having two separate codes? Geoffrey Moorhouse, writing in last year's British Coal *Rugby League Yearbook*, made it clear that he thinks not. He recognises that any merger will take a long time but argues that once the division on payments disappears the continuation of two separate codes would be seen as wasteful and obsolescent: 'I now believe that the reconstitution of rugby football is as inevitable as was the great schism of 1895', he said.

Similar thoughts have been aired from the Union side of the fence by the columnist Alan Watkins. The quality of such advocacy compels attention. It is a seductive idea – not least to those of us who follow both codes but would also like the occasional free Saturday or Sunday between September and April. And you don't yet need to accept the view that the main difference between top League players and their Union counterparts is that League men pay tax on their rugby earnings to believe that Union is well on the way to professionalism.

Professionalism is an outlook, an attitude of mind and a level of commitment as much as a definition of economic status. As long ago as 1929 the former Cambridge University RUFC captain, Rowe Harding, spread horror in Union circles by saying of his team: 'We played rugby, talked rugby, thought rugby and dreamed rugby. For one term we were professional gladiators, devoting all our time and energies to winning the Varsity match.'

Oxbridge students were a special case, but today most top Union players would recognise Harding's description as their own reality. A few years ago the Harlequins and England centre, Jamie Salmon, described his week: 'On Saturday we're playing London Welsh, then there's an England squad session on Sunday. On Monday there's a London squad evening, on Tuesday there's a Quins training session, then on Wednesday I'm playing for the Barbarians at Newport and Thursday is Quins again. Then next Saturday we've got another match'.

That may have been a heavier than average week. But it was also before the arrival of leagues, forcing clubs to take training much more seriously, and of the intense, highly organised regime that has brought England success in the last couple of years. Salmon wasn't getting paid – at the time he was earning his living as a teacher – but the commitment implicit in such a timetable can only be termed professional.

That sort of commitment is now unavoidable for players who want to compete at the highest level. A few years ago a midweek interview with an England player might have been conducted over a quick half, today he is likely to have emerged from a tough lunchtime session in the gym and to demand nothing more intoxicating than mineral water.

The Rugby Football Union, upholder of amateur traditions, is a highly successful commercial operation with a lucrative and professional marketing division. Executive boxes have arrived at Twickenham. The England team, cashing in on success like any professional club, will wear a new specially-designed kit in this season's World Cup. The well-paid professional manager has arrived. Barrie Corless's full-time efforts have helped transform Northampton from decaying Huddersfield-style relics of past history into Pilkington Cup finalists inside three years. Brian Thomas's ten-year contract at Neath is believed to be worth £360,000, while Swansea are prepared to top that annual salary for the right man. It sometimes seems that the players are the only people not making anything out of top-level Union.

At the same time the International Board is tying itself into glum knots in an attempt to redefine amateurism without actually allowing the game to go open. The line may hold, but the experience of other sports including League, amateur for precisely three years after the schism of 1895, is hardly encouraging.

So, if the two codes simply differ over money, there should be few obstacles to amalgamation. But is it that simple? It may have been the root of division in 1895, but a lot has happened to both codes since.

The League-Union split wasn't the only bifurcation in rugby's 19th-century tracks: American Football also shares common roots, means of scoring and some skills with the two codes. But nobody would suggest that it too should rejoin the mainstream. And both League and Union are now played very differently from the game that split in 1895. League started the divergence almost immediately, significantly dropping the bothersome line-out in 1899. That process has speeded up over the last twenty years – which is one reason why fewer Union players have been able to convert to League with any success.

Union has become a game of division of labour and specialist skills, with great attention played to ball-winning and set-pieces. It wasn't always so – as late as the 1920s Welsh forwards often packed down for scrummages in the order in which they arrived. Last year it just looked as though that was happening; in fact prop forwards develop specialised scrummaging skills, lock forwards are expected to win line-out possession and the hooker plays the key role in both set-pieces. With the specialist skills come physical characteristics – props as squat, rugged endomorphic, locks markedly ectomorphs. Bob Mordell once commented that anyone who is 6ft 6in and can jump will be capped as an England lock; whether or not that was fair, it is unlikely that anybody significantly shorter will don the No. 4 or 5 shirt again for England.

Differentiation by position is most dramatic among the tight five forwards, but specialisation runs throughout Union. Players such as Swansea's Tony Clement, who has played for Wales in four different positions, or the Neath prop, Brian Williams, who has the occasional game on the flank are regarded as unusually versatile. To switch from pack to backs or vice versa as Ellery Hanley or Mal Meninga have done is unheard of at top level. League has moved in the opposite direction towards a stripped-down game eschewing the technical ball-winning set-piece in favour of the basic skills of handling, running and tackling. Concentration on fewer skills has allowed them to be developed to a far greater degree.

As a consequence, League players are much more homogeneous. The decline in the importance of scrummaging has made even the specialist skills of the hooker marginal – Wigan's John Monie for one is highly sceptical of the need for a specialist hooker. League has no need of the physical extremes seen in Union – 20-stone props, such as South Africa's Flippie van der Merwe, or 6ft 10in locks, such as Sean O'Leary of Wasps. Its answer to the Welsh outside-half factory has marketed giant prototype forwards, identifiable by the codename Harrison, but players are much more interchangeable. Two examples from Fulham – Russell Bridge's conversion from a utility back most often found on the wing into a hooker, and Greg Pearce's alternation between full-back and second-row or loose forward – show shifts that are unimaginable in Union.

Successful conversion between codes remains possible: one of the heaviest concentrations of ex-Union talent in League is in Widnes's dexterously inventive back division. Pace such as Martin Offiah's or the natural gifts of Jonathan Davies prosper in either code. But for forwards the conversion is desperately difficult. Both Stuart Evans and David Young sacrificed their basic skill, set-scrummaging, when they moved over. Both are fast-moving and good handlers – by the standards of Union props. But in League those are the essential skills, rather than a desirable addition to a bedrock of ball-winning abilities.

Fans will always debate the relative merits of the two games. Here League has had rather the better of it. There is a steady supply of ex-Union players ready to testify that League is harder, faster and requires greater involvement, fitness and concentration. Union naturally lacks such propagandists – on the one occasion when they had a player, Steve Ford, who returned from League trials saying that he preferred Union and was staying put, the Welsh Rugby Union chose to ban him! A more imaginative organisation would have videoed an interview and sent copies to every club in Wales for compulsory viewing by first-team squads.

Featherstone Rovers scrum-half Deryck Fox continued to turn in consistently impressive performances at club level, which would have earned him a recall to the national colours against France had it not been for his work commitments.

So perhaps the money issue is only part of the argument. In the last ninety-six years two separate games have developed, each with its own virtues and adherents. Union fans can point to the potential for fluency implicit in their tackle rule – that the ball stays alive. Teams who match mastery of ruck or maul to quality backs, such as the 1970s Welsh or the best French teams, can produce breathtaking flowing rugby. The downside, as League fans will tell you and honest Union followers admit, is that risks involved in the ball being live ensure that percentage-playing teams kill it at every opportunity. Too many games degenerate into a morass of set-pieces, most being less a means of restarting play than the prelude to a further scrum, line-out or penalty, punctuated by endless kicks to touch.

League's tackle rule ensures that the game stops continually, but never for any length of time. There are few set-piece interruptions. Knowing that a player held on the first five tackles will retain the ball encourages aggressive running and risk-taking in all parts of the field. An open-minded Union fan will admire the athleticism and the handling skills, but may also point to a lack of variety. Strange though it may seem, Union fans enjoy the variety of specialisms in their game, and derive entertainment from fine rucking, line-out play or scrummaging – particularly when they link directly with fluent handling movements.

My own view, subjective as anyone's, is that a follower of both codes who watches twenty first-division games of each a season will see sixteen entertaining games of League against six of Union. But one or two of the Union contests will exploit the code's latent fluency to produce a more satisfying all-round spectacle than any of the League games. This may simply confirm northern suspicions that the Welsh are ineducable.

Like many rugby followers I enjoy both games, for different reasons. Combine the best of both and you might have a great game. Or might you have an unsatisfactory hybrid that pleases nobody? We can all start to think of ways in which a graduated merger of the rules might start. Much as I admire League's view that a set-piece's only purpose is putting the ball back into play as fast as possible, if we're going to have scrums let's do it properly. If the line-out is going to be an incoherent jungle leading as often as not to a scrum or penalty, has it outlived its usefulness? Union should long ago have adopted the kick to touch and tap for penalties, so there's no problem with that.

How many players? There's a strong case for thirteen – advocated by some Union followers who feel that their game's problems relate to overcrowded pitches. But is the less stable six-man pack one reason for League's lousy scrummages? How about fifteen men and a bigger pitch? This can be negotiated. But what do you do about the tackle rule? Herein lies the fundamental difference between the codes, and no obvious middle way: it has to be a choice, not a compromise.

Easy, League followers might say, we'll play League – it's obviously the better game. At the moment it is. League is in an unquestioned Golden Age. Union had its last Golden Age in the 1970s, on the back of rule changes adopted from League (although they'd never admit it), and is still arguably on the downswing. Is the rivalry between the codes the only thing stopping Union from adopting a whole range of League rules? Maybe for minor issues like the kick and tap-penalty it is. But on major differences Union is the way it is because Union people like it that way.

Any battle between proponents of the two codes over combined rules would be fierce – and the odds are against League. Remember Brunel's fate – and there's no doubt in this case which code equates to Brunel and which to the big battalions on the other side. In England, Union has 2,000 affiliated clubs with more than 200,000 players – compared to League's 686 clubs and 23,000 players. It already has the nationwide network pursued by League through the national development scheme – and can still afford to employ thirty-one development officers, a concept it hasn't been too proud to copy from League, against the League's dozen.

Union's World Cup attracted thirty-three entries, and will give the game an immense publicity boost in the first few months of this season. League's World Cup was clearly planned by the winners of a competition to find the format most guaranteed to destroy coherence, marketability and interest – but its real problem is that there are only five candidates.

But let us suppose that the codes have merged and, wonder of wonders, have taken the Brunel option of the League's tackle rule. What shape of competition can we look forward to? Not, I suspect, a very large one. Without some quantum leap in public demand, rugby crowds simply aren't large enough to support a large-scale professional competition. How many League clubs are serious professional businesses on any scale, really? Six, eight maybe? Oddly enough that is the sort of number that have emerged ahead of the pack in the Rugby Union's leagues and are starting already to do the same in Wales. Let's assume two national divisions of fourteen each, at the most.

How would former League clubs fare? Pretty well, one would hope. Wigan's massive support and endless flow of local talent would make them competitive in any system. Leeds's local population base would matter, as would Humberside's. But in the long-term could they compete financially with the big-city clubs who would emerge from Union professionalisation? The prospect of Will Carling playing for Leeds certainly appeals, but bear in mind that its possible concomitant would be Ellery Hanley – or more likely some descendant of his – appearing for Harlequins.

In four years of Union leagues a lively transfer market has grown up, favouring the London clubs with their superior financial backing. There were two London clubs in the first division three years ago. Next season there will be five. In Wales the transfer market favours their financial and business centre, Cardiff, who acquired an entire international front row in the space of six months a year or so back. In combined rules Widnes, Wigan and the like might find their star players similarly tempted to the big cities. Of course, just now they pull in bigger gates than the London clubs, but so do any number of provincial Union clubs who have still seen their stars leave.

Pessimistic? Maybe. I share Geoffrey Moorhouse's exhilaration at the thought of Wigan playing Bath, or Llanelli Widnes. But I can't help believing that in ninety-six years the differences have become much more fundamental than the simple issue of money – and that in any merger, whatever the timescale, League has much more to lose.

TWELVE

Two Great Australian Coaches: John Monie and Brian Smith

John Whalley

'Clipboard men with negative minds, overrated, overpaid and over here.' With welcoming noises like that to greet him any Australian coach taking a job in England has got to be equipped with a fairly thick skin and Henry Kissinger-type diplomacy. Ultimately and most relevantly, he must be successful.

Failure for an English coach can result in depression. Failure for an Australian can bring depression and ridicule. After all, if we cannot win a Test series, at least we can console ourselves by saying their coaches are no good. They have an endless production line of top-quality players, good weather and even independence. Sure, there may be one or two tricks we could learn from them but is it really necessary for them to come here and try to teach us their ways? Maybe the game in Sydney is technically good but is it better than ours in terms of excitement? We are much better sticking with our own.

Yet, despite the views of the bigoted or those who feel concern that the appointment of an overseas coach deprives an Englishman of a vital opportunity, Australian coaches have, in general, done more for the British game than their players who, in too many instances, seem to have treated their visit as a holiday with a nice fat pay-packet thrown in. Too many, asked to adapt to a different style, have looked ordinary when removed from their own environment. There have been exceptions, of course, such as Mal Meninga at St Helens, Peter Sterling at Hull and Andrew Ettingshausen at Leeds, who all adjusted to the British style and, in the mid-1980s at least, to different standards.

After the heavy influx of Australian players, it was natural that coaches would follow. But they cannot go out on the pitch and score breathtaking tries, and they are working with players here who have had a totally different upbringing from their Australian counterparts. Understandably, British supporters are at least suspicious when an Australian is given the task of taking charge of a leading club.

Certainly appointing an overseas coach has its dangers. It is not just a question of whether he can select a team which can perform to a degree of competence. The environments in Australia and England are as alike as chalk and cheese and not just meteorologically. In order to reach the top in both countries, a coach must have character. He must be adaptable and have the ability to instil loyalty and trust in his players. In short, they must want to play for him. Employees will always put in that little bit extra if the boss is a man they respect. That applies in all walks of life.

Two clubs which did their homework were Wigan and Hull. For different reasons, both needed men who could produce results as quickly as instant coffee. Wigan's requirements were for someone who could handle a team of highly talented individuals, keep established stars happy and yet provide an incentive for an exciting crop of young but untried talent. Oh, and he had to ensure that the team kept manufacturing silverware at the rate of two major trophies a season!

None of those conditions was specified in John Monie's working agreement but Wigan's vast number of demanding supporters were not prepared to let standards slip. They could appreciate the problems after three years of continuity under Graham Lowe . . . just so long as Monie kept on winning.

Hull, a former giant in danger of dying in its sleep, needed more than just a specialist coach. A miracle-worker, more like; someone to rouse a club which had fallen on hard times and did not have the finance to match its ambitions.

Two Stones Bitter Championships, two Silk Cut Challenge Cups, a Regal Trophy and two coach-of-the-year awards later, and Monie can say, with some pride, that he has done rather well. He did not equal, he surpassed, the incredible feats of Lowe. He had, in the words of Smith, 'batted after Bradman' and found what many had regarded as a greenish-looking wicket to be one that was near perfect. Perfect, that is, for a man with an absolutely sound batting technique.

Brian Smith failed to win the trophy he so desperately wanted for the Humberside public he fell in love with. But, when he returned to Sydney in January 1991 to coach St George, he left Hull as league leaders and he had had the satisfaction of taking the side to a Premiership final. Most important, he had given the club its pride back.

By returning home, Brian Smith has chosen to start all over again. Just as some over here are suspicious of men who have made their reputations in Australia, so some of the Antipodean public, and the media, are wary of men who have received their accolades in Britain. Monie always has, and always will be, held in high esteem in the southern hemisphere, having established his own high standards at Parramatta before joining Wigan. Smith had done a good solid job with Illawarra in the mid-1980s, earning a reputation as one who could make the most of limited resources. He was an intelligent half-back with an above-average ability to read the game before injury wrecked his career before he was 30. He had experience as a teacher, and coaching seemed a natural progression in the game. But could such a man, who would not look out of place behind a bank manager's desk, really have stirred such deep emotions on Humberside that he was chaired off the pitch like a monarch after his final game at the Boulevard against Leeds?

A measure of the bond between Smith and his team was felt by the Leeds scrum-half, Paul Harkin, who, even as an outsider, noticed the effect Smith's pending departure had on the team. It was, in Harkin's view, as if the entire Hull team were on a high that night, wanting to leave Smith with a memory he would never forget as Hull romped to a 34–14 victory.

Monie and Smith have supplied a rich part of the cream out of the Australian coaching bottle and it is perhaps significant that, outwardly at least, both seem to have similar styles. Neither is a bellower. Neither appears anything other than cool, calm and collected in public. Both are impeccable at dealing with the media and both keep internal wranglings, an inevitable occurrence at most professional institutions, within the confines of their club's four walls. Neither will tolerate indiscipline on or off the field and both have received wide acclaim for their work as summarisers on television, a role that requires confidence and authority. Both are expert at spotting weaknesses in opposing teams and, coming from a land where one game a week is the accepted norm, they share disenchantment at the overcrowded British system which puts such an unacceptable amount of wear and tear on players.

Yet neither took their jobs with a belief that their sides should play in a so-called 'Australian way'. Neither Wigan nor Hull could be described, even by their fiercest critics, as boring but both teams have made significant improvements defensively during the regimes of Monie and Smith. In addition, both have made further improvements in the fitness levels of their players.

Hull do not possess an Ellery Hanley, an Andy Gregory or a Shaun Edwards. Such quality players gave Monie a start over Smith, but expectations at Hull were running nowhere near as high as at Central Park, or at least they were not before Smith took over, and there is no question as to which coach endured the greater pressure. Nevertheless, Hull looked strong relegation candidates a month into Smith's first season in charge, and a hopeful, if not too expectant, Humberside public could have been forgiven for having serious misgivings about the new coach.

Smith's English coaching story can be looked at later. Tracing the short, spectacular career of Monie provides a perfect lesson in handling pressure. Coaches seem to be better prepared for the demands of the media in Australia, where the game in New South Wales and Queensland receives the sort of coverage usually reserved for soccer in this country. With hindsight, after seeing Wigan in operation during two glorious seasons, there was no way Monie was naive enough not to expect to be put under the microscope of public expectancy. His first press conference, in front of some fifty journalists representing all sections of the media, might have raised self-doubts. If so, none was apparent.

There seemed a tone of sympathy as well as curiosity in the questions. To most reporters, Lowe's act seemed impossible to follow. Wigan had not only won their second successive Challenge Cup but had also finished as runners-up in the Championship after being narrowly pipped by Widnes in a thrilling decider in the final match of the season. There was genuine shock in the town when Lowe announced that the game against Wigan's fierce rivals, St Helens, at Wembley was to be his final match after three remarkable seasons in charge.

How could Monie, this smartly dressed but jet-lagged Australian, possibly follow Lowe's seemingly unique formula of success plus high entertainment value? The players had turned on the style for Lowe as Wigan set standards which forced the rest of the domestic game to follow. But what would the reaction of those same players be to Monie? He seemed to be in an impossible situation even though he had a playing squad whose quality and depth was the envy of the country. He said he liked a challenge, but was this a fair one when success in only one major competition could still be branded as failure?

In retrospect, that press conference revealed more about Monie than anyone

Opposite
Full-back Richard Gay was a typical product of the nursery developed by Brian Smith at the Boulevard for young local talent. Gay underlined his potential with a forceful try in the Premiership final, as part of Hull's 14–4 victory over Widnes.

originally realised. It was not simply a case of making the right noises. He was starting as he intended to go on in his own quiet, but authoritative, manner. He did not make the mistake of setting targets nor did he pretend he knew more about Wigan than he really did.

Instead, he promised only that his own particular style would become apparent as the season progressed. There was no beating of drums yet no appeals for settling-in periods either. Monie wisely never put any unnecessary pressure on himself or the players by extravagant public statements which might have endeared him to supporters in the short term but would have done nothing for the club's long-term future.

He now has deep feelings for the Wigan public and an intense pride in his players' professionalism. He has gradually introduced younger players into the first team on a regular basis and, as his older stars approach 30, Monie has included David Myers, Ian Lucas, Martin Dermott, Denis Betts, Phil Clarke, Bobby Goulding and Ian Gildart in the first-team squad. When he finally decides to leave England, possibly at the end of the 1991–92 season, the club will not be weaker than when he arrived, although Ellery Hanley, Andy Gregory, Steve Hampson, Dean Bell and Andy Goodway will be approaching the twilight of their careers.

Like Bradman, Monie started with a duck. Wigan, after going so close in 1989, started the following season determined to win the Championship and earn a crack at the Australian Grand Final winners in the World Club Challenge. Widnes had already signalled their intentions by proving worthy winners of the Charity Shield at Anfield and many bookmakers made them favourites to retain the Championship.

Wigan began Monie's reign by losing to Warrington, who have enjoyed more success than most against them in the last five years. Although six successive victories followed, Wigan's defeat in the semi-final of the Lancashire Cup at Oldham was a bitter pill for Monie to swallow.

However, despite that set-back and another home defeat in the league, by Castleford in October, Wigan's form was such that they did not lose again until January when Smith's Hull side pulled off a spectacular victory at the Boulevard. But Wigan's consistency was already proving the dominant feature at the top of the table. Such was their command that even late-season defeats by Castleford, Widnes and St Helens only delayed the inevitable. Wigan clinched the title on the final day of the season with an emphatic success over Leigh, who were thus condemned to the second division.

Defensively, Wigan were much stronger than in previous seasons and had a greater mobility in the pack. Monie had his sights on his first Wembley final and on a first Championship-Cup double since the reintroduction of two divisions in 1973. Victory would have given them also the final leg of an unprecedented treble, with the Regal Trophy already won.

Warrington, despite the forecasts of many pundits that it would be a close final, were never in the hunt at Wembley with Wigan effectively wrapping up the game before half-time. They won 36–14, failing by only 2 points to equal Wakefield's record score thirty years earlier. After such feats, Monie was the only real contender for the much coveted coach-of-the-year award, despite Doug Laughton's superb Widnes team taking the World Club Challenge against Canberra on an unforgettable night at Old Trafford and retaining the Premiership. Laughton seemed to be the only Englishman capable of thwarting Monie's ambitions.

Monie possibly faced a more daunting challenge at the beginning of the 1990–91 season as Wigan paid the price of success. Ten of his players, not all by any means first-team regulars, were selected for Great Britain's successful tour of Papua New Guinea and New Zealand in the summer of 1990, and his top men, Ellery Hanley, Andy Gregory, Shaun Edwards, Andy Platt, Denis Betts and Steve Hampson were all to feature in the autumn against Australia.

The World Club Challenge was cancelled because of the Australian tour and such a series, with the whole of Britain's pride on the line after the demolition job carried out by Australia's invincible sides of 1982 and 1986, would stretch the home players to their mental and physical limits. It also meant that Wigan's best men missed preparation for club games while they spent a week away on international duty before each of the three Tests. Even though Monie, as he has always done, made full use of the substitute's quota during games to give players a much-needed breather whenever possible, surely it was too much to ask for Wigan to equal the previous season's exploits.

Instead, Monie's side settled for winning just the two most important trophies in the domestic game. In the circumstances, winning the second double was even more difficult than the first, even for a side which was making the exceptional appear normal.

At the start of the season Wigan had recruited Kelvin Skerrett from Bradford Northern to replace the departed Adrian Shelford, with Frano Botica switching codes from New Zealand Rugby Union and David Myers, a talented, but relatively untried, youngster, joining the club from Warrington, having started his career with Widnes. Botica proved the most significant signing, ensuring that Wigan were finally armed with an accurate goal-kicker. It put even more pressure on teams tempted to stop Wigan's flow by any means possible.

A combination of postponed fixtures, brought about by international calls, and indifferent form, put Wigan nearer the bottom than the top in the early stages of the season. The nadir came when Bradford Northern ended Wigan's hopes of retaining the Regal Trophy, fully deserving their victory in the quarter-finals in December. The champions were struggling and fortunes needed to change quickly for them to stand even a remote chance of challenging for the league.

Wigan started the new year unconvincingly and were beaten by Warrington. It was virtually their last disappointment as they started on a winning run which, even in Monie's experience of Rugby League in two hemispheres, had never been equalled. Wigan failed to win only one match, and that was drawn, in eighteen successive games, and they produced arguably their best performance during Monie's reign by hammering Castleford in the snow in the opening round of the Silk Cut Challenge Cup. Even when faced with ten games in the last thirty-two days of the season, the numbers backing against their retaining the Championship gradually dwindled, such was their momentum. It was like a thoroughbred racehorse getting into top gear in the final furlong, and taking the lead for the first time inches from the line.

At the outset of that truly remarkable but horrendous run-in, Monie wisely made only two promises: the first was that his team would give the title its 'best shot', and the second that he would field his strongest team for every game. He and Wigan kept both. After all, they could ill afford to do anything else. They could not risk losing a single game. As the pressure and the stakes increased with each victory, Monie's players turned out with various types of injury to all parts of the body. Monie had shown his faith in them and his players were prepared to return the compliment with blood and sweat if not tears. The result was devastating.

It took Wigan until the final game at Leeds to clinch the title but still Monie, deprived of proper training sessions because of the hectic Championship run-in, was not allowed to prepare his side properly for the Wembley final against St Helens. Not many coaches in the history of the competition have gone into the final week with doubts hanging over so many key players.

By the Tuesday it was down to two, Ellery Hanley and Joe Lydon. Twenty-four hours before Wigan took the field there was only one imponderable and that was because Lydon was forced to withdraw. Hanley faced a fitness test an hour before the kick-off. He wanted to take the risk and Monie agreed.

Playing Hanley when he was nowhere near full fitness was a calculated gamble but Monie knew his value to the team and the effect his presence would have on St Helens. The level-headed coach would not have considered such a course with any other player. Hanley played, Wigan took the Cup, and Monie was named coach-of-the-year for the second successive time after one of the most remarkable seasons in history.

Monie – and he has had extensive experience – had never known anything remotely to compare with Wigan's schedule in the final months of the 1990–91 season. Like Smith, he had been a half-back, on Cronulla's books as a stand-off. He moved to Parramatta as assistant to Australia's coaching guru, Jack Gibson, and took over the senior coaching position there in 1984, meeting with the sort of instant success that was to serve him well later in his coaching life.

He took Parramatta to the 1984 Australian Grand Final where they were narrowly pipped 6–8 by Canterbury-Bankstown. Two years later his side turned that bitter experience to good effect when they won through to another Grand Final, again dominated by defence, and once more against Canterbury.

It was because of Monie's feats in Sydney and his general reputation in Australia, both among the players and with the public, that led Wigan to him. Smith enjoyed nothing like Monie's high reputation but he was sufficiently well thought of for Wigan to look at his record before they appointed Graham Lowe in 1986, and his decision to join Hull two years later had Wembley exerting a strong influence, or at least that is how the story goes.

Smith was very much undecided about coming to Humberside and was inclined to try coaching in England at a later stage of his life. He knew Hull's position. They had been a major force in the early 1980s but had fallen on hard times and the possibility of taking them to within even viewing distance of the elite was remote. But Hull was a big club as Smith saw it from 12,000 miles away and it was basically a question of whether he wanted to uproot his young family and come to England.

The chance to watch the 1988 Challenge Cup final between Wigan and

Halifax, an offer Smith was given by a Hull official, was too good to turn down. Smith came over, thought long and hard about the English challenge and decided it was one worth taking. It was the beginning of a relationship with the Hull supporters which made Smith as big a hero on Humberside as Monie was to become in Wigan.

Unlike Monie, who merely failed to make an auspicious beginning twelve months later, Smith's start was a disaster as Hull lost their first four league games of the 1988–89 season. It set the alarmists talking about second-division obscurity, while Smith remained calm, quoting the famous phrase, 'What crisis?' It was not so much that Smith was to bring about a 180-degree turn in the club's fortunes which made him so popular. It was the way he did it. Smith simply said there was no crisis; and he had the confidence in his own and his players' ability to believe it.

When Brian Smith left Humberside at the beginning of 1991 to coach St George in Sydney, Hull were top of the league and on their way to success in the Premiership final. His last match in charge, a 34–14 victory over Leeds, was a night he will never forget.

A young player called Lee Jackson, later to become a full international, was drafted into the side as a regular and with the Australian, Craig Coleman, proving a good organising scrum-half, Hull gradually became a compact team and one difficult to defeat. Despite a lack of true pace in the backs Hull lost only five other league games during the rest of the season and finished fourth. And as a bonus they won through to the Premiership final.

Smith could not quite bring about a fairy-tale ending to the season. Playing the powerful Widnes side in the Premiership final, the Humbersiders did not have the best of luck, losing their scrum-half, Phil Windley, after twenty minutes through injury. Then, with the score at 8–6 in their favour minutes before the interval, the game's turning point came when Richard Price tried a hopeful kick through on the last tackle deep inside the Widnes 25. The ball bounced perfectly for Andy Currier and, even from ninety-five yards out, he was always going to be odds-on for a try. Martin Offiah's 100th try for Widnes early in the second half effectively settled the match.

Widnes finally won 18–10 but it had been a highly creditable performance by the underdogs whose noisy contingent left no doubt about their warm feelings for the team. The chant of 'There is only one Brian Smith,' coming from the direction of the famous Stretford end, may have been a popular cry on the soccer terraces but was strange to Australian ears; the coach was not only surprised by the acclaim but it brought a lump to his throat. He was bitterly disappointed not to have rewarded those supporters with a trophy after they had reacted to the team's improving displays by turning up in increasing numbers.

Because of limited financial resources, a legacy he had inherited, Smith could not indulge in any extravagant expenditure; perhaps his most significant signing came in the summer of 1989 when Karl Harrison arrived from Featherstone at a cost of £55,000. He was to give Hull arguably the most powerful front three in the country, with Andy Dannatt the other prop and the mobile Jackson at hooker.

With the Australian international, Noel Cleal, also coming into the pack, Hull were expected to achieve even greater things in the 1989–90 season after the previous year's exploits. Indeed, many felt they were a solid outside bet for the title. Sadly for Smith, it was not to be. Hull made another dreadful start, losing their first three games, and with Monie's Wigan in total command, the title was virtually beyond Hull after only a month of the season.

They suffered surprise set-backs in the Yorkshire Cup and Regal Trophy against Halifax and Salford respectively, and a superb display by St Helens ended their hopes of Wembley glory in the first round of the Challenge Cup. As in the previous season, Hull ended their fixtures with a defeat at Widnes, except that this time it was the quarter-finals and not the final of the Premiership.

Yet Smith's standing on Humberside remained high. The public seemed fully to understand what he was trying to achieve and had the faith in him to achieve it. They had not forgotten that talk of relegation rather than championships was the subject of most conversations before the start of Smith's first season. Smith had also made it his policy to concentrate on young talent. Jackson had already gone through to the first team but such players as Dean

Busby, Richard Gay, Ian Marlow and Steve McNamara all came through under Smith. He was also shrewd at bringing in overseas players, taking a chance, in the opinion of many, with the French international, Patrick Entat, who had a fine first season in 1990–91, and also in acquiring the finished article in the Australian Greg Mackey who had started the 1989–90 season with Warrington.

Rumours that Smith was wanted back in Australia persisted during the summer of 1990. It should have been an easy decision to return home yet Smith did not want to leave without at least one trophy to show for what had been a touching relationship between himself and the club. His family, wife Karen, two young sons and a newly born daughter, had settled on Humberside. He had agreed a new and improved contract with Hull in his first season and had played a regular part in Granada television's live Rugby League commentaries, where he was a popular, if at times a controversial, summariser.

Eventually, Smith decided for several reasons that he would return to coach St George for the 1991 Australian season. It was to be a challenge as big as the one he had faced at Hull but Smith at least left the club in a much healthier state than when he joined it.

For the first time in three seasons, Hull made a tremendous start in the league Championship at the beginning of his last season. Smith's target – making sure they would not be involved in the relegation struggle – was achieved by October. His second, finishing in the top eight, was sealed by December. And his third and, at the time of his departure, most likely, a top four spot, was how, in the event, Hull finished.

Smith always knew there was ground to be made up to reach Wigan and Widnes, but Hull are a team to be feared again and I believe Smith may return one day. A final tribute to his popularity was that after Hull's great Premiership win against Widnes in May – their first in five attempts – he received phone calls from Humberside at 4 a.m. so that he could share the good news. That was in no way insulting to Noel Cleal, Smith's successor. The former coach is not interested in any reflected glory. It was Cleal's side from the day Smith left for St George. Indeed, Smith is now as big a supporter as any who chanted his name from the Stretford end after the whistle had blown on the 1989 Premiership final.

Making the type of impact which Monie and Smith have made is exceptional. Both are outstanding coaches who, in different circumstances, have shown that they are characters of depth. Of course, there have been cases of Australians being failures when put in charge of English teams yet without doubt Australian coaches have added to the game in England; indeed, many have helped its progress. As long as there is a Smith or a Monie available, they will always be in demand. Supporters of Hull and Wigan are a testament to that. More important, players under Monie and Smith have undoubtedly benefited from the experience. The players of today are the coaches of tomorrow and the influence of these two outstanding Australians seems certain to be felt for several years to come.

THIRTEEN

Messages from St George

Brian Smith

The expectations of all associated with Rugby League in Britain ran high at the beginning of the 1990–91 season. Not only were we looking forward to the special entertainment of a Great Britain versus Australia Test series, but a number of other questions had to be answered too.

Was that third Test victory in Sydney in 1988 just a fluke? Had British standards really improved sufficiently at national level for Great Britain to win the series or even another Test? Could a club side hope to compete or even, the unthinkable, beat the touring Aussies? Would the Kangaroos repeat their unbelievable unbeaten whitewash of everything British for the third successive tour?

Linked to these questions were doubts about Rugby League's place in British sport. A trouncing from the Aussies would bring out those few remaining socially bigoted ghouls who love to hate all that is (or more precisely what they say is) Rugby League.

Many of us were concerned that poor performances at this level might set us back a long way in lifting our sport's image in Britain – after all, it's hard to promote a heavy loser. In the event, almost every immediate doubt and question was answered at the best possible place – at Wembley Stadium. October 27th 1990 was a date to remember in Rugby League's history. The game's international credibility returned, and with it came renewed hope for the sport in Great Britain. In fact, all three Tests provided hard-fought entertaining contests of the highest calibre, going into the last with opinions almost evenly divided on the likely outcome.

The first Test, when Britain were written off by almost everyone, resulted in a comprehensive victory for the underdogs. The home side enjoyed an edge seemingly from the time the teams strode on to the pitch to strains of *Land of Hope and Glory*. While many of us remain critical of Australia's preparation and performance on that occasion, international Rugby League returned with a vengeance. Moreover, the competitive nature of the series achieved an enormous amount for a sport that had threatened to become polarised through an imbalance of standards. That Australia went on to win the series after two more epic and controversial battles naturally was a great disappointment to the British players and coach, but for all who are fair-minded about our sport Britain had achieved a far greater victory. So much so that Australian clubs are now in competition to host a fixture with the touring Lions of 1992 – what a turnaround!

So at international level British Rugby League is almost back to an acceptable standard: 'almost' because nothing will really satisfy the fans until a Test series has been won. How can Britain achieve that?

First, there is a need for players to face higher levels of pressurised performance on a weekly basis. A high-standard domestic competition, the Winfield Cup, has been the springboard for Australia's supremacy over the last ten to fifteen years. To graduate to national selection every player must run the gauntlet of the Sydney premiership or bust. How does the Stones Bitter Championship, Britain's equivalent domestic platform, compare? As one who has jumped out of the latter into the former I can offer an insider's evaluation.

'Favourably' is the immediate word that springs to mind but 'not quite' follows shortly after. In my term as manager/coach of Hull FC (July 1988 to January 1991) I believe the competitive level of the Championship increased noticeably. True, Wigan and Widnes, for quite a number of seasons, have been the only clubs to have competed seriously for the title but a large group of other teams are now putting considerable pressure on them.

My reasons for qualifying what I said with 'not quite' and 'considerable' as opposed to the Winfield Cup's often used 'unrelenting' and 'ever increasing' need to be explained. In the first place, every fixture in Australia is set down before the season begins – nothing short of earthquake or flood can change the programming. Unfortunately the Stones Bitter Championship is an interchangeable hotch-potch of pencilled-in dates where teams may meet if nothing else arises along the way. Thus, proper physical conditioning, skills and mental programmes which need to be implemented for one date are often hopelessly out of order for another.

Second, there are twenty-two fixtures in an Australian season plus play-offs to make an absolute total of twenty-six. Compare this with the matches that Wigan have to play or, indeed, any team which meets with reasonable success. Don't listen to anyone from yesteryear – listen to our players of today. They will tell you without any doubt that there are too many fixtures in a season. Together these factors lead to a lessening of the intensity at which matches are played, which in turn inevitably leads to a lowering of standards. The weekly pressure needed to develop long-term standards of excellence is reduced.

Another real worry for those who truly want Rugby League to prosper in Great Britain is the financial problem faced by all but a couple of the very big clubs. Wigan are to be congratulated on their incredible performances on the field again last season: Championship winners in the most glorious of circumstances. But what a way to win the war – battle fatigue would surely have stopped a club with fewer resources. Their win was undoubtedly the highlight of the domestic season but much of the credit for their success must go to their off-field 'commandants'. No club could have assembled such an arsenal of expensive warriors without great business acumen behind the scenes.

What about Leeds? Well, I am afraid they deserve our scrutiny for yet another season of on-field failure. With a wage bill that most other clubs would like to use as their meal ticket for the next three or four seasons, the Loiners provide one very valuable lesson to the less fortunate (or less wealthy) clubs. Money is not the only answer to the problems facing British Rugby League. However, I am sure that while others will go on enjoying their moments of glory from time to time Leeds are certain to break through to a continued run of success one day soon. Will it be Doug Laughton who leads the way? It will take a strong man but it will be fruitful when it happens.

Hull FC's magnificent triumph in the Premiership final at Old Trafford gives great hope to other similarly stricken competitors. Noel Cleal's black and white battlers broke the Wigan–Widnes stranglehold on major trophies, despite many financial pressures and constraints. A third place on the Championship ladder was a tremendous achievement for all on Humberside who have worked so hard. The money tree does not grow on the east coast and the plight of their neighbours, Hull KR, shows just how much work has been done by so many at Hull FC not only to keep the club afloat and competitive, but to make them now Premiership winners!

Can clubs regularly achieve such levels of success without the huge financial support enjoyed at Wigan and Leeds? Those of us in whom hope springs eternal (the definition of any Rugby League supporter) may answer 'yes', though the number may be trimmed to those few who look in their dictionaries for 'impossible' under 'challenge'. But for how much longer can a handful of clubs provide the finance to mount a challenge to the top guns? In this current financial battle, who is the foe? Players are demanding more money than ever before, causing many officials to call them 'greedy'. But with the increased levels of fitness that are needed to remain competitive, players today must devote more and more time to preparation. And the increased intensity of matches leads to an increasing number of injuries so that even more time must be set aside for preparation and for the treatment of injured bodies. 'Greedy'? I think not.

Spectators at today's fixtures are far more varied in social background than those of the past. Granted, clubs still have a great deal of valued support on the terraces and should never forget that. However, uncovered standing room is not the type of facility to lure many non-fanatical supporters to a night match – or a day match come to that – in cold and rain. Today's supporter may wish to take his wife and children, his company boss or valued clients. Comfortable seating, parking and other facilities are minimum requirements to attract such valuable, if not historical, support. Is this an unreasonable expectation on the spectators' behalf? Certainly not, but with most grounds belonging to pre-war days it is expensive, sometimes not even viable, to consider such basic facilities.

Many sports and recreations compete for players' and spectators' leisure time these days. We can no longer expect the ritual of 'Sunday afternoon is rugby time' to coerce the tepid supporter. To make him or her eager for our sport is much more of a challenge than in bygone days and requires a total rethink of how to attract an audience.

Television and radio also cause great consternation in British Rugby League. Do they keep people away from our game by providing home entertainment? Is the game's future in jeopardy because our spectators may become lounge lizards? These questions were asked in Australia about ten to fifteen years ago. Perhaps the record levels of interest in the game there today provide the long-term answer. Changing kick-off times is sometimes difficult to come to terms with but the influence of television and radio in generating a positive image for Rugby League must not be underestimated.

Now let's get all of this in order. Standards of performance have improved but Britain must aim higher still. Remember that improvements will continue in Australia and New Zealand as well so a much greater rate of improvement is necessary in Britain to overtake the southern hemisphere. If these higher standards are to come from the domestic competition, then all the clubs taking part must be competitive and preferably more or less equal in standard. And to be competitive in the long term all clubs must have a solid administrative and financial basis.

It is the last of these requirements that makes me anxious about the measures that are necessary to improve the game in Britain. Many clubs really do want to be competitive and not just to sit about dreaming of the good old days or what might be if only Mr X would drop in a portion of his wealth to bale them out of trouble. What, then, is holding these clubs back? In some cases it is the clubs themselves or, more correctly, those who are at the wheel. Some simply have not realised that running a professional Rugby League club is a complex business and simply do not know how to act when they discover how vulnerable they are.

More often, though, I feel that it is the way the game is organised that is holding back the clubs in Britain. It must be very difficult, near terrifying sometimes, for many club officials to go about their business aggressively without a lead from somewhere. It would be a monumental break from past traditions for Chapeltown Road to don an authoritarian cloak (as was the case in Australia when the change was made several years ago from beers and pies and jobs for the boys to shape up or ship out) but with such a great product to sell I believe the risks of failure of any aggressive marketing and development programme are very slim. The rewards for those clubs able to break free from their financial shackles would lift the spirit.

With help from above I'm sure many other aspects of the code would prosper. There is still a need for the vast majority of British and European sports followers to realise that our game is vastly different from Rugby Union – that 'rugby' is as different as chalk from cheese when it comes to League and Union. We are not Union players being paid! If we can only get people to become aware of the excitement that is Rugby League, the entertainment value of a game tailored for the spectator, we may then start to enjoy all the fringe benefits of the sport.

'I saw it on telly; the teacher asked me to play it at school; Dad, can we go on Sunday?' or 'Mum, would you buy me one of those shirts? That man from the Rugby League who came to our school had one on the other day, you know, we saw him in the magazine.' Development of this awareness at junior level is where the greatest benefit can be gained, improving overall playing standards. It will take time but the result is a greater quantity of playing talent. While quantity does not always provide quality it does give it a kick start.

I find it amazing that professional clubs in Britain are not required to spend time and money on developing the game in their own locale. The short term answer from clubs is, 'What do we get out of it? Other clubs will just come and sign our best youngsters.' This overlooks all the other benefits that development brings. If all clubs were made to develop and foster this potential talent, wouldn't this make them all the richer?

In producing quality players, at junior or senior level, standards of coaching are a critical factor. Intensive coaching and better preparation in all aspects of athletic performance has seen the acceleration of standards in all sports all over the world. Why, then, do we in Rugby League have dinosaur coaches decrying the coaching accreditation scheme? Fear of change and of being left behind? Perhaps some of those in charge of the scheme may not be everyone's cup of tea but does that make the system wrong? More and better coaches will inevitably lead to more and better players. One of the problems of attracting good young men (and women) to the coaching ranks of school and junior teams is the lack of incentive. To what do they aspire? Few have graduated to positions of coaching prowess, at any rate among the professional clubs.

Indeed, at professional level there has been an outcry over the high number of New Zealand and Australian coaches in the British game. Why have clubs not appointed local home-grown coaches? One factor is that the 'coach the coaches' system has been accepted in the southern hemisphere for very much longer, leading to improved standards all round. And that will happen in Britain, too, if coaching schemes for coaches are supported wholeheartedly.

Another problem is the criteria on which clubs base their coaching appointments. A close look at the playing backgrounds of the sixteen Winfield Cup coaches would in most cases leave the British fan saying 'Who?' Unfortunately this cannot be said of professional coaches at first-division level in Britain. What counts there are the applicants' achievements and years of service as players.

So on what criteria do Aussie clubs base their appointment of coaches? Results! 'What results?', the young aspiring British coach will say. 'How do I get results without the opportunity?' The production of quality players is seen as a major plus for coaching credentials in the southern hemisphere as well as producing winning teams at a lower level. In fact, every head coach (except Alan Jones – a Rugby Union rarity) has proved himself at a lower level before graduating to the top. Most, by the way, have used the Australian coaching scheme along the way.

In Britain, this graduation from a lower level is difficult because so little attention or credit is given to the lower levels of Rugby League. The development factor of both players and coaches is overlooked. This must change. In fact, for Rugby League's continued progress in Britain I would put the fostering of elite youth or A-team competitions as a very high priority. Providing a high-quality competition recognised by all as a truly important part of the season's programme, rather than the present system where these teams are seen simply as an extra expense, would enable ambitious coaches and players to go forward in a properly structured way.

As better-quality coaches, with the right qualifications, move up the ladder of achievement (not just on paper), so too will their charges. What happens at present is that a failed coach at one club moves on to fail at another club seemingly because there are no other candidates at the second club. This is what I call the band-aid method – it covers up the problem for a while but eventually the nasty sore which lies beneath will be exposed. Unfortunately, by then the sore will have grown much worse. The development method will take longer but its effects are long-lasting and far-reaching.

This is the main problem with most British professional clubs at present – the need to create immediate success while laying the foundations for future security. Look at the first division and each season you will see two or three clubs which are destined for the second division before a ball is kicked. They have not built a secure foundation for themselves. At the same time you will see the Rugby League's engraver practising his Ws for the Championship trophy. The rest of the clubs have aims ranging from simple survival (in the first division or sometimes just in the game) to a top-eight position at the season's end. This is an unhealthy, unbalanced situation.

What the code needs is a levelling-off of standards. No, rather a levelling-up of standards. Perhaps some financial restraints could be placed on the money-spinners (one club with seventeen internationals while others are in danger of bankruptcy is unfair) but it's not the top clubs which need to come down. Again, the Rugby Football League's administrators could show a lead for all clubs, not just for those in the first division. A minimum standards policy is supposed to operate. Let them make it effective. Give each club guidelines, a blueprint, for what the Rugby Football League sees as the way forward for that club. If the majority of the clubs gain in stability and support, then standards must surely rise. Those clubs who elect not to follow the guidelines could then justifiably be asked to please explain themselves when the next distribution of funds takes place from Chapeltown Road.

In summary, the 1990–91 Rugby League season which promised so much lived up to that and then some more. The most important question of continued competition with Australia was answered with an emphatic affirmation. This alone must give not only those who are charged with the responsibility of administrating the game a renewed mandate to revolutionise and innovate but also a major boost in enthusiasm to all of us who live and love the game.

Now a new set of challenges and questions is posed. For players, the 1991–92 season offers the ultimate challenge and prize – a tour down under. As well, there will be the trophies to be won and week-by-week obstacles to be overcome but only by the most committed.

The even bigger challenges sit immediately opposite the administrators at all levels. Will they be like our top players and coaches in being able to lift their heads above the ruck to find the winning plays? As in many of life's challenging situations, strong leadership (or lack of it) will determine the future of British Rugby League.

FOURTEEN

Beyond the Fringe

Philip Fearnley

Promoting Rugby League football beyond international boundaries, and across cultural, linguistic and fiscal barriers, has often proved to be a traumatic, confusing, costly and anticlimactic experience. Moreover, overzealous, and thus at times blurred, reporting has fogged any serious analysis of the topic. Shirking the labour of verification has restricted positive discussion and constructive interpretation to marginalia. As a consequence, oral tradition (a strong undercurrent in League circles), encouraged by the paucity of literature, has reinforced ambiguities and misconceptions which will not stand the test of close inspection.

Let us take four past and present examples where misunderstandings seem to abound. First of all, Italy and Yugoslavia: any examination of Rugby League's abortive development there requires a brief look at FIRA (Fédération Internationale de Rugby Amateur). This body, formed significantly in the year Rugby League was born in France, in 1934, is responsible for secondary-level national Rugby Union in Europe. Dominated by France, it naturally acts as a sounding board and social agent between European countries. Thus, crossing 'la diagonal' by French Rugby Union players to Rugby League in the early days almost certainly spread the idea, if only vaguely, of 'paid rugby' to a European fraternity.

Those regional neighbours, Piedmont in Italy and Provence in France, have

In late August and early September 1950 an Italian Rugby League team, largely drawn from Turin, played six matches in the north of England in front of large and fascinated crowds. Here Cale of St Helens is seen tackling a Turin player, with Moss, Aston, Whittaker and McCormick following up.

always enjoyed close cultural connections. So Jean Galia's efforts in the mid-1930s to persuade his fellow countrymen in southern France to adopt 'paid rugby' soon became known to a trainee commercial lawyer in Turin, Vincenzo Bertolotto. After the Second World War, discontent with the policies of the Italian Rugby Union led to thoughts of alternatives and Rugby League was born there. The *Wigan Examiner* revealed in 1950, '... talks between the RFL's secretary, Mr Fallowfield, and a group of Italian rugby dissidents have been proceeding for several years ...' Eventually, no less than 4,000 spectators attended an exhibition RL match in Turin by two French sides. A local resident, Dennis Chappell, once of Wakefield, helped foster the rebels. Bertolotto, then an elder statesman of Italian rugby at 38, motivated and organised an educational tour to England. Chappell was a steadying hand at stand-off. Six games took place in late August and early September 1950 in which the tourists, mainly from Turin, were outclassed in good spirited encounters before some healthy crowds.

On their return to Italy, a slow expansion took place but the breakaway movement was always to be dogged by the adversarial nature of its evolution. The wish to outface the Union establishment was not a noble objective. Its repercussions at government level, together with strong Union lobbying, meant it never received all-important ministerial assent, and the state subsidy and insurance cover that accompanied that assent. Despite this, progress of a sort continued. Realising the gravity of the situation, the RFL threw out a financial lifeline, spending £16,000 plus, a considerable sum at that time, indicative of the RFL's determination to aid development. Sadly, however, depending as they did on the RFL continuing to underpin their insurance costs, once that support was removed, because no Italian government bill was in sight, the Comitato Italiano Rugby XIII collapsed in 1962.

Watching these events had been representatives from the Balkans. In contrast to Italy, government approval had never troubled Ragbi XIII in Yugoslavia. But war's postscript was their eventual undoing. Acting on his own initiative, Dragan Marsicevic, secretary of the Yugoslav Sports Council, approached the French RL Federation to explore the possibility of establishing Rugby League in his country. Two French university selections departed in 1953 for a four-match propaganda trip. In September, Rugby League made its debut at the Army stadium in the capital, Belgrade. Further fixtures were held in Novi Sad, Subotica and Ljubljana near the Italian border. Well attended and entertaining, an excellent impression was left.

In Belgrade, the famous Partizan club accepted Rugby League as a section member. Elsewhere keenness was frustrated by war reconstruction projects taking priority; housing in particular swallowed any available flat land for apartment blocks. Suitable playing surfaces proved to be a major difficulty along with cash. However, brittle localised expansion began. International club competition with Italy and France stimulated the pioneers. Sadly, Marsicevic's influence was lost at the end of the decade and he was succeeded by an ex-Romanian RU international.

Problems were compounded by the compulsory purchase order for a ground

Polutka melea ubacuje loptu između dva prva reda igrača protivničkih ekipa u tzv. hodnik melea. Polutka melea obvezna je da loptu ubacuje sa one strane gde se nalazi sudija, da loptu ubaci pokretom ruku odozgo na dole, tako da se lopta ne kotrlja. Odmah po ubacivanju lopte polutka melea neizostavno mora otići iza svog poslednjeg igrača u meleu.

Pravila igre predviđaju da se igrači ne smeju prikupljati tj. formirati mele, pre nego što bude dosuđen, kao i da ne smeju gurati niti podići noge pre nego što je lopta ubačena u hodnik melea. Dozvoljava se igračima prve linije (krilima) sa suprotne strane od ubacivanja lopte da mogu svojim spoljnim nogama zatvoriti hodnik melea kako lopta ne bi prošla kroz hodnik melea. Posle izvršenog ubacivanja lopte od strane polutke, i kada lopta dodirne tlo hodnika melea dozvoljeno je privlačenje lopte.

Igrači koje nazivamo privlakači (slika 20 br. 2) nastoje da svojim nogama privuku loptu čim ona dodirne tlo u hodniku melea. Međutim najstrožije se kažnjava ako bilo koji od privlakača istovremeno digne obadve noge ili pak pokuša da oslobodi svoje ruke sve dok je lopta u meleu.

Postoje i pravila koja određuju da ni jedan od igrača u meleu ne sme da klekne, legne ili rukama dodirne loptu u meleu.

Lopta može biti korišćena po izlasku iz melea od igrača čija je polutka vršila ubacivanje i to: kod melea sa 6 igrača — može biti igrana od strane igrača treće linije, tj. po prolasku druge linije, ili ukoliko je mele bio formiran od 5 igrača, loptu može odigrati jedan od igrača druge linije, tj. odmah po prolasku prve linije.

Ukoliko lopta izađe iz trougla melea posle pravilnog privlačenja i izlaska lopte iza prve linije, lopta može biti odigrana od bilo koga igrača, pod uslovom da ovaj ne bude u položaju van igre.

Treba napomenuti da pravila obavezuju sve igrače koji ne učestvuju u meleu da moraju biti iza poslednjeg igrača njihove ekipe u meleu.

ZADRŽAVANJE TENI

Ranije je rečeno da se prilikom obaranja ide na protivničkog igrača koji nosi loptu sa namerom da se obaranjem i zadržavanjem zaustavi akcija toga igrača.

36

Zadržavanje je izvršeno i oboreni igrač nalazi se u položaju zadržavanja kada su ostvareni sledeći uslovi i to: — oboreni igrač je zadržan od strane protivničkog igrača prilikom obaranja, a lopta je bila u dodiru sa zemljom (vidi sliku 17).

Ukoliko igrač koji poseduje loptu bude blokiran (sl. 18) od strane jednog ili više protivničkih igrača, pa mu oni onemogući da se kreće ili da doda loptu sudija obično priznaje zadržavanje, te naređuje vraćanje u igru odnosno izvođenje zadržavanja.

Dešava se da oboreni igrač nije dodirnuo zemlju sa loptom, prilikom obaranja, pa mu je dozvoljeno da tu loptu može odmah dodati.

Pošto je zadržavanje izvršeno sudija naređuje nastavak igre komandovanjem »u igru«, jer zadržavanje ne pretstavlja prekid igre.

Sl. 24. — Izvođenje zadržavanja-tenija

37

Pages from a Yugoslav Rugby League coaching manual, c. 1955.

shared by several Belgrade teams. Money was tight. And what little was available had to be divided because of the rise of Rugby Union. Renewed attempts were made to maintain interest. One final fling of the dice was invested in an international with France at Banja Luka in June 1961. A squad drawn from six sides was cheered on by 5,000 fans. Formidable France won 13–0. But Yugoslav RL was a spent force. The years between 1962–64 were shrouded in apathy and a feeling of isolation and FIRA were to take advantage of these factors. Gripped by helplessness, the Yugoslav Rugby Federation eventually listened to overtures from FIRA in the form of general assistance and international matches. Voting at the annual general meeting in the summer of 1964 came out in favour of switching to Rugby Union and rebuilding, even though League was more popular nationally. The light had gone out of Marsicevic's 1953 dream.

Elsewhere in 1953, there were whispers that a South African syndicate based in Johannesburg would soon be ready to open negotiations with Chapeltown Road. A spokesman visited London to seek advice. The RFL secretary, Bill Fallowfield, presided at an informal conference. Obtaining pitches for demonstration matches looked impossible for four years until the autocratic president

SOUTH AFRICAN RUGBY FOOTBALL LEAGUE

INTRODUCTION

We at the "SOUTH AFRICAN RUGBY FOOTBALL LEAGUE" wish to pass on and promote several important guidelines.

Primarily we emphasise a totally non-racial stance of the SARFL. The fun and enjoyment which can be gained from not only playing the game and developing the skills, but also the importance of team work, team spirit and fair play on and off the pitch.

As the game grows and develops the principles of fair play and acceptable social behaviour become even more important.

The "message" is not winning at all costs but being a good sport and a valuable member of your team.

of the South African Rugby Board, Danie Craven, publicised Rugby League by calling League people, 'Reptiles.' Offers of pitches quickly followed.

Following the 1957 World Cup, France and Great Britain played each other in a series of matches at Benoni, Durban and East London. Great Britain's casual style was surpassed by a nonchalant Gallic outfit. Spectator reaction was limited. Fortunately, awareness among the Springbok community of the monetary rewards available encouraged South African players to journey to northern England. There were failures and successes; in the latter category none more so than the man born in Bethlehem (Orange Free State) on Christmas day, Tom van Vollenhoven.

Spurred by his achievements, South African consortia started recruitment in 1961. But silently the tourniquet that is South African RU was tightening to stem the pulse of the rival organisations, Rugby League South Africa and the National Rugby League, each with its own tiny combination of clubs. The Ashes-winning 1962 Lions returned from the Antipodes via South Africa, ominously minus one Billy Boston, his talent not in doubt: apartheid's first RL victim. A Springbok RL team jetted out to tour Australasia in 1963 only to hear on leaving Auckland's muddy Carlaw Park, victorious over New Zealand 4–3, that everything was lost. The infant League clubs, each with a proportion of costly former Springboks, and playing on unsuitable grounds for which they were charged hugely inflated rents, began to founder. At the same time the SA Rugby Board offered amnesty for the former players if they gave up the professional game there and then. Thus Kode-Rugby was eclipsed in the Republic. Considerable public support at the turnstiles and an incredible £750,000 spent on development counted for nothing.

Today, as a result of much nocturnal activity in Houghton, a Johannesburg residential area, the resilience and commitment of South Africa's RL fans will once again be put to the test. Centred around the Vaal triangle, where 60 per cent of the population live, exiled League people and Afrikaner colleagues are trying to bring sanity to African rugby and the emotional and mental virus of apartheid. Informal meetings have been held, and a small newspaper advertisement has been placed to test the water. Immediate response is first-rate though the media exaggerates to the point of an instant professional league. The buzz-word is multi-racial, an antibiotic to heal the diseased soul. Danie Craven's lurid picture of Rugby League bears little resemblance to today's game. The miracle of satellite has bypassed the tyrant – and him a descendant of Yorkshire mill-owners too! Not that all is yet clear sailing for Rugby League South Africa 1991.

Now the good news is that the RFL has recognised SARL (1991) and that practical assistance is on the way. On the playing front, their PRO, Tony Lane, has spoken to Bev Risman, one of the British Student RL administrators, to air views on a South African invitation to the Student World Cup in Australia in 1992. Physical education lecturers in academic institutions are monitoring the situation while Wits Technikon have forwarded assurances of their intention to sponsor a South African presence. Expectations are high that Australia will extend a cordial hand, providing an avenue for a return to normality in international rugby relations.

A further chink in the armour of the SARB is the decision to disband the Transvaal sub-union, roughly a provincial second division. As a result there are ten South African Rugby Union squads currently kicking their heels, including talented young men without the privilege of the vote. Forcing teams to amalgamate or disband in order to strengthen first-division standards is as disruptive to Rugby Union as the effects of boycott. Generally, the clubs are unhappy and among this division curiosity about Rugby League has grown. Need I say the rand is more convertible than the rouble? Can we deal SARL (1991) a card to trump mere moral agreement?

In 1987 Terry Bourke, a Widnesian but long-time resident of the Netherlands, in his capacity as chairman of the Drechtstreek RU club offered to play a Hull amateur RL team. Lack of confidence in Dutch Rugby Union administration, and the Union's constant rejection of shirt advertising, drew a narrow line between rugby's survival and failure in Holland. Eventually, the Netherlands RL Commissie was formed to promote the 13-a-side code.

November 1988 saw a propitious start thanks to the hard work of RL officials. High on euphoria a Dutch tournament outlined the potential until realities hit home. Hotel damage; one arrest. Goodwill evaporated. A decline set in. Progress was slowed by work commitments. The original NARL way forward, setting up a small amateur league, was abandoned. Instead they gambled on increasing student co-operation after a pleasing performance in the Student World Cup in July and August 1989. Expected results did not materialise; threats of expulsion from RU teams (so much for the free gangway) ended any hopes of growth. Tas Baitieri's withdrawal as European development officer was a huge blow, and many contacts with various RL bodies have been lost. Are the Dutch fading off the International Board agenda as there are bigger fish to fry in the Soviet Union?

However, a ray of hope has emerged; a group of players have asked Terry Bourke to form a national RL roster, bearing in mind quality rather than quantity. Outside their RU duties they have undertaken to prepare a national selection for instructional games at home and abroad. In fact, Rugby League continues to grow thanks to BBC and Sportsnet's coverage of English and French RL matches. Emma Islanders, formerly Drechtstreek, entertained another Humberside RL amateur team on May 25th this year. After this friendly encounter Bourke, who has resigned from NARL in frustration, will speak to the Dutch Rugby League president, Hans Modderman, to try to resolve the situation and plan for next year.

Elsewhere on the continent, in Germany in 1987, television presented Stefan Niehaus with the chance to enjoy Australian Rugby League. He was hooked. Assuming it to be exclusively an Australian game, Niehaus corresponded with his sister who lives in Australia. Eventually the League network via Tas Baitieri linked up with Niehaus in May 1988. Under Baitieri's guidance and with a large contribution from David Kelly, an accountant at the British Consulate in Düsseldorf, Bocholt RLFC came into existence. A short distance from Holland, the question of fixtures seemed easy but the lack of activity in the Netherlands has brought about something of a lull. Temptation in the form of German Rugby Union is already on the horizon, and one Bocholt player has joined a Berlin Rugby Union club. However, a hard core want to carry on. What a pity that units of the Rhine Army (BAOR) are unable to play against them. In the early months of 1991 there were at least ten regiments, with 10,000 men, relatively close. When will the all-party Parliamentary group tackle Services' Rugby League?

3

The International Scene

FIFTEEN

The 1990 Kangaroos Tour

David Hadfield

Before the announcement of the twenty-eight names to make the trip, there were no delusions in Britain that the Australians would bring anything but a very powerful party. Nonetheless, with players such as Peter Sterling and Gene Miles retired from representative Rugby League and with men with massive British reputations, such as Gavin Miller and John Ferguson, either out of favour or on the point of retirement . . . well, there might just be a chance.

By Grand Final week in Australia, forwards of the calibre of Bradley Clyde, Ian Roberts and Sam Backo were also out of the reckoning. Clyde, a loose forward of the very highest quality, had been side-lined for most of the season with a dreadful knee injury. Roberts, snared for Manly from South Sydney by his former Wigan coach, Graham Lowe, had looked the best forward in Australia but had suffered groin problems which made those of Ellery Hanley on the other side of the world look trivial; and Backo – so devastating against Great Britain in the 1988 series – had struggled with leg ailments that ultimately forced him to give up the game.

Next to be ruled out was Michael O'Connor, the Manly and former St Helens centre or wing, who would have been close to a Test certainty. But these absences were small beer compared to the storm that was about to break over the exclusion of a player who had become synonymous with Australian supremacy on the Rugby League field throughout the 1980s.

It had been a miserable 1990 season in Australia for Wally Lewis. He had lost the captaincy and even his place at stand-off for the Brisbane Broncos; he had fallen out so badly with his coach, Wayne Bennett, that he was destined to leave the club. He had missed a big slice of the season with a badly-torn hamstring, had been fined £2,000 for swearing at a touch-judge and had been widely criticised for his behaviour on and off the field. Almost as an afterthought, he had broken his left forearm.

One thing that remained constant throughout this chronicle of disaster was Lewis's determination to go on his third Kangaroos tour. He believed he had proved his recovery from his arm injury by playing for Brisbane against Canberra in the play-offs, and hell knew no fury like his when the Australian Rugby League doctor, Nathan Gibbs, ruled that the injury had not healed sufficiently for him to tour. Gibbs became the target for abusive calls and even death threats, but he stuck to his diagnosis; Lewis would not be fit for a month and should not be allowed to tour. Lewis's anger extended to others within the ARL, and his public statements on how he believed himself to have been wronged suggested that this would be the last act in a great Test career.

Opposite
The difference between two extremely well matched teams in the 1990 Ashes series was always going to depend on their respective coaches, Mal Reilly of Great Britain and Bobby Fulton of Australia. The first Test at Wembley reflected better on Reilly.

Bob Fulton, Warrington-born but raised in Woollongong and refined at Manly and Eastern Suburbs, had been earmarked all season as the Kangaroo coach. He made no secret of the fact that he wanted Lewis aboard – if fit. Gibbs's verdict took that issue out of his hands; in other respects, he got the squad that he wanted. On paper, an Australian coach has no say in the choice of the twenty-eight players he takes to Europe. In practice, his views were the main yardstick used by the selectors.

There were few surprises, and success in the domestic season was reflected accurately in the choice of five members of the Winfield Cup-winning Canberra Raiders side, including the tour captain, Mal Meninga, and four from the beaten Grand Finalists, Penrith. The Broncos might not have sent Lewis, but six others from the Brisbane club were on the plane. Benny Elias was named as vice-captain and Kerrod and Kevin Walters guaranteed a degree of confusion by becoming the first twins (and identical ones at that) to tour. Brad Fittler became, at 18, the youngest-ever Kangaroo, but he was surrounded by players who had either toured before or who had played club rugby in Britain.

The full party was: (backs) – Gary Belcher (Canberra), Andrew Ettingshausen (Cronulla), Greg Alexander (Penrith), Michael Hancock (Brisbane), Dale Shearer (Brisbane), Mal Meninga (Canberra), Brad Fittler (Penrith), Mark McGaw (Cronulla), Laurie Daley (Canberra), Chris Johns (Brisbane), Cliff Lyons (Manly), Kevin Walters (Brisbane), Des Hasler (Manly), Allan Langer (Brisbane), Ricky Stuart (Canberra); (forwards) – Steve Roach (Balmain), Martin Bella (Manly), Mark Sargent (Newcastle), Glenn Lazarus (Canberra), Kerrod Walters (Brisbane), Ben Elias (Balmain), Bob Lindner (Wests), Mark Carroll (Souths), Paul Sironen (Balmain), John Cartwright (Penrith), David Gillespie (Canterbury), Mark Geyer (Penrith), Brad Mackay (St George).

As a squad, it looked a little light on specialist full-backs – the selectors had decided against sending Garry Jack – and wingers. On the other hand, it seemed overloaded with half-backs; it was already clear that some of them would have to find employment in other positions.

Fulton's line was that every player was a potential Test match performer. 'In my time, I can't remember a Kangaroo outfit leaving this country with twenty-eight genuine Test candidates. It is a marvellous squad of exceptional talent,' he said, stopping just short of congratulating himself on a job well done. Much comment was aroused in both Britain and Australia by the sheer physical presence of the squad. It would have to prove whether it was the best; it was undoubtedly the biggest. Malcolm Reilly, the Great Britain coach, sounded suitably impressed. 'It's an awesome squad,' he said. 'The strength in depth there is unbelievable. I'd hate to be in Bobby Fulton's shoes picking the best side out of that lot. The second team could turn out stronger than the first.'

In fact, for all the talk of the unpredictability of the pecking order on the tour, Fulton stuck very closely to the status quo for the first match against St Helens, picking a side as close as possible to the one which had played against New Zealand in Australia's last Test. The exceptions were the Penrith second-rower, John Cartwright, his claims enhanced by being the only accredited ball-handling forward in the squad, and Andrew Ettingshausen, in for Dale

5
30

Penrith's utility back Greg 'Brandy' Alexander was considered to be the best all-round footballer in the Kangaroo touring party, yet his versatility may well have told against him in the selection of the Test team.

Shearer after the latter had fallen victim to a back injury. They were the two players to stand out in a disappointingly one-sided 34–4 victory over Saints, Cartwright forming a highly effective second-row partnership with Paul Sironen, and ET starting his tour in spectacular style with a hat-trick of tries. Others who played particularly well were Belcher, McGaw, Bella and Lindner, but nobody could be said to have blown their chance to establish first claim on a place in Fulton's top side. The Test team was taking shape early.

It was a big day for St Helens, with the celebration of 100 years of rugby at Knowsley Road. A cavalcade of past stars was paraded before the kick-off. It was a shame that the public address system rendered many of them anonymous, but the 15,260 crowd had no difficulty in recognising old heroes such as Tom Van Vollenhoven and Alex Murphy; those two, in particular, were given a huge welcome.

The present-day Saints had a less satisfactory afternoon. Their defence was never up to the job of putting Australians on the ground, and only Paul Groves enhanced his reputation. As their coach, Mike McClennan, admitted, the Kangaroos had hardly needed to get out of second gear.

The midweek side had an altogether rockier ride at Wakefield Trinity. Although the 36–18 scoreline looked sufficiently clear-cut, it was a stormy match with an equally stormy aftermath. Three Australians were sent off – Stuart for punching, Carroll for fighting and Gillespie for abusive language after full-time – along with John Thompson of Trinity. Three other players were sin-binned by the referee, Kevin Allatt, of whom Fulton said: 'I've been to England on three tours now and that is easily the worst piece of refereeing I have ever seen here. You'd have thought we were in France.'

Any hint that a lack of discipline had contributed to the Kangaroos' problems were given short shrift. Fulton's radio interview with the BBC's Harry Gration, who suggested that the Australians had not exactly covered themselves with glory, had been a collector's item. His outburst was so remarkable that it was played by a Radio 1 disc jockey, and, whatever the rights and wrongs of his case, Fulton sacrificed a great deal of goodwill by the intemperance with which he stated it. Close followers of his coaching career in Australia were less surprised, but the venom of his comments shocked many in Britain.

On the field, Glenn Lazarus had started the campaign to force his way into the Test side. Mark Sargent, Brad Mackay and – until his dismissal – Stuart were also impressive. By what is now a seemingly unbreakable tour convention, none of the three Australians sent off was suspended.

John Monie had never gone along with the theory that the Kangaroos game at Wigan was any sort of unofficial fourth Test match. His view was that club against country should always be an uneven struggle, but that did not blunt the sense of anticipation when the tourists met Britain's leading team. It was perhaps unfortunate that neither Wigan's form nor their injury list put them in the best possible shape for the encounter, but they still gave Australia plenty to think about – if only for the first quarter. Within six minutes they were 6 points up, Shaun Edwards being awarded a penalty-try after Lindner hauled him down as he pursued his own kick, with Joe Lydon adding the conversion. Sadly for the 25,000 crowd, that was it for Wigan. By half-time the tourists

Opposite
Kangaroo second row Paul Sironen gets the ball away to centre Mark McGaw as the tourists demolish Wigan 34–6.

were 20–6 ahead and the final score of 34–6 did not flatter them. The problem, as Monie acknowledged, was that Wigan could match them for intensity for twenty minutes but not for eighty. Ettingshausen continued his remarkable start to the tour with a second hat-trick, Langer showed that he intended to remain first-choice scrum-half, and Roach and Kerrod Walters were the pick of what was, ultimately, a dominant Aussie pack.

Australia's four-yearly trip to Cumbria ended in the predictable manner, although there was little disgrace in Cumbria's 10–42 defeat. Elias pulled the strings and it was Shearer's turn to go in for a hat-trick.

Giant prop Steve 'Blocker' Roach splits Leeds forwards Cavill Heugh and Paul Dixon with a mighty charge. Leeds gave the Kangaroos a real fright on the eve of the first Test, finally going down 10–22.

Leeds's performance in the last tour match before the first Test was a major surprise. They presented their distinguished guests with a real challenge, leading 10–0 after half an hour and putting up a tremendous struggle before going down 10–22. It was a hard-fought Kangaroo victory, but the general view afterwards was that Leeds had done them a favour by giving them such a vigorous work-out the week before the Test. Fulton had seen little to change his mind about his best line-up, although with Daley out injured, Stuart was selected to play stand-off outside Langer – two natural scrum-halves in partnership.

Loyalty to the men in possession also played a major role in Great Britain's team selection. The Wigan trio of Steve Hampson, Andy Gregory and Ellery Hanley – all of whom had missed the tour to Papua New Guinea and New Zealand during the preceding summer – were recalled and Karl Harrison was

Hull prop Karl Harrison (now with Halifax) won a richly deserved Great Britain début alongside his club-mate Lee Jackson in the first Test at Wembley, and played a full and rumbustious part in the historic 19–12 win.

selected for a Test debut at prop. Otherwise, the team was built on the foundations laid on that summer tour, with players who had emerged then – such as Paul Eastwood, Daryl Powell and Carl Gibson – holding their places. There was one exception: Jonathan Davies, who had certainly proved his worth on tour, was conspicuous by his absence. He had originally been in the squad of nineteen, but, as a decision had been made not to name him among the seventeen for the match, he was released in order to visit his sick father in South Wales. Great Britain would play their most intriguing Ashes Test for years – the one they had to win if they were to show that the apparent progress of the past five years was real – without arguably the 'form' player in the first division.

First Test
Wembley Stadium, 27 October

Great Britain 19 Australia 12

There was a feeling of 'now or never' about the Wembley Test; a sense that here was a big stage for Great Britain and that they might never have the same chance. So it proved. A performance which combined tremendous commitment – which was to be expected – and the ability to seize upon chances – which could not be predicted so confidently – was enough to beat an Australian side which looked, as a few lonely Australian voices had suggested, badly selected and vulnerable.

The sense of occasion was greatly to Britain's benefit. The crowd in the stadium was big enough to give it the required atmosphere. The idea of a massed choir singing *Land of Hope and Glory* as the teams came out sounded one of the more dubious gestures, but as Britain filed out to the rousing sound of its archaic sentiments you could see chests swell.

That fervour was carried on into the play. There was no great secret about Britain's tactics; they would kick deep and try to pen Australia in their own territory and force mistakes. That part of the plan worked magnificently from the start. The Kangaroos looked rattled and the only British worry was that the pressure did not produce much in the way of points, with Andy Gregory missing with a drop-goal and Paul Eastwood with two penalties. The one that he did kick, as Australia continued to be harried into mistakes and infringements, put his side into the lead midway through the half.

On Australia's rare thrusts upfield, they found Steve Hampson in typically secure form under the kick. A penalty he conceded running the ball out, however, gave Meninga the chance to kick an equalising goal. A huge British effort had yielded, for practical purposes, nothing; but, early in the second half, Eastwood made up for his kicking lapses by going in for the first try of the match. The chance came from a rarely-seen aspect of Ellery Hanley's skills, his tantalising kick floating over the defensive line for him to re-gather and go within a couple of feet of scoring. The damage was done; the Australian defence was nowhere to be seen and, from the next pass, the strong and unpretentious Eastwood put his head down and smashed through Hancock and Cartwright's efforts to retrieve the situation.

Britain had been in this position – of leading early in the second half – before, and had lost. History threatened to repeat itself when McGaw – arguably Australia's best player – worked the opening for Meninga to put them level. But Hanley's new-found enthusiasm for putting boot to ball came up trumps

Mal Meninga was the perfect captain of the 1990 Kangaroos: courteous and diplomatic off the field, he was dynamic and dangerous on it, scoring vital tries in all three Test matches.

again, Belcher dropping his high kick and Offiah scooping it up to score, with Eastwood adding the conversion.

Schofield's drop-goal gave Britain an extra cushion, but that was unceremoniously yanked from beneath them when McGaw did superbly to ride a series of tackles down the right touchline and score a try which Meninga converted from a wide angle.

Once more it looked as though the prize would be dashed from Britain's grasp, but this most determined of sides dug deep to find the resources to complete the job. Schofield, another outstanding figure for Britain, was the man this time to find the kick that could embarrass Australia. The admirable Daryl Powell backed him up and then timed his pass to Eastwood perfectly. The winger was in no mood to be stopped. The last few minutes would have been even more nerve-wracking if the same player had not landed another penalty after Hanley was obstructed in pursuit of yet another astute kick.

Celebrations on and off the pitch were intense and emotional. Spectators and players had all waited a long, long time for this, and – despite Fulton's predictable complaints about the penalty count – it had been a classic Test, won by the better side.

The crowd of 54,569 was the biggest for an international in Britain. To speculate about what the attendance might have been if more money had been spent on promoting the event in the south of England seemed churlish under the circumstances.

Great Britain: Hampson (Wigan); Eastwood (Hull), Daryl Powell (Sheffield Eagles), Gibson (Leeds), Offiah (Widnes); Schofield (Leeds), Gregory (Wigan); Harrison (Hull), Jackson (Hull), Dixon (Leeds), Roy Rowell (Leeds), Betts (Wigan), Hanley (Wigan)

Substitutes: Ward (St Helens) for Roy Powell after 46 minutes, Fairbank (Bradford Northern) for Harrison after 72 minutes; David Hulme (Widnes) and Edwards (Wigan) not used

Scorers: tries – Eastwood (2), Offiah; goals – Eastwood (3); drop-goal – Schofield

Australia: Belcher; Ettingshausen, McGaw, Meninga, Hancock; Stuart, Langer; Roach, Kerrod Walters, Bella, Sironen, Cartwright, Lindner

Substitutes: Lazarus for Bella and Hasler for Cartwright after 72 minutes, Alexander for Langer after 76 minutes, Shearer for Hancock after 78 minutes.

Scorers: tries – Meninga, McGaw; goals – Meninga (2)

Referee: A Sablayrolles (France)

Attendance: 54,569.

Suddenly, it was Australia who were under pressure. Their domestic press, while giving due credit to Britain, was scathing in its criticism of their side's composition and application. It was going to be back to the drawing-board for the Old Trafford Test a fortnight later, and the intervening games had instantly taken on a new significance.

The first of those games was at Warrington, where Ben Elias, Australia's most constructive forward by far in the British view, virtually booked his place in the second Test side by creating two tries and posing problems throughout. The final margin of 26–6 rather flattered Australia, two late tries from Hancock and Fittler stretching the scoreline. Warrington had left out Paul Bishop – prompting his departure for St Helens – and their Welsh recruit, Kevin Ellis, had a chance to show his potential.

At Castleford, it was Brad Mackay, the versatile St George man playing at loose forward, who put forward an unarguable case for a Test place. The first joint outing for the possible half-back combination of Lyons and Stuart was also promising, but Cas really presented little threat. Their inability to hang on to the ball meant that Australia were rarely extended in their 28–8 victory. It was, however, interesting to see Twickenham or Wimbledon-style hospitality tents on the training pitch at Wheldon Road.

The fixture formula for the tour gave Halifax, with their continuing high level of loyal support, a match against the 1990 Kangaroos. At the time it looked as though the fixture could have been better used elsewhere – for a match against Yorkshire at the Don Valley Stadium, perhaps. As it turned out, Halifax acquitted themselves rather well; indeed, very well, considering their unimpressive league form at the time. There was never any danger of Australia losing, but Halifax, well led by the massive Brendan Hill, scored enough points in the second half to embarrass them severely. The final score was 18–36, and Fulton – unsurprisingly – blamed a heavy second-half penalty count imposed against his side by the referee, Brian Galtress. The Kangaroos allowed their frustration to affect their discipline, and only a handful of players, Alexander and Sargent among them, performed close to their best. Langer had a strong defensive game, but did not quite do enough to hang on to his Test place.

Second Test
Old Trafford,
Manchester
10 November

Great Britain 10 Australia 14

While Bob Fulton shuffled his cards, making the obvious changes by bringing in Shearer, Daley, Lyons, Elias, Mackay and Lazarus, Malcolm Reilly – apart from the addition of a fit-again Andy Platt – stood by the players who had served him so well at Wembley, hoping that they would be able to complete the job at Old Trafford. They could not do so; but they came within seconds, within inches, within one lapse of concentration and one missed tackle of guaranteeing themselves a share of the Ashes for the first time in twenty years.

In the second minute of time added on for injuries, Ricky Stuart, far from comfortable at scrum-half in this match, was penned in his own 22, apparently with nowhere to go, and the scores were tied at 10–10. But he swept past an exhausted Lee Jackson and found himself, to his own surprise, with an invitingly open corridor down the right flank. Offiah had gone off injured early in the second half; he might not be the world's most feared defender, but it is fair to assume that, had he been on the pitch, he would have caught Stuart. As it was, the British cover was caught cold and Stuart was almost over the try-line before he was hauled down. By that time, Meninga was on the scene and there was no stopping him.

Despite a reputation for being vulnerable to the pressures of the big occasion, stand-off Cliff Lyons was drafted into the Australian team for the second and third Tests and produced two inspired performances.

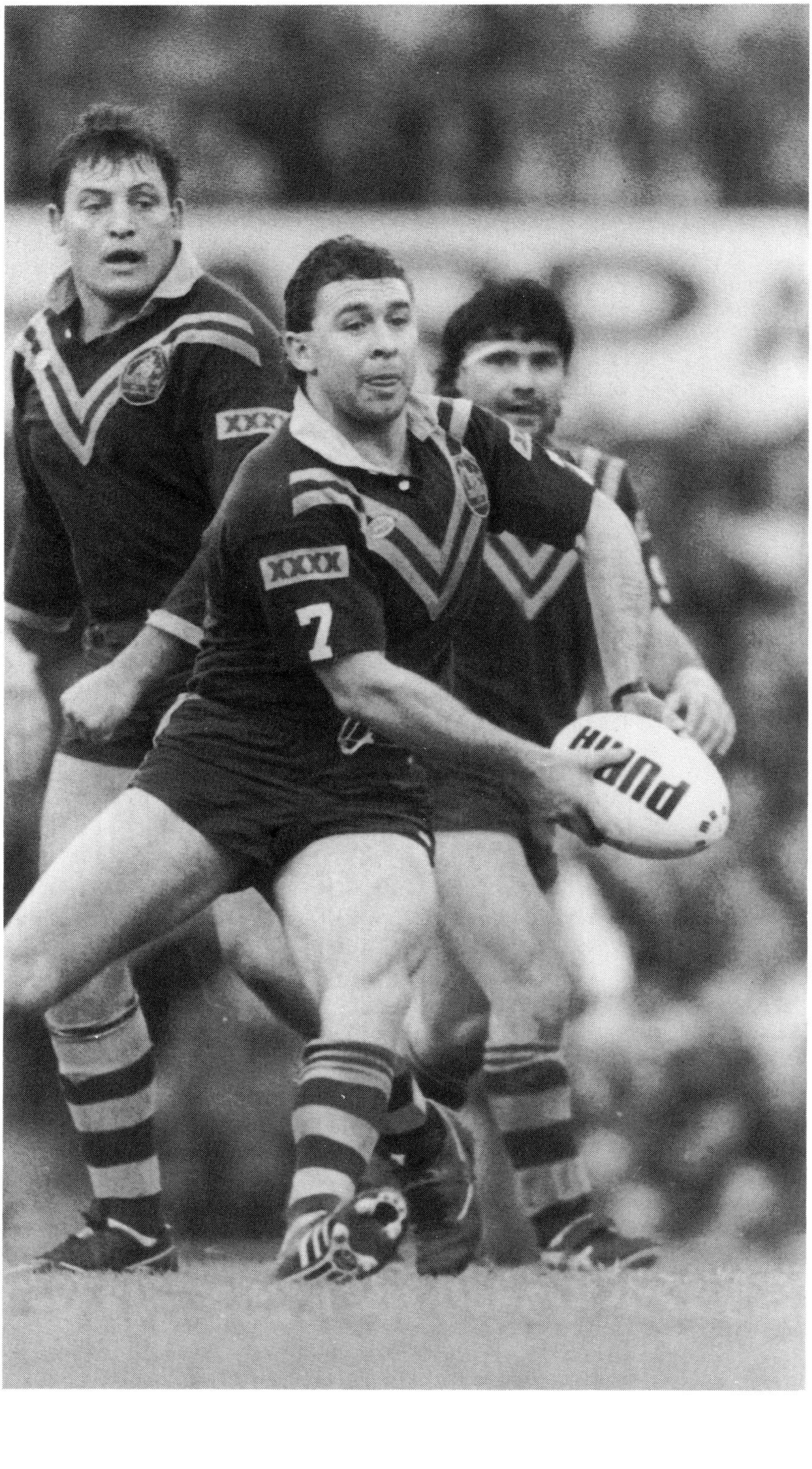

Canberra half-back Ricky Stuart was hero and villain in the second Test at Old Trafford, his intercepted pass giving Great Britain a lead they looked like holding until his last-minute, seventy-metre break gave Meninga the winning try.

It was a cruel way to lose a Test match, especially when a draw would have brought such a glittering prize, but Australia were in no way unworthy victors. Their revamped side functioned better in all areas than it had at Wembley, with the man-of-the-match, Elias, and Lyons, despite his reputation for blowing up in the big matches, both having excellent games. It was Lyons who sent Laurie Daley away to give Dale Shearer an ominously easy first try, and Britain suddenly looked as though they could be swept away. To their great credit, they steadied the ship and held the score to 2–4 at half-time. A try by Paul Dixon, a player whose fierce determination epitomises so much that the Great Britain side has achieved over the last two years, put them ahead after fifty-one minutes, but Australia hit back with a glorious effort, picking the ball up from substitute Paul Loughlin's weak clearance kick and moving it spectacularly through several pairs of hands before Ettingshausen's imaginative cross-kick found Lyons with the time and space to complete the move.

Stuart's one bad moment of the match – a loose pass that was intercepted by Loughlin – brought a fifty-yard try to put Britain level, and the stage was set for that heart-breaking finale. Denis Betts summed up the disbelief in the British camp that one trifling imperfection, so late in the game, should have proved so costly. 'Eighty-two minutes,' he kept repeating. 'We held them for eighty-two minutes.' It wasn't quite enough, but it had been, whether you were celebrating or lamenting in the eighty-third, a quite magnificent Test.

Great Britain: Hampson (Wigan); Eastwood (Hull), Daryl Powell (Sheffield Eagles), Gibson (Leeds), Offiah (Widnes); Schofield (Leeds), Gregory (Wigan); Harrison (Hull), Jackson (Hull), Platt (Wigan), Betts (Wigan), Dixon (Leeds), Hanley (Wigan)

Substitutes: Loughlin (St Helens) for Offiah after 45 minutes, Ward (St Helens) for Harrison after 51 minutes; David Hulme (Widnes) and Roy Powell (Leeds) not used

Scorers: tries – Dixon, Loughlin; goal – Eastwood

Australia: Belcher; Ettingshausen, Meninga, Daley, Shearer; Lyons, Stuart; Roach, Elias, Lazarus, Sironen, Lindner, Mackay

Substitutes: Alexander, Hasler, Sargent, and Cartwright not used

Scorers: tries – Shearer, Lyons, Meninga; goal – Meninga

Referee: A. Sablayrolles (France)

Attendance: 46,615.

In theory, the two club matches between the second and third Tests should have given Australia the hardest run-in imaginable, pairing them as they did against the first and second-placed sides in the league. The theory only turned out to be half-true, because the league leaders, Hull, were a shadow of the team that had been playing so forcefully in the first division. Brian Smith, pragmatic Aussie as he is, had made it clear that the tour game was a sideshow, not serious business. That approach communicated itself to the players, who performed without their usual intensity. Having said that, the Kangaroos turned it on,

9

Opposite
Balmain hooker Ben Elias gave Australia an imaginative and penetrative edge around the ruck in the last two Tests, won the man-of-the-match award at Old Trafford and defied a cracked rib to score the clinching try at Elland Road.

Right
Referee Alain Sablayrolles, heavily criticised throughout the series by the Australian camp, leaps in to quell a flare-up between Steve Roach and Andy Gregory in the second Test.

with the understanding between the Walters twins at the centre of much of their best work. They won in a canter, 34–4, on a night when Hull's efforts on the pitch never lived up to the sense of occasion created by the opening of their new Threepenny Stand.

Widnes were a different proposition, and their contest was the best club match of the tour. After trailing 0–10 at half-time, Widnes, inspired by Kurt Sorensen, hurled themselves at Australia, but their try from Jonathan Davies, who also kicked two goals, came a little too late to give them a realistic chance of repeating their 1978 victory – the last over the tourists by an English club side. Bob Lindner, an expressive tourist from the outset, stood out for Australia. It was interesting that the Australian press contingent was unanimous on one point: that Davies had looked the most likely of all British players to disconcert Australia in the third Test six days later and that the British management should be certified if they failed to select him.

Third Test
Elland Road, Leeds, 24 November

Great Britain 0 Australia 14

The management team presumably would be regarded in Australia as semi-certifiable, because the most significant change for Elland Road – a late switch to Wembley being deemed administratively impossible – was the inclusion of Davies, but only as a substitute. It was a wary compromise, made in a mood of deep conservatism and with a feeling that the only way to proceed was through more of the same.

In fact, Davies was brought into the game after only nine minutes, to replace the injured Carl Gibson. Before he could come on, however, Stuart's long pass took advantage of the overlap created by the one-man shortage and Ettingshausen scored.

Opposite
Andy Gregory struggles to control a wet ball in the third and deciding Test at Elland Road. Gregory was unable to exert the influence he had had at Wembley, and Australia ran out worthy winners by 14–0.

Britain had two good chances to get back on terms, but the excellent Stuart scampered back to tackle Davies and then Betts failed to sense Schofield in support after he had made a break. After that, Australia took control in a way more redolent of the processional early 1980s than the new, competitive Ashes era which seemed to have dawned since. Another adventurous Stuart pass drew Schofield out of the line in search of an interception; it was a worthwhile gamble, but a losing one as Australia clinically exploited the gap to score. A late try from Elias, playing with a series of injections to deaden the pain of a cracked rib, just served to emphasise the fact that the men in green and gold were once more in control.

For Britain, the game was a dreadful anti-climax, and the suspicion that the chance to deny Australia the Ashes had been created and lost at Old Trafford proved all too accurate. That particular Great Britain team had given all it had to offer in the first two Tests. Elland Road cried out for a change of approach, for a team to confuse and conquer rather than contain. Sad to say, and despite all the glorious achievement of London and Manchester, I know of nobody who was genuinely surprised by the loss of the series at Leeds.

Great Britain: Hampson (Wigan); Eastwood (Hull), Daryl Powell (Sheffield Eagles), Gibson (Leeds), Offiah (Widnes); Schofield (Leeds), Andy Gregory (Wigan); Harrison (Hull), Jackson (Hull), Platt (Wigan), Dixon (Leeds), Betts (Wigan), Hanley (Wigan)

Substitutes: Davies (Widnes) for Gibson after 9 minutes, Mike Gregory (Warrington) for Dixon after 55 minutes, Roy Powell (Leeds) for Harrison after 73 minutes; David Hulme (Widnes) not used

Australia: Belcher; Ettingshausen, Meninga, Daley, Shearer; Lyons, Stuart; Roach, Elias, Lazarus, Sironen, Lindner, Mackay

Substitutes: Alexander for Shearer, Sargent for Lazarus, Gillespie for Sironen and Hasler for Mackay all after 76 minutes

Scorers: tries – Ettingshausen, Meninga, Elias; goal – Meninga

Referee: A. Sablayrolles (France)

Attendance: 32,000.

Much of the credit for that sense of inevitability must go, of course, to Australia for the way they had regrouped after what, by modern touring standards, was a cataclysmic disaster at Wembley. The feeling that this was a squad which was going to peak later on its tour than some of its predecessors was confirmed by events in France.

Despite unmistakable signs of a French revival the previous season – although it is amazing how many people have completely forgotten that victory at Headingley – the Gallic section of the Kangaroo tour was more one-sided

than ever. It opened with a 46–18 win over a President's XIII, staged for development motives at Corbeil on the outskirts of Paris and watched by a relatively encouraging crowd of 3,000. France B were swept aside 78–6 in Lyon and the stage was set for a humiliating Test in Avignon.

Paul Dixon of Leeds was perhaps Great Britain's most consistent performer in the Ashes series, his non-stop grafting at both prop and second row catching the eye in all three Tests.

Opposite
Mal Meninga proudly displays the Ashes trophy after Australia's third Test win at Elland Road.

First Test
Avignon,
2 December

France 4 Australia 60

Students of midweek form in Britain had long since come to the conclusion that Greg Alexander, perhaps the most gifted and versatile footballer in the party, was unlucky not to command a place somewhere in the Test side. In Avignon, he got his chance when Stuart was injured after eighteen minutes and he seized it in remarkable style. The Penrith player, already a prime target for English clubs pondering their import situation for the following season, scored 26 points from three tries and seven goals; not a bad effort for a reserve.

France, with a number of enforced changes from the side which had played so well against Great Britain at the start of the year, simply could not cope with him, nor with the power and pace of his team-mates.

France: Roses (Le Barcarès); Bouzer (Toulouse Olympique), Bienes (St Gaudens), Bret (XIII Catalan), Pons (St Gaudens); Fraisse (Carcassonne), Entat (Hull); Titeux (Avignon), Valéro (Lézignan), Calvo (Toulouse Olympique), Divet (Carcassonne), Verdes (Villeneuve), Moliner (XIII Catalan)

Substitutes: Tisseyre (Pamiers) for Calvo after 55 minutes, Bouscayrol (Pamiers) for Pons and Marginet (St Estève) for Bienes after 74 minutes; Lope (Toulouse Olympique) not used

Scorer: try – Fraisse

Australia: Belcher; Ettingshausen, Meninga, Daley, Shearer; Lyons, Stuart; Roach, Elias, Lazarus, Sironen, Gillespie, Mackay

Substitutes: Alexander for Stuart after 18 minutes, Hasler for Daley after 40 minutes, Geyer for Sironen and Sargent for Gillespie after 61 minutes

Scorers: tries – Alexander (3), Belcher (2), Ettingshausen (2), Sironen, Shearer, Gillespie, Lazarus; goals – Alexander (7), Meninga

Referee: J. Holdsworth (England)

Attendance: 3,329.

The tour reached its nadir in Carcassonne, when only 500 spectators turned up to see a weak Languedoc–Roussillon selection beaten, but not disgraced as it happens, by 9–38. Minds, as they always do at this stage of the tour, were turning to home.

Second Test
Perpignan,
9 December

France 10 Australia 34

In the context of what had gone before, France got off lightly at the Stade Gilbert Brutus. They deserved to do so, because they put up a greatly improved performance, with their captain, Patrick Entat, showing the benefit of his British experience and lifting many of the players around him. For much of the match they gave as good as they got and it was only a series of silly defensive errors that undermined their effort.

France: Fraisse (Carcassonne); Bouzer (Toulouse Olympique), Bret (XIII Catalan), Delaunay (XIII Catalan), Pons (St Gaudens); Moliner (XIII Catalan), Entat (Hull); Tisseyre (Pamiers), Valéro (Lézignan), Buttignol (Avignon), Divet (Carcassonne), Lope (Toulouse Olympique), Verdes (Villeneuve)

Substitutes: Bienes (St Gaudens) for Bret after 69 minutes, Marginet (St Estève) for Fraisse after 74 minutes; Rémirès (Carcassonne) and Titeux (Avignon) not used

Scorers: tries – Pons, Entat; goal – Tisseyre

Australia: Belcher; Ettingshausen, Meninga, Shearer, Alexander; Lyons, Stuart; Roach, Elias, Lazarus, Sironen, Lindner, Mackay

Substitutes: Gillespie for Lindner after 21 minutes, Johns for Alexander after 57 minutes, Sargent for Lazarus and Hasler for Stuart after 73 minutes

Scorers: tries – Mackay (2), Shearer, Meninga, Alexander, Ettingshausen, Roach; goals – Alexander (3)

Referee: J. Holdsworth (England)

Attendance: 3,428.

With that, the 1990 touring party headed for home and Christmas on the beach, leaving students of comparative Kangaroo-ology to ponder their place in the scheme of things.

First impressions were that the advance claims made for them were exaggerated, but this was a squad that grew into the job once it identified the precise nature of that job. If it lacked a truly dominant figure – a Sterling or a Lewis – it had more than its share of success stories. There was Stuart, beating off the competition to make himself Australia's number one scrum-half; Elias, a shining light in the game for what seems like a generation but only on this tour establishing himself as a Test player; Lindner, for his sheer consistency perhaps the man-of-the-tour; and Ettingshausen, despite his oft-stated distaste for the wing, giving a series of seminars on how to stay involved for eighty minutes from wide out. Young players, such as Lazarus and Mackay, came good and lived up to all their promise. Not least, there was Meninga. Not only did he continue to look the world's most damaging centre, he was also an exemplary captain, his easy manner a priceless antidote to the abrasive Fulton.

The Australian coach will be remembered with little affection in Britain; he played up to his reputation as a whinger too enthusiastically for that. The low points of his 'world against us' mentality were his diatribes about the refereeing at Wakefield, Halifax and Wembley. There were also allegations of gouging – which he declined to substantiate – after the game at Widnes.

There is much to be said in his defence, however. He had given no promises to depart from his lifelong practice of complaining when he thought he had something to complain about, and some of the refereeing – although not that of M. Sablayrolles in the Tests – was dire. He also deserves credit for doing what no recent Australian coach has had to do – rethinking and regrouping in mid-tour. When fresh decisions were forced on him, he made the right ones. Perhaps the greatest achievement for Fulton was the way he conquered his own nature and personality during the run-up to the deciding Test. There was a popular theory, and a reasonable one on the face of it, that his own tension would communicate itself to the players and that they would be unable to perform to their best at Elland Road. But he kept the lid on; the build-up was relaxed, and Australia went out and saved him from the ignominy of losing an Ashes series.

There were unsavoury stories of vandalism, of a cricket centre in Manchester and a hotel in Perpignan damaged by players, but those incidents were not typical of the behaviour of the tourists. They were under pressure and under the spotlight and they found little peace in their hotel in Manchester, which was always bulging as well with parties of supporters.

If they made a less stunning impression than the parties of 1982 and 1986, that was because Britain had a clearer idea of what to expect. These were the Kangaroos who stared disaster in the face – had they lost at Old Trafford, all their obituaries sixty years on would have led off on the fact that they played in the side that lost the Ashes – and went home intact. They did it the hard way – or at least a much harder way – and many will say now that the 1990 tour is the more satisfying in hindsight for that fact.

SIXTEEN

The British Coal Tests against France 1991

Mike Rylance

Like everything else in the middle of the 1990–91 season, the annual Great Britain–France encounters suffered by comparison with what had gone before. The Kangaroo tour had probably contained more drama and had been exposed to a wider public than any previous Australian tour and when the visitors departed there was an undeniable atmosphere of post-Australian *tristesse* that the French were unable to dissipate. The French were left looking like the support act who have to wind up the show after the star has left the stage to raptures of applause.

Of course, in an ideal world, the French should provide the warm-up act for such a tour. They had spent a nervous couple of months waiting to see what damage the Australians would inflict on their already minimal self-confidence, only to emerge drained from that ordeal and then to concede even more points to the British.

To Great Britain's credit they treated the two matches with appropriate seriousness and resisted the temptation to treat these Tests as trials, as had sometimes happened in the past. The key to their highly competent performances was twofold: their professionalism had been tempered in the heat of the series against the Australians, and they were also fired by the humiliation of their defeat by France in the previous year's series. The memory of a scrambled 8–4 win in Perpignan followed by a numbing defeat at Headingley, needed to be dispelled; and having just failed to take the series against the world's best, the British were now in no mood to lose face and two World Cup points against the country at the bottom of the table.

The French turned out to be more acquiescent opponents than those who had turned the tables at Headingley in that famous victory of the year before. The Australians had just put 94 points past them in two Tests. Such experienced players as Jean-Luc Rabot and their captain, Hugues Ratier, had retired from international football, though Guy Delaunay had been persuaded to return against Britain. Their influential play-maker, Gilles Dumas, had been injured for half the season, as had their strong-running second-rower, Didier Cabestany. His partner, Daniel Divet, seemed no longer interested in the tricolour jersey. Their resources were looking not so much thin as transparent. After they had played against the British they had conceded 199 points in their last four Tests. Their one consolation was the Espoirs' revenge victory over Great Britain Under-21s at Wigan on the eve of the senior international.

The Headingley Test would have been cancelled if Malcolm Reilly had had his way. Great Britain's coach, who had recently been appointed on a full-time basis, thought that the match would be 'of no relevance'. While asserting that 'international competition is very important for the general welfare of the game', he clearly felt that he was being prevented from fulfilling his duty towards it. As national coach his immediate aim was to improve on his team's performance in their last match in Perpignan. But the conflict between club and country arose when, as a result of many players' midweek commitments, notably the Castleford v. Wigan Challenge Cup match, he had just two days in which to prepare, as well as redesign, the team. It was yet another addition to the catalogue of evidence of too much football for the top players. As it turned out, he need not have worried.

What a contrast with the opposite camp! To suffer a record defeat, a year after achieving a record victory, was a poor way for Jacques Jorda to end a memorable four-year spell in charge of the national side. One of his major difficulties was to bring French players into line with methods current everywhere in the world except in the French Championship in which they played week in, week out. But he brought a much-needed discipline to the national side, as well as trying to maintain a fine balance between traditional French improvisation and the increasingly organised game of their opponents. The French management has always been prone to debilitating bouts of nostalgia for past glories, but Jorda was only too aware that romanticism is rarely a match for percentages, weight-training and game plans. And yet his teams did go some way to restoring French attacking values, as they showed at Headingley in 1990. The pity for them was that it had to be followed by Headingley, 1991.

FRANCE v GREAT BRITAIN – THE FIRST TEST

Gilbert Brutus Stadium, Perpignan, 27 January

France 10 Great Britain 45

Two World Cup points were intended to give added meaning to this first Test match, but the points were in Britain's bag well before half-time, after which the British did little more than go through the motions while the French tried to stop them. It was an impressive, if slightly flawed, British performance on the ground where they had struggled so much a year before. The pragmatism which the French always associate with the British style of play was obvious in the logical way Britain approached this game, except that they could have made it even harder for the home side by making better use of the stiff breeze in the first half.

Outstanding for Great Britain was Denis Betts, who again confirmed his huge international potential by filling the role once played by his Wigan team-mate, Andy Goodway. It was Betts's pass that put Garry Schofield over for the first try before France had got out of their own quarter. Then the Schofield–Betts partnership put Martin Offiah in for the second, before the Wigan second-rower was himself awarded an obstruction try from a kick ahead at the play-the-ball. With a fourth try from Shaun Edwards, who was making the most of his recall to the scrum-half position, following Andy Gregory's international retirement and David Hulme's unavailability, Britain were 25–0 up after as many minutes.

Denis Betts, supported by stand-off Garry Schofield, prepares to drive the ball up. Great Britain won the first Test in Perpignan by 45–10.

The forwards set up good positions for the backs to plunder from. Among them Ian Lucas, replacing the suspended Karl Harrison, and Les Holliday, playing his first game for Britain at Perpignan as his father, Bill, had done in 1964, had sound debuts. All in all, the British were just too solid for their brave but outgunned opponents.

So long as the French are capable of scoring a try as inspired as the one set up by David Fraisse they will find their admirers on the international scene. The Carcassonne centre stormed through a gap before Jacques Moliner and Christophe Auroy continued the move to give Cyril Pons a run to the corner. As the winger was bundled into the corner flag by Paul Eastwood, he flipped the ball up for the supporting Auroy to dive over for a fine debut try. Fraisse added another before half-time as he intercepted and sprinted some seventy metres to touch down.

In the second half, France showed more commitment in defence, but even so could not prevent further tries from Edwards and Andy Platt. The inevitable Offiah put his seal on the game by dashing over for his 200th try, a remarkable record established in less than four seasons.

France: Auroy; Rémirès, Fraisse, Delaunay, Pons; Dumas, Entat; Buttignol, Valéro, Tisseyre, Magnac, Verdes, Moliner

Substitutes: Chamorin for Verdes after 8 minutes, Biénès for Dumas after 34 minutes, Baba for Valéro after 50 minutes; Roses not used

Scorers: tries – Auroy, Fraisse; goal – Buttignol

Great Britain: Hampson (Wigan); Eastwood (Hull), Gibson (Leeds), Powell (Sheffield Eagles), Offiah (Widnes); Schofield (Leeds), Edwards (Wigan); Lucas (Wigan), Jackson (Hull), Platt (Wigan), Betts (Wigan), Holliday (Widnes), Hanley (Wigan)

Substitutes: Fairbank (Bradford Northern) for Holliday after 50 minutes, St John Ellis (Castleford) for Hampson and Eyres (Widnes) for Jackson after 70 minutes, Aston (Sheffield Eagles) for Schofield after 79 minutes

Scorers: tries – Schofield (2), Edwards (2), Offiah (2), Betts, Platt; goals – Eastwood (6); drop-goal – Schofield

Referee: G. McCallum (Australia)

Attendance: 3,249.

Hull hooker Lee Jackson took up against the French where he had left off against Australia, giving two displays of lively and energetic commitment.

Patrick Entat brought all the experience he had garnered over the season at Hull to bear on a depleted and inexperienced French side, but he could not prevent disaster in either of the Tests against Great Britain.

Opposite
Widnes second row Richard Eyres returned to the national side for the second Test against France at Headingley, a match won by Great Britain by the record margin of 60–4.

GREAT BRITAIN v FRANCE – THE SECOND TEST

Headingley, Leeds, 16 February

Great Britain 60 France 4

'It's not easy building up to the French Tests, especially the home one,' said Martin Offiah, just before the event, 'because I'll play a lot of games with bigger crowds and a better atmosphere over the course of a season.' Certainly the intensity of Wembley, Old Trafford or Elland Road seemed a long way away from this Saturday afternoon at Headingley. A record aggregate of 131,000 had watched the series against the Australians, but just 5,284 spectators turned up to watch a very similar British side play against France.

Martin Offiah scored a record five tries for Great Britain in the 60–4 rout of France at Headingley.

But Offiah must have found inspiration from somewhere as he ran in a record-breaking five tries in Great Britain's biggest Test match victory. He didn't begin to find the try-line until the second half, but after he had helped create Garry Schofield's second try he went on a personal rampage to score what Malcolm Reilly called 'real winger's tries'.

The Great Britain coach said afterwards: 'We knew that the first fifteen minutes of the second half would be vital. I asked the lads to be patient. Our support play, awareness and opportunism were superb.' It went like clockwork. Within twenty minutes of the restart, Britain had trebled their half-time score to lead by 48–0.

It could have been very different. In the opening period of play France had looked the more enterprising in attack, with scrum-half Patrick Entat calling most of the shots. It was unfortunate that it should be his pass that Schofield intercepted to open Britain's account and that his Hull team-mate, Paul Eastwood, should be on form with his kicking, before adding a try just before half-time. The 16–0 interval lead flattered the British and disheartened the visitors. 'I knew that last year's team would have been leading at half-time instead of losing,' said Jacques Jorda, 'but the new players couldn't take the shock psychologically. They weren't physically or mentally strong enough to compete for eighty minutes.'

But the British team was also a different proposition from the previous year's. They had developed a new quality – ruthlessness. In this, their fifth Test of the season, they might have been expected to wind down or not play to their capacity. That they maintained their concentration and keenness throughout and punished any error of the opposition's was yet further evidence that they were drawing level with the Australians at the top of the international tree.

Great Britain: Hampson (Wigan); Eastwood (Hull), Daryl Powell (Sheffield Eagles), Loughlin (St Helens), Offiah (Widnes); Schofield (Leeds), Edwards (Wigan); Dannatt (Hull), Jackson (Hull), Platt (Wigan), Eyres (Widnes), Fairbank (Bradford Northern), Hanley (Wigan)

Substitutes: Roy Powell (Leeds) for Eyres after 56 minutes, St John Ellis (Castleford) for Hampson, Kevin Ellis (Warrington) for Loughlin and England (Castleford) for Fairbank after 62 minutes

Scorers: tries – Schofield (3), Eastwood, Offiah (5), Edwards, Hampson; goals – Eastwood (8)

France: Auroy; Bouzer, Fraisse, Chamorin, Pons; Moliner, Entat; Montgaillard, Valéro, Buttignol, Cabestany, Verdes, Saumitou

Substitutes: Magnac for Cabestany after 50 minutes, Rémirès for Bouzer after 54 minutes, Tisseyre for Montgaillard after 61 minutes, Alésina for Auroy after 71 minutes

Scorer: try – Pons

Referee: G. McCallum (Australia)

Attendance: 5,284.

Garry Schofield scored a hat-trick at Headingley to add to the brace he scored in Perpignan, and generally proved too hot to handle for the outgunned French.

Two matches against France were played at Under-21 level, with Great Britain sharing the spoils

Limoux, 26 January

France Espoirs 2 Great Britain Under-21 48

France Espoirs: Van Brussel; Correira, Ricard, Garcia, Millet; Despin, Koob; Stéphane Martin, Gayral, Sautrice, Grandjean, Durand, Mons

Substitutes: Texeido, Hébert, Giorgi Martin, Gagnon

Scorer: goal – Millet

Great Britain Under-21: Moxon (Bradford Northern); Myers (Wigan), Rudd (Warrington), Newlove (Featherstone Rovers), Fawcett (Leeds); Martyn (Oldham), Goulding (Wigan); Chambers (Warrington), Southernwood (Castleford), Richards (Bradford Northern), McNamara (Hull), Price (Wakefield Trinity), Clarke (Wigan)

Substitutes: Darbyshire (Warrington), Forshaw (Wigan), Lumb (Hunslet), Jackson (Hunslet)

Scorers: tries – Goulding, Southernwood (2), Martyn, Fawcett, Clarke, Forshaw, Lumb; goals – Rudd (8)

Referee: B. Galtress (Bradford)

Attendance: 1,800.

Wigan, 15 February

Great Britain Under–21 6, France Espoirs 16

Great Britain Under-21: Connolly (St Helens); Myers (Wigan), Rudd (Warrington), Darbyshire (Warrington), Hunte (St Helens); Smith (Castleford), Goulding (Wigan); Chambers (Warrington), Southernwood (Castleford), Richards (Bradford Northern), McNamara (Hull), Price (Wakefield Trinity), Clarke (Wigan)

Substitutes: Martyn (Oldham), Forshaw (Wigan), Spruce (Widnes), Burgess (Salford)

Scorers: try – Myers; goal – Rudd

France Espoirs: Carvet; Correira, Despin, Ricard, Van Brussel; Fages, Delgado; Grandjean, Torreilles, Hébert, Costes, Teixido, Amat

Substitutes: Sautrice, Gayral, Millet, Gagnon

Scorers: tries – Fages, Van Brussel (2); goals – Torreilles, Millet

Referee: M. Chanfreau (France)

Attendance: 3,005.

SEVENTEEN

The Season in France 1990–91

Harry Edgar

On May 26 St Gaudens, with their strong Australian contingent, achieved a defensive win over Villeneuve by the narrowest of margins, 10–8, to carry off the French Championship. The weekend before they had beaten a young and comparatively inexperienced Pia side, 30–4, in the final of the Lord Derby Cup in Carcassonne and so achieved the double.

Those lucky enough to be present at the Toulouse stadium that day in May saw a crowd of 10,000 enjoying a great Rugby League occasion. There were bands and country dancing, firecrackers going off in all directions, a forest of waving flags all over the stadium and some good rugby played out under a blazing sun. It was a day to be cherished.

Villeneuve, player-coached by the Australian Mark Wakefield, were unlucky to lose. They played much the more thoughtful, aggressive rugby but failed to break down the St Gaudens defensive wall and lost by a penalty-goal, the deciding try coming from the second-row, Richard Clarke, the player-of-the-season in French Rugby League.

St Gaudens's double was largely due to the discipline brought to the side by their Australian players – at times they featured no less than six Australians – including the goal-kicking stand-off, Chris Hastings, and the experienced centre, John Maguire, as well as Richard Clarke. In addition to the Australians they were able to rely on the brilliant finishing of the international winger, Cyril Pons, and the long experience of Gilles Dumas and Philippe Fourquet. They were certainly France's team of the season.

That great Toulouse occasion seemed also to be a celebration of the revolution that had swept away the old administrative regime in the Rugby League elections at the beginning of the month. On May 4 Jean-Paul Verdaguer was replaced in the French game's highest office by the long-serving council member, the much-loved Gilbert Dautant, and suddenly a new wave of energy and optimism swept over the game in France.

Gilbert Dautant, now 63, is well known to British RL followers after his many years of supervising exchange visits and tours between the two countries. There seems no doubt that he has galvanized the French League into action: a fresh wind is blowing through the new offices in Toulouse. Certainly the crowd at the Championship final showed their affection for him and their hope that, under his leadership, the game might really begin to achieve something in France.

Dautant has already brought several capable officials back from premature retirement. Among them is Charles Zalduendo, the former international prop forward. Now a senior police inspector in Toulouse, 'Za-Za' is only one of a team of officials working hard to win a new, positive image for French Rugby

League. He was quickly appointed manager of the French touring team to New Zealand and Papua New Guinea which set off in early June.

Of course, despite all the optimism and activity, it still remains desperately difficult for French RL to win over the media to the game and thereby recruit sponsors and more support from the public. As ever, the key to everything is achieving success at international level – and this still promises to be a hard road for France to tread.

Certainly the announcement of their team for the tour to New Zealand and Papua New Guinea at the end of the season only served as a cruel reminder of how tough things are going to be for France to win international credibility against such hardened professional opposition as Great Britain, Australia and New Zealand.

The French selection looked ominously weak, even by its own standards, from the day it was announced. Captained by Gilles Dumas, who had struggled against injuries throughout the season, it was missing many of France's most talented players – and, to fill the gaps, included several players with little international experience largely to make up the numbers and not because they offered any genuine hope of building a successful Test team.

Of the talented absentees, the best of the lot, Jacques Moliner, was injured, and the enigmatic attacking genius, David Fraisse, had been tragically cut down in a motorcycle accident. The full aftermath of Fraisse's injuries is not yet known, but after lying in a coma for two weeks in a Marseilles hospital it is highly unlikely that he will ever play Rugby League again.

Losing any of their handful of genuine top-class Test players is a burden that France, with its inconsistent club competition, can hardly be expected to carry. Yet that was the Achilles heel that dogged the French at international level throughout the 1990–91 season.

Coming fresh from their exploits of the previous season, that emotional victory over Great Britain at Headingley in April 1990 and a highly respectable three wins and three losses tour of Australia, France had high hopes of keeping up that momentum. The early part of their domestic season did nothing to change that with the new Pool of Aces format in the Championship providing a series of excellent games, many of them televised on the Eurosport channel, and drawing some of the best attendances for early season club games for many years in French Rugby League.

Carcassonne, who won the Pool of Aces competition 28–16 in a thrilling replay to the final against St Estève drawn 22–22 after extra-time, regularly attracted crowds of over 4,000 to the Stade Albert Domec for their home games. Sadly for Carcassonne, and for the treasurer of the French League, their players were unable to produce the results their large payments (compared to all other clubs with the possible exception of XIII Catalan) should have justified, and the Canaries failed to reach the play-offs in both Cup and Championship.

But the strands of optimism started to filter away as soon as the national coach, Jacques Jorda, and his selectors tried to put together a team to face the Australians at the end of the Kangaroos tour. The experienced threequarters, the former captain Hugues Ratier and the centre Guy Delauay, had announced their retirement from international football, as had the tough and talented front-rower, Jean-Luc Rabot. Dumas and Didier Cabestany had long-term injuries, and other experienced players had had disagreements with Jorda and were ruled out of selection.

Having to throw in either half-a-dozen new caps, or to pluck players from a previous era of test football, whose regular Rugby League diet nowadays was in the French Championship, and, in some cases, Pool B of that Championship, was like leading lambs to the slaughter against Australia. And that's how it turned out at Avignon on December 2nd. The Aussies won 60 points to 4, and the whole world of French Rugby League caved in once again.

A stronger French side, boosted by the recall of Thierry Buttignol, Francis Lope and, following an S.O.S. from coach Jorda, Guy Delaunay, managed to show much more control and overall effort in the second Test a week later at Perpignan. The Aussies won 34–10, but French heads were held a lot higher as aperitifs were sipped in the Stade Gilbert Brutus clubhouse. France had shown they could at least compete and, in Moliner and Patrick Entat, growing visibly in confidence after proving himself as a professional in the English League with Hull, they had individuals who could excel in even the highest company.

After their better showing in the second Test against Australia, it was not without confidence that Jorda's team prepared for their annual encounters with Great Britain – against whom the French had done so well in the previous season. But a terrible opening quarter against Mal Reilly's revitalised British team in the first Test at Perpignan, in which France displayed a tactical naivity and skill deficiencies that defied belief – certainly it was hard to believe that so many of the very same players had looked so good only twelve months before against Great Britain – washed all the optimism away with the force of a tidal wave.

Two shattering defeats by Great Britain, 10–45 at Perpignan and 4–60 at Headingley, left French Rugby League on its knees. Crucified by a media that refuses to acknowledge the athletic prowess of Rugby League, preferring instead to doff its cap at all things Rugby Union, and staring bankruptcy in the face, the French Rugby League Federation was in crisis. Jacques Jorda, whose relationship with the national coaching director, Louis Bonnery, had been strained for some time, finally resigned. He had offered his resignation after the two Tests against Australia, but had been persuaded to stay by President Verdaguer.

But now Verdaguer himself was under severe pressure to quit. The *coup de grace* finally came at the Federation's elections on May 4 when Verdaguer polled only 102 votes, and thus did not even win a place on the League's 24-person council. The former president finished no higher than in joint 28th place and so was gone, along with the long-serving Federation secretary, Pierre Rayssac, who won only enough votes to register at 37th place!

The man who polled most votes was Fernand Soubie, president of the St Gaudens club, and manager of French international teams back in the 1970s. Monsieur Soubie, however, declined the office of President of the Federation, preferring to concentrate his efforts on his own beloved St Gaudens club – and he had much to celebrate with their first ever double. So it was that Gilbert Dautant, second in the voting, took over as the new president, declaring as he took office, 'I have been married to the game for over half a century . . .'

The passing of Jean-Paul Verdaguer's presidency should not be allowed to happen without some credit being paid to a man of great honesty and integrity. Verdaguer always appeared to be a reluctant president – he stepped into the breach twice when the Federation was facing severe crisis, and on both occasions provided a calming, healing effect. First, he won over from René Mauriès after the debacle of the aborted Championship final in 1981, and then again in 1987 when Jacques Soppelsa was ousted in disgrace by angry Rugby League council members.

Verdaguer was a good man. His problem was that to be the president of the French Rugby League, a great deal more arrogance and aggression is required unfortunately. The League needs dynamic leadership now if it is to make any progress, especially in the face of much unpleasant behaviour from many areas of the Rugby Union game.

Gilbert Dautant is wisely building a team of workers around him, rather than continuing the French tradition of an all-powerful president who makes all the decisions. His first task was to ensure that France went ahead with their tour and fulfilled their World Cup commitments in both New Zealand and Papua New Guinea. The British Rugby League have recognised the vital need to support their European neighbours during their current financial difficulties, and with the prospect of more international successes next season in the

Wigan's Phil Clarke captained Great Britain's Under-21 team to a comfortable victory over France Espoirs by 48–2 in Limoux. In the return, however, Clarke suffered defeat on his home ground as a revitalised French team won 16–6.

home World Cup match against Papua New Guinea and, hopefully, fixtures against Wales and Russia, brighter days should lie ahead.

This summer's tour brought the predicted heavy defeats in New Zealand, but was not without optimism. As captain Gilles Dumas said on arrival in Auckland, 'Before May 4 we did not even know whether there was going to be a tour. Our sole aim is to prove to the rest of the world that France can still play Rugby League.'

Whether they could was open to doubt after the first Test when they were thrashed 6–60 by the Kiwis at Carlaw Park, as Dumas and his men suffered painfully for the hopeless itinerary agreed to by the former French regime: most of their Test players were forced into battle against New Zealand without having had a game for over a month.

France showed their courage, tenacity and no little skill, ten days later when they improved out of sight in the second Test against New Zealand in Christchurch. France led the Kiwis after Entat and Daniel Verdes had fashioned a try for the Villeneuve second-rower, and were hanging on to New Zealand at only 10–18 midway through the second-half. Then a solo try by the Kiwis' replacement half-back, Clayton Friend, sparked a late points burst by New Zealand to win the game 32–10. 'France could be proud of their game,' said an impressed New Zealand coach, Bob Bailey.

Indeed, the French team could take much credit for their effort against the same New Zealand team which, two weeks later, were to thrash the Australians on their own soil.

France's tour managers, Zalduendo and Bonnery, were pleased with the improvement in their team's application, especially in defence. Bonnery's comment that, 'It took the coach four games on tour to realise that defence is just as important as attack' may have been a hint that Jorda's replacement with the national team, Michel Mazaré, may have a short reign as French coach.

At the start of the tour Louis Bonnery, aware of the weaknesses in the hastily assembled French team, declared that, with several young players in the team yet to play in Tests, the tour could be deemed worthwhile if those youngsters benefitted from the experience and started to emerge as full internationals. On that score, France could take some satisfaction from their journey to the southern hemisphere, particularly in a long-awaited World Cup win, achieved with a last-minute try and conversion against Papua New Guinea in Goroka on July 7.

To achieve any kind of Test win against the Kumuls in the rarified atmosphere and hostile environment of Goroka is not easy, as Great Britain found to their cost last year. That a French team, following their battering in New Zealand, could hang in and win 20–18, with the game going right down to the last minute, after being 10–16 behind at half-time, reflects great credit on their spirit and powers of endurance.

Significantly, bearing in mind Bonnery's pre-tour comment, all France's points in their World Cup win in Papua New Guinea were scored by youngsters new to Test football, by the threequarters David Despin (Villeneuve) and Jean-Marc Garcia (St Estève) and the hooker, Patrick Torreilles (Pia). All three had earlier starred in the one bright spot of France's international season, when their Under-21 team had won a memorable 16–6 victory over Great

Bobby Goulding kicks through the French defence during the Under-21 international in Limoux. Goulding ended an unsatisfactory season at Wigan with a brief and controversial spell with Eastern Suburbs and a transfer to Leeds.

Britain, just three weeks after being mercilessly hammered 2–48 by the same opposition at Limoux.

If the promise of Despin, Garcia and Torreilles can be matched by the emergence of other exciting young talents such as the utility back, Pascal Fages (Pia), the winger Eric Van Brussel (Carcassonne), the full-back Daniel Calvet (Villeneuve) and the back-rower Jean-Luc Bardes (XIII Catalan), the French national team could have much to look forward to. But then the production of talented young players has never been a problem for French Rugby League. The problem is providing the players with an administration and a competition worthy of their talents.

The national coaching director, Louis Bonnery, finds himself very much in the middle of French League's struggle for improvement. Bonnery has as many detractors as supporters, and the challenge for Louis must be to be able to work alongside the other more capable individuals in French Rugby League, all with the common aim of improving coaching, administration, and thereby playing, standards.

Bonnery believes that more young French players need to spend time in England and Australia, exposed to the training and preparation required to play professional Rugby League. Certainly Patrick Entat has returned to France with glowing reports of the work put in by his Hull team-mates in the

English first division. Patrick thrived on the pressure, and there's little doubt that many of his French colleagues would do likewise if they got the opportunity.

The belief that the French Championship had too many Australians in it, with many clubs using Aussies merely as a stop-gap instead of putting in the effort to develop their own players, has been manifested in the decision to cut next season's import quota from five to three overseas players.

The need is for French clubs to recruit Australians (or any other overseas players) who will bring leadership qualities and impart coaching knowledge to their new team-mates. That was evident in the 1990–91 season at Villeneuve, where Mark Wakefield, ably assisted by the former Workington Town player, Philip Hurst, guided the 'green and whites' from one of the lower pools to within two points of the Championship of France.

At St Estève, the loose forward, Steve Robinson, took over as player-coach, while the interesting progress made by Cannes in Pool B was spearheaded by the Australian player-coach, Tony Vella. Of course, the Australian influence was the key factor in St Gaudens taking the double, although as a matter of unavoidable protocol their coach, Pierre Surre, was named as France's coach-of-the-year. Runners-up were Luc Mendez of Pia and Jacques Jorda of XIII Catalan and, formerly, of France.

Jorda's Perpignan side proved to be a major disappointment. They flourished for a while under the influence of the Australian imports, Steve Robinson (a stand-off-half formerly with St George and Castleford) and the big Tongan forward, John Fifita. But, with a number of established players, among them the former international captain, Guy Laforgue, reacting to disagreements with the volatile coach by leaving to play their rugby with lesser teams in the Catalan area, Perpignan just weren't good enough to win the games that counted in their semi-finals against Pia in the Cup, and Villeneuve in the Championship. Their publicity coup of signing the Rugby Union international forward, Alain Carminati, proved to be a flop as soon as the big man actually got on to the field of play. Carminati looked exactly what he is, an ex-Rugby Union forward, and was only marginally more successful than Leeds's Welsh recruit, David Young. There is some hope, however, that Carminati may yet manage to provide some useful rôle in Rugby League, if he can harness his huge bulk into laying the ball off for supporting colleagues. But his lack of mobility was quite startling, and another reminder of the vastly different athletic requirements for forwards playing the two rival codes of rugby today.

So, with St Gaudens the winners of both the Championship in Pool A and the Lord Derby Cup, it was the re-emerging Albi club who took the Pool B Championship, defeating FC Lézignan 23–18 in a thrilling final played at Carcassonne before a 5,000 crowd. A star for Albi was their Australian stand-off, Sean Mullins.

Leading scorers for the season were, in Pool A, tries: Hurst (Villeneuve) 17, Rémirès (Carcassonne) 16, and Pons (St Gaudens) 16. Goals: Delbert (Villeneuve) 64, Hastings (St Gaudens) 59 and Tisseyre (Pamiers) 50. In Pool B, tries: Ratier (Lézignan) and Roses (Le Barcarès) 26 and Nickling (Limoux) 23. Goals: Abadie (Lézignan) 86, Perez (Toulouse) 65 and Richard (Paris Chatillon) 56.

EIGHTEEN

The Season in Australia 1991

David Hadfield

The game in Australia rarely stands still, but the last twelve months have included more jolts and changes of direction than most in the code's history down under. Apart from the small matter of losing a Test match in England for the first time since 1978, Rugby League has gone through a series of domestic upheavals which have radically reshaped it. Hard on the heels of the salary cap came the draft system, designed to spread the talent on the market more evenly across the competing clubs. It was always bound to lead to problems, and it did. The most celebrated case was that of Terry Hill, a young back with plenty of potential but little experience, from South Sydney. He wanted to go to Wests, and when Easts got in first to claim him, he was adamant that he would not play for them. By mid-season, however, he was wearing a Roosters jersey and enjoying considerable success. Others stuck to their guns and eventually got what they wanted, which in the case of Ron Gibbs – the destructive forward who spent two seasons at Castleford – was a move from Gold Coast to Wests.

Overall, it went more smoothly than might reasonably be expected of the imposition of an entirely alien system. The main beneficiaries looked to be Wests, who, apart from Gibbs and a revitalised Graeme Wynn, picked up, courtesy of their new coach Warren Ryan, the backbone of the Canterbury side, and Norths. The North Sydney Bears worked the draft system beautifully, going for quality rather than quantity and coming away with Mario Fenech, Phil Blake (both from Souths) and Peter Jackson (Brisbane) in their shopping trolley. They also got in ahead of Manly for Emosi Koloto, but the limitations of the system were exposed when Koloto voted with his feet and decided, as he could not go to the club of his choice, to go home to New Zealand instead.

As for the salary cap, that arm-twisting directive towards good housekeeping that is now starting to gather support from some in England, it too had its effects and its limitations. It was the reason, for instance, that neither Eastern Suburbs nor Cronulla could get anywhere near the deal Martin Offiah was seeking in order to go to Sydney; demands which, interestingly, included a return air ticket for his friend Ellery Hanley. Offiah later joined St George for a lower figure and one which they could accommodate within their budget.

It will surprise no one who appreciates the ingenuity of an Australian faced with a rule book that talk of fiddles and abuses – encapsulated in that fine Australianism 'rorts' – became increasingly rife as the season went on. Everybody seemed to know of some player who was getting cash or benefits under the table to bypass the restrictions of the cap, and many have already come to the conclusion that the idea is one which is impossible to police.

On the field of play – or, rather, just off it – in-goal touch-judges became part of the game. As if by magic, matches started to throw up any number of incidents on which only they could rule with authority, and it was not long before people started to ask how they had ever managed without them.

The new interchange rule was a more contentious matter. The unlimited use of substitutes recommended itself to many in Australia because of the ever-increasing speed and intensity of the game; still, despite the great strides that have been made in Britain, a couple of notches up the scale from the tempo here. In the first week of the new rule in the Winfield Cup, however, Graham Lowe of Manly and Wayne Bennett of Brisbane made a total of forty-one changes during the match between their two sides. Newcastle and Cronulla were not far behind with thirty-five. Everyone apart from some coaches disliked those excesses; players and fans alike found it frustrating and confusing – to say nothing of the poor old match commentators and reporters. It called for a compromise, and a limit of four men on the bench and a total of six changes – plus the head bin and the blood bin, the latter of which is soon to be a part of the British game as well – seems to cater for most eventualities.

THE NISSAN SEVENS

Seven-a-side Rugby League has been a late-comer on the Australian scene, but the crowd of 29,213 at the Parramatta stadium for the 1991 tournament showed that it has arrived in a big way. The event – the last before it becomes a truly international contest next February, when Wigan will be the British representatives – was won by Newcastle Knights. Along with a very worthwhile cheque for $70,000, the Knights were receiving their first trophy since being admitted to the Sydney competition in 1988.

Newcastle beat the reigning Premiers, Canberra Raiders, in the first round and then accounted for Parramatta and Easts to set up a final against St George. Saints, in their first competitive outing under their new coach, Brian Smith, had beaten Wests, Souths and then the surprise team of the early rounds, the Illawarra Steelers. They seemed to be on their way to winning the final as well, until the Newcastle forward, Marc Glanville, forced his way over in the corner with ten seconds to go to tie the scores at 22–22. Ashley Gordon – one of the Knights stars of the day, along with Glanville, Michael Hagan and John Schuster – put over the winning goal-points in eccentric fashion with a drop-kick.

THE LOTTO CHALLENGE

Australia's main knock-out competition got yet another new name in 1991, but stuck with the pre-season, take-it-to-the-people formula which had proved such a success the previous year. Bundaberg in North Queensland was the venue for the opening double-header, Brisbane beating Norths 24–10 and Newcastle following up their Sevens victory by edging out Balmain 22–20.

Illawarra beat Gold Coast and St George downed Parramatta at Toowoomba; Easts beat Wests and Canterbury defeated Manly at Lismore; and Port Macquarie saw Canberra beat Cronulla and Penrith thrash Souths – with the additional drama of a section of temporary grandstand collapsing.

The first two quarter-finals at Tamworth rather tarnished the concept of Sydney football 'going bush'. Illawarra beat St George 36–6 and Brisbane outlasted Newcastle to win 28–13 in the country town which is, among other claims to fame, the centre of the Australian country and western industry, but the results were overshadowed by bad feeling. Another collapsed stand, fighting on and off the field, sendings-off and the failure of three of the four clubs to attend a function afterwards left a sour taste. In Dubbo, Penrith were comfortable winners over Easts by 20–0, and Canterbury beat Canberra 11–10, thanks to a last-minute try from Darren Brown, just back from a stint with Trafford Borough.

In the first semi-final at Orange, Brisbane trailed Illawarra 0–12 after fifteen minutes, but got back on terms thanks to Allan Langer's party-piece of stealing the ball out of the tackle – something he is now precluded from doing by the latest round of rule changes. The Broncos eventually nicked it 16–14 after their winger, Brett Plowman, scored his second try.

Over at Wagga Wagga, Penrith proved far too good for Canterbury, with Steve Carter scoring three tries and Greg's little brother, Ben Alexander, two in a 34–6 win.

Brisbane had to come from behind again to claim the $200,000 first prize in the final at Broken Hill, the mining town at the very edge of the known Rugby League world. Penrith were 16–2 up after half an hour, but Brisbane fought back to only 2 points behind early in the second half and won a compelling match 20–16 when Kevin Walters went over for a try and Terry Matterson kicked the goal six minutes from time. Brisbane seemed to have shown that, even with Wally Lewis gone, they could win big matches. Penrith, resplendent in their new kit, had to put up with a lot of jibes to the effect that the colours might have changed but their habit of folding when the pressure is on had not.

CITY v COUNTRY

The annual selection trials for the New South Wales state team saw the City Origin side – consisting of players who played their first Rugby League in Sydney – beat their Country-bred counterparts 22–12. The all-Manly triangle of Cliff Lyons, Geoff Toovey and Des Hasler took an early grip on the game, and the pace and finishing power of Andrew Ettingshausen, who scored two tries, supplied the killer touch.

A crowd of 21,466 at the Sydney Football Stadium also saw a City Firsts side including big names like Steve Roach, Mario Fenech and Les Davidson beat Country Firsts – the team drawn from NSW's hundreds of rural clubs – by 36–20. It was a creditable performance by the country boys, who led at half-time and drew level again midway through the second half.

STATE OF ORIGIN SERIES

If every State of Origin series is tough, fiercely competitive and basically unpredictable – and so far they all have been – then 1991 was distilled essence of State of Origin: an unmistakable form of football at its purest and most characteristic.

Lang Park, Brisbane, May 8

First State of Origin
Queensland 6 New South Wales 4

This was a match in which the Maroons of Queensland, for all their proud record at Lang Park since State of Origin football began, had no chance. The imbalance between the two sides seemed just too great. Whereas Tim Sheens, in his first match as NSW coach, was able to name an all-international starting line-up, with more on the interchange bench, the Queensland side was full of players with little or no representative experience. Against the NSW pack, they had just one Test forward – Martin Bella – in their side; some Queenslanders, like Norths' loose forward, Gary Larson, and the Newcastle second row, Mike McLean, making his representative debut at an age when many Australian players are thinking of retirement, were not even assured of first-team places with their clubs.

For once in State of Origin history, you could get long odds against a Queensland victory, and some south of the border were talking confidently of record scores. What they forgot to take account of is what might be called the L factor: Lang Park, Wally Lewis and Graham Lowe.

Between them, the ground with its fanatical local support, the captain with so much left to prove and the new coach with the proven ability to create just the right mood for a big occasion inspired the Maroons to one of the great Origin victories. The scoreline might suggest a dour, defensive struggle, but it was anything but that. Both sides played with plenty of attacking intent and it was only brilliant defence that kept them at bay, with no one doing better than the Queensland full-back, Paul Hauff, in the side for the injured Gary Belcher. The only points of the first half came from a Mal Meninga penalty, but the crucial moment arrived just after the hour when Lewis, more and more influential as the game went on, suddenly split the NSW defence and slipped an inside pass to Meninga.

The Blues came back in determined fashion, bombarding the try-line but finding no way through. Finally, Queensland's exhaustion gave them their chance and Laurie Daley scored wide out to set up a dramatic finale. Michael O'Connor missed the conversion, but Meninga's kick-off went out on the full, giving Greg Alexander an opportunity to tie up the score after the hooter with a penalty from half-way. It dropped short, and Queensland kept the spoils they deserved.

Queensland: Hauff (Brisbane); Hancock (Brisbane), Peter Jackson (Norths), Meninga (Canberra), Carne (Brisbane); Lewis (Gold Coast), Langer (Brisbane); Bella (Manly), Steve Walters (Canberra), Steve Jackson (Wests), Gee (Brisbane), McLean (Newcastle), Larson (Norths)

Substitutes: Kevin Walters (Brisbane), Renouf (Brisbane), Coyne (Canberra), Allen (Brisbane)

Scorers: try – Meninga; goal – Meninga.

New South Wales: Alexander (Penrith); Johns (Brisbane), Ettingshausen (Cronulla), Daley (Canberra), O'Connor (Manly); Lyons (Manly), Stuart (Canberra); Roach (Balmain), Elias (Balmain), Roberts (Manly), Geyer (Penrith), Sironen (Balmain), Hasler (Balmain)

Substitutes: McGaw (Cronulla), Fittler (Penrith), Gillespie (Wests), Lazarus (Canberra)

Scorer: try – Daley

Referee: W. Harrigan (Sydney)

Attendance: 31,500

Sydney Football Stadium, May 29

Second State of Origin
New South Wales 14 Queensland 12

This year's second match will be remembered as a classic game of Rugby League and as an outbreak of war. The physical intensity of State of Origin is legendary, but there were times at the Football Stadium when even the staunchest admirer of the way the two states confront each other thought it was all going a bit too far.

The controversy centred on the giant figure of Mark Geyer – once with Sheffield Eagles – who seemed to go into the match as psyched-up as Gazza at Wembley. While he kept the lid on his aggression and tackled within the rules, he was devastating; the most crippling hitman in a match of mighty hits. But an attack on Steve Walters just before half-time enraged Queensland and Wally Lewis in particular, and the two did their best to keep their argument running all the way down the tunnel. When Geyer elbowed Paul Hauff in the second half there was more fury, although the referee, David Manson, took no action. Geyer was later cited and banned for six matches, and opinions on whether he was villain or scapegoat depended very much on which side of the border your sympathies lay.

The violence aside, the game was full of excitement and tension. New South Wales were 8–0 up, but Queensland took the lead for the first time with thirteen minutes to go. Ten minutes later the Blues, with John Cartwright and Ricky Stuart doing the difficult bits, somehow managed to keep the ball alive, and Mark McGaw found just enough space on the outside to go in for the equalising try. That left Michael O'Connor with the daunting task of kicking the conversion from wide on the right touchline to win the match and leave NSW with a chance of winning the series, and his shot was right on target.

New South Wales: Ettingshausen (Cronulla); Johns (Brisbane), Daley (Canberra), O'Connor (Manly), Wishart (Illawarra); Lyons (Manly), Stuart (Canberra); Roach (Balmain), Elias (Balmain), Gillespie (Wests), Roberts (Manly), Geyer (Penrith), Clyde (Canberra)

Opposite Martin Offiah joined former Hull coach Brian Smith for a summer stint with St George, and immediately caused problems for opponents with his blistering pace.

Substitutes: Hasler (Manley), McGaw (Cronulla), Mackay (St George), Cartwright (Penrith)

Scorers: tries – O'Connor, McGaw; goals – O'Connor 3

Queensland: Hauff (Brisbane); Hancock (Brisbane), Peter Jackson (Norths), Meninga (Canberra), Carne (Brisbane); Lewis (Gold Coast), Langer (Brisbane); Bella (Manly), Steve Walters (Canberra), Steve Jackson (Wests), Gee (Brisbane), McLean (Newcastle), Larson (Norths)

Substitutes: Kevin Walters (Brisbane), Shearer (Brisbane), Coyne (Canberra), Allen (Brisbane)

Scorers: tries – Carne, Shearer; goals – Meninga (2)

Referee: D. Manson (Queensland)

Attendance: 41,520

Lang Park, Brisbane, June 12

Third State of Origin
Queensland 14 New South Wales 12

At the end of a series which many who had seen the whole, turbulent history of State of Origin football were calling the best ever, it was only fitting that the drama should continue to the final whistle and beyond.

As in the first two games, NSW started the stronger, and the new stand-off Brad Fittler's kick-through created a try for Chris Johns after only one minute. Meninga drew McGaw and sent in Hauff – again outstanding at full-back – for a quick equaliser, and Queensland led at half-time due to Stuart's failure to deal with Langer's kick-ahead and Michael Hancock's decisive finish.

NSW's replacements put them in a winning position after the break. Brad Izzard, playing his first Origin game since 1982, combined with the new prop, Craig Salvatori from Easts, to put O'Connor across in the corner. Then Norths' second-row David Fairleigh's break allowed Des Hasler to slide over the line. With the strong man of their pack, Martin Bella, in the sin bin, Queensland were up against it, but they came back with fourteen minutes to go: a complex move, in which Langer twice threw the important pass, saw Dale Shearer tie up the scores. Meninga needed to land the first goal of the match to put the Maroons in front and did so, but the action was far from finished. NSW had chances to apply pressure in the remaining minutes, and, with only seconds remaining, Rod Wishart dropped a difficult pass with a gap along the touchline beckoning.

For all the hairs-breadth closeness of the scorelines in all three games, the more convincing side had undoubtedly won the series. The matches had seen the emergence of young players, such as Hauff, Carne, Steve Walters and Gee, as men of genuine international calibre, and also marked the departure of players who had become synonymous with State of Origin football. Wally Lewis, influenced by the news that very day that his daughter had been diagnosed as profoundly deaf, announced after the game that it had been his last in an Origin career of heroic proportions. Michael O'Connor, NSW's leading points-scorer in Origin matches, had his nose smashed in a tackle with Meninga and also decided that he had had enough.

Queensland: Hauff (Brisbane); Hancock (Brisbane), Peter Jackson (Norths), Meninga (Canberra), Carne (Brisbane); Lewis (Gold Coast), Langer (Brisbane); Bella (Manly), Steve Walters (Canberra), Steve Jackson (Wests), Gee (Brisbane), McLean (Newcastle), Larson (Norths)

Substitutes: Lindner (Wests), Shearer (Brisbane), Coyne (Canberra), Kevin Walters (Brisbane)

Scorers: tries – Hauff, Hancock, Shearer; goal – Meninga

New South Wales: Alexander (Penrith); Johns (Brisbane), McGaw (Cronulla), O'Connor (Manly), Wishart (Illawarra); Fittler (Penrith), Stuart (Canberra); Roach (Balmain), Elias (Balmain), Gillespie (Wests), Clyde (Canberra), Cartwright (Penrith), Mackay (St George)

Substitutes: Izzard (Penrith), Fairleigh (Norths), Salvatori (Easts), Hasler (Manly)

Scorers: tries – Johns, O'Connor, Hasler

Referee: W. Harrigan (Sydney)

Attendance: 31,500.

New South Wales lock Bradley Clyde and Queensland stand-off Wally Lewis compete for a loose ball in the third and deciding State of Origin match, won by Queensland 14–12. Both Clyde and Lewis missed the 1990 Kangaroo tour through injury.

THE WINFIELD CUP

A Sydney Premiership table with Norths, Wests, Easts and Illawarra in or around the top five? With Balmain and Parramatta – seven Grand Finals over the last decade between them – struggling at the bottom? And reigning Premiers Canberra and would-be Premiers Brisbane treading water in the middle reaches? Some mistake, surely.

The theme of the first half of the Winfield Cup season seemed to be that the last should be first, and the first last. North Sydney had shown signs of improvement last season, but the addition of proven campaigners such as Fenech, Blake and Jackson to the rich promise of Fairleigh, Billy Moore and Jason Martin made them look a good deal stronger this time. A place in the top five play-offs was strictly the lower limit of their ambitions.

Western Suburbs, with the formidable expertise of Warren Ryan and an expansive recruitment policy, were expected to lift their game, and they duly did so. Eastern Suburbs and Illawarra were rather more surprising successes. Easts pulled out of their recent slump in startling style, the new team of Jack Gibson as supremo and Mark Murray as coach seeming to generate the right chemistry. Two distinguished veterans found a new lease of life, Paul Vautin and Hugh McGahan inspiring the pack with their best football for years.

The Illawarra Steelers, the slow starters of the expansion entry that also brought Canberra into the Winfield Cup in 1982, finally established themselves as a power in the game nine years later. With Alan McIndoe back from Penrith to join Rod Wishart and Brett Rodwell in a potent threequarter line, a hugely talented scrum-half in John Simon, and Ian Russell showing all the consistent class that he frustratingly failed to produce for Sheffield Eagles, the Steelers had the look of a club heading for their first semi-final.

If these were dramatic changes of fortune, then the plight of Balmain was even more sudden. Those who found the appointment of a coach with no Rugby League experience – former Wallaby mentor Alan Jones – bizarre had their views endorsed by the Tigers' deplorable early form. There was more controversy when Jones signed the Australian-Irish Rugby Union international, Brian Smith, and preferred him to Gary Freeman at scrum-half. The much-publicised signing of the Olympic athlete, Darren Clark, produced little but the publicity as the runner tried to learn his new job in reserve grade. There were signs of a revival in a good 21–8 victory over Wests, but Balmain's hopes of claiming their usual play-off place had already been dead for weeks.

Parramatta's season effectively died when Peter Sterling aggravated his old shoulder injury and resigned himself to missing most of the campaign. The great force of the early 1980s, the Eels have some good youngsters, a few notable veterans – including Brett Kenny, now at loose forward – and a great stadium with guaranteed support. But it is a sign of the times that they simply do not have the depth of ability to compete these days.

Only Gold Coast looked likely to spare Parramatta the indignity of the wooden spoon. Despite the signing of Lewis – and he missed more games through injury and representative commitments than he played in the first half of the season – Daryl Powell and Paul Dixon, the Seagulls continued to

Opposite Sheffield Eagles centre Daryl Powell, along with Leeds forward Paul Dixon, guested for Gold Coast in the summer of 1991, yet neither could prevent the Seagulls from struggling in the Winfield Cup.

struggle along, with the meagre gates at Tweed Heads demonstrating local disappointment with their progress all too clearly.

Up the road, Brisbane were almost as big a disappointment to their considerably more numerous fans. Brilliant on their day, they were also maddeningly inconsistent; and that was something which was only partly attributable to their uniquely heavy burden of representative depletions.

Astonishingly, after their domination of the previous two seasons, Canberra Raiders slipped into no-man's-land alongside the Broncos. The retirement of veterans such as John Ferguson – who made a brief comeback playing for Newtown in the 'non-league' Metropolitan Cup – and Dean Lance left gaps that were not filled. Injuries to such as Glenn Lazarus and Laurie Daley compounded the difficulties. The club ran into severe financial problems, and their decline showed that, in a competition as merciless as the Winfield Cup, nothing can be taken for granted.

Into the vacuum created by Canberra's decline came Penrith. Beaten in the previous season's Grand Final, the Panthers at last looked ready to go all the way. A big, powerful pack and solid team-work were their strong suits. The prodigious Brad Fittler hit form again after a post-tour slump, and even Greg Alexander's absences were capably covered by his equally talented younger brother, Ben.

If the Panthers were everybody's first choice as likely Grand Finalists, then Manly had plenty of backers as well. Despite the dislocation created by Graham Lowe's serious health problems and by the heavier than usual injury toll, Manly began to emerge as a real threat, especially if Kevin Iro could get fit and stay fit.

The two other likeliest challengers for a place in the top five were both heavily indebted to their English connection. St George, under the former Hull boss, Brian Smith, made a sensational start to the season. They then lost their way, and only found it again with the arrival of Martin Offiah. His ability to score tries out of nothing began to win matches for the Dragons which they would otherwise have lost and they started to move in the right direction again.

Canterbury, also coached by a man – Chris Anderson – who had cut his coaching teeth in Britain, had to adjust to life without many of the players who had contributed to their successes in the 1980s. There were compensations, like the exciting running of Ewen McGrady and the power of their new Kiwi centre, Jarrod McCracken, but it was not until the arrival of Jonathan Davies that the whole pattern started to slot into place. Like Offiah, he was criticised for one or two of his British habits, but he was also undeniably a match-winner.

Newcastle threatened to come good but won too few games away from home, and South Sydney, despite the emergence of a much-needed new generation of first-graders, still have a long way to go. Both performed rather better, however, than Cronulla. The Sharks, always there or thereabouts in recent seasons, went into a precipitous dive. Despite the presence of players of the calibre of McGaw, Ettingshausen and Gavin Miller, they looked short of teeth; and the Winfield Cup in 1991 was no place for sides which could not chew what they bit off.

NINETEEN

The Seasons in New Zealand and Papua New Guinea 1991

David Hadfield

It says virtually all that needs to be said about the mood of Rugby League in New Zealand this year that a Test match should be postponed because of a clash with the televised State of Origin decider from Australia.

Kiwi League knows exactly where it stands. The real thing – in the shape of an international against France – has no hope of competing with the second-hand experience of armchair football from across the Tasman Sea. Delaying the France Test for a day was in one sense a humiliating decision, but it was an inevitable and a logical one.

Most people in the game in New Zealand know the answer to their conundrum; they need a side in the Winfield Cup, and the sooner the better. But progress towards that goal has become more, rather than less, complicated over the last year. Fears in the rest of New Zealand that an Auckland entry into the Winfield Cup would serve to increase 'big brother's' domination of the domestic scene has led to moves in Wellington and Christchurch to stake a claim for inclusion as well. The city of Wellington has moved particularly rapidly since deciding that it wants a slice of the action, hosting and impressing a high-powered Australian delegation and going so far as to name Salford's Kevin Tamati as their prospective coach if they were to be admitted.

Apart from the red herring of inter-city rivalries, it hardly matters which New Zealand side wins the right to play in the competition that the whole country is already watching. What matters is that one of them should do so before the peak of public interest passes – as it will if the business is played out for too long – and before majority opinion in Australia swings against the radical plan of a trans-national competition.

WAINUIOMATA – WELLINGTON'S TOP CUP-WINNING SIDE

Wellington's bid to represent New Zealand in the Winfield Cup can only have been helped by the remarkable rise of their club side Wainuiomata. After a mere two seasons as a first-division team in Wellington, Wainui began the 1991 campaign as New Zealand's top club side. After losing the Lion Red Cup final to Northcote in 1989, they went one better in 1990, beating two of Auckland's other leading clubs in the process. They beat Te Atatu 20–16 in the semi-final, with two second-half breaks from their Maori representative prop, John Lomax, proving decisive.

Wainui trailed 4–12 midway through the final to an Otahuhu side for whom Des Maea – later to make his name in England with Sheffield Eagles – wore the loose forward jersey which has belonged, in a remarkable succession, to Mark Graham, Hugh McGahan and Tawere Nikau. The superior power of their pack and the ingenuity of their man-of-the-match, the scrum-half, Ali Davys, saw them turn that into a handsome 34–12 victory. Despite the lack of a single New Zealand international in the side, Wainuiomata had proved themselves the most effective combination in the country.

Part of their reward was a pre-season fixture against the glamorous – and heavily Kiwi-influenced – Australian side Manly. The chance to see in the flesh the players who figured so prominently in the nation's television habits drew a capacity 10,000 crowd to Fraser Park on the outskirts of Wellington, once more raising the question of what could be expected for competitive matches in Wellington, Auckland or Christchurch. The presence of three illustrious Kiwis – Tony Iro, Darrell Williams and Matthew Ridge – in the Manly side no doubt helped, and Iro and Ridge both played significant roles in a 20–8 victory. Iro, in the second-row position he had been trying for size at Leigh, ran powerfully and to good effect, while Ridge scored a try and three goals. Wainui's points all came from the boot of their stand-off, Jason Gilbert, showing again that, Ridge and Frano Botica notwithstanding, he is as reliable a kicker as any New Zealand has produced in recent years.

THE NATIONAL CHAMPIONSHIP

The six-week competition between the four strongest Rugby League areas in New Zealand has too often followed a processional course, with Auckland far too good for the rest from first to last. It was a refreshingly different story in 1991; before the last round of matches, it was possible for the Championship to finish in a three-way tie.

That tight contest was largely created by one of the biggest shocks of recent years – Canterbury's largest-ever winning margin over Auckland. Mark Nixon, back from his second season at Rochdale Hornets, was the star of a 33–24 victory at the Addington Showgrounds in Christchurch, scoring two tries and setting up one for Carl Hall, formerly with Doncaster. English second-division experience was a strong element in Canterbury's win; the scrum-half, Aaron Whittaker (Chorley), and their loose forward, Logan Edwards (Swinton), were the other outstanding performers on a night to remember for Rugby League on the South Island. Esene Faimalo also made a welcome return to form after a slow start on his reappearance from Widnes.

Canterbury had also beaten Wellington at the Showgrounds, with Nixon and Hall again standing out in a 27–18 win, and had little difficulty in twice beating the perennial wooden-spoonists, Bay of Plenty. Where their challenge fell down was in one of several close and exciting matches in this year's Championship. Wellington won 26–24 thanks to a late try from Sonny Whakarau, who played with Batley last season and came on, along with the Leeds and Test loose forward, Mike Kuiti, as an important pair of second-half substitutes.

It was some consolation to Wellington for an even narrower defeat by Auckland the previous week, 25–24 being the result that night. Their two seemingly inevitable wins over Bay of Plenty left them needing to win at Carlaw Park to take a share of the Championship. Auckland, under their new coach, Owen Wright, had started by beating Bay of Plenty 44–8, with the former Sheffield Eagles prop, Se'e Solomona, leading the charge. Solomona was again the eye-catcher in the 24–4 beating of Canterbury, which was followed by that single-point win over Wellington and a 58–14 thrashing of Bay of Plenty in which their ex-Featherstone Rover, Iva Ropati, scored four tries. Their defeat by Canterbury in Christchurch had suggested that Auckland's whole season might fall apart but they responded in a very Auckland way, hammering Wellington 56–8 to demonstrate that it will be a while yet before they release their grip on the National Championship.

Jonathan Davies scores a try for Canterbury-Bankstown against Norths in a summer spell down under that confirmed the impressions he had made in the 1990–91 season.

Wellington and Christchurch had both had their moments and were left to wonder what might have been if key matches had gone just slightly differently. Even Bay of Plenty could point to some games which were relatively close at half-time and a points-against column which was slightly more modest than usual. It was ironic that their coach, Tony Gordon, the former Kiwi Test coach, was unable to get any appreciable assistance from the players he had been instrumental in rerouting from New Zealand Rugby Union to Rugby League in England. The Bradford Northern scrum-half, Brett Iti, made just one appearance, and that a distinctly unimpressive one in the 14–58 defeat by Auckland. He, his brother Clarrie and Darrall Shelford were then sidelined because of Bradford and Featherstone's insistence on heavy insurance cover on their investments. At least Warrington's Gary Mercer was able to return to the representative scene for the battered Bay after missing last year's Champion-

Brisbane full-back Paul Hauff stood in for injured Kangaroo tourist Gary Belcher in the Queensland side for the State of Origin matches, and ended the season by replacing Belcher also in the Australian team to face New Zealand.

Canberra hooker Steve Walters (*left*) emerged as a player of genuine international calibre during Queensland's successful State of Origin campaign, and he won his first Test cap against New Zealand in July 1991, replacing the incumbent, Benny Elias.

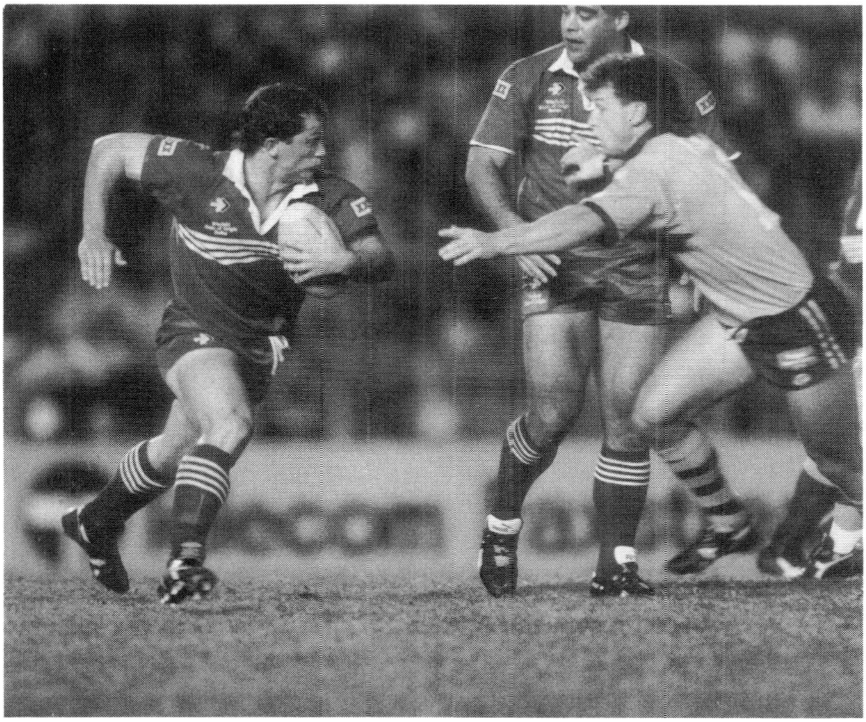

ship with injury. Even in badly beaten sides, he managed to stand out in his new British position of second row. The final placings were: Auckland 10 points; Canterbury 8 points; Wellington 6 points; Bay of Plenty 0 points.

NEW ZEALAND v FRANCE

For a fixture which does not usually produce a fever-pitch of excitement, this year's first Test against France yielded more than its share of headlines, long before a ball was kicked.

The increasingly irrelevant Test trial had less effect on the shape of the Kiwi side than politics and injury. Long-term injuries ruled out the Iro brothers, creating the chance for first caps for Jarrod McCracken and Richard Blackmore. McCracken, who had previously played in country football in Australia, had impressed in the centre since joining Canterbury-Bankstown. Blackmore, the Otahuhu winger, had not even come into the Auckland team until the last round of the National Championship, but his performances in that match and in the trial – when Probables beat Possibles by a convincing 31–8 – were enough to impress the New Zealand Test coach, Bob Bailey.

Parramatta's Mark Horo was also kept out of the reckoning by an injury, but the fun began when three other Test candidates were eliminated by a row between their Australian clubs and the New Zealand League. Matthew Ridge would have been an automatic choice at full-back, but Manly, while willing to release him to play, would not allow him to miss a competition round in Sydney merely to go into camp with the Kiwis. Newcastle, whose former All Black John Schuster had been in outstanding form in the Winfield Cup, took the same attitude, as did North Sydney over their goal-kicking winger Daryl Halligan. Had the players been signed from Rugby League, their releases from the NZRL would have specified that their country would have first call on them. There is no such ruling to cover players signed from Rugby Union, but the NZRL decided that they must have 'all or nothing' and ruled all three ineligible for selection if they could not attend the build-up. Feelings ran high, and accusations about the role played by Manly and the former New Zealand coach, Graham Lowe, added to the acrimony.

Ridge's place went to Frano Botica, although he had played full-back just once in his first season with Wigan. With McCracken and Blackmore, that made it three new caps in the backs, plus Emosi Koloto, finally getting his call-up in the pack. Two notables re-appearing among the substitutes were Mercer and Clayton Friend, fresh from his season with Carlisle.

Carlaw Park, Aukland, 13 June

New Zealand 60 France 6

Jarrod McCracken and Richard Blackmore both celebrated their selection with two tries in their debut Test, but the French did not present any sort of yardstick against which to gauge the potential of the newcomers. Heavy defeats in their warm-up games had already suggested that France were not going to be up to the job, but few expected them to cave in quite as quickly as they did at Carlaw Park.

Their new coach, Michel Mazaré, summed up the difference between the two sides. 'New Zealand were too big, too strong and too fast,' he said. The Kiwis were 32–0 ahead at half-time, and only eased up slightly after the break, with the French captain, Gilles Dumas, getting the try and the goal that provided scant consolation just two minutes from the end.

It was an undemanding Test for all the newcomers, and one in which Emosi Koloto should have epitomised the 'too big, too fast and too strong' verdict. However, the general view of him was that he had not shone quite as he should have done, and he was replaced by George Mann early in the second half. Frano Botica had a happier debut, playing steadily and kicking smoothly to finish with eight goals.

New Zealand: Botica; Panapa, McCracken, Watson, Blackmore; Shelford, Freeman; Brown, Duane Mann, Todd, Lonergan, Koloto, Nikau

Substitutes: George Mann for Koloto and Patton for Blackmore after 48 minutes, Friend for Shelford and Mercer for Todd after 70 minutes

Scorers: tries – McCracken (2), Todd, Blackmore (2), Shelford, Nikau, George Mann, Freeman, Panapa, Lonergan; goals – Botica (8)

France: Auroy; Despin, Chamorin, Bienes, Pons; Dumas, Entat; Storer, Valéro, Buttignol, Cabestany, Verdes, Plante

Substitutes: Campana for Pons after 40 minutes, Tisseyre for Verdes after 58 minutes; Romano and Fages not used

Scorers: try – Dumas; goal – Dumas

THE CLUB SCENE

Auckland. The rivalry between Northcote and last season's champions, Otahuhu, continued this year as the two leading clubs in New Zealand Rugby League scrapped it out for top spot. Northcote took a handy 3-point lead when they beat Otahuhu 24–22 in the key match of the first half of the season. Stuart Galbraith (ex-Trafford Borough and Rochdale Hornets) was the key figure in that match. Otahuhu, with such forwards as Francis Leota (ex-Sheffield Eagles and Salford) and Aaron Palelei (Nottingham, Featherstone Rovers and Keighley) in form, will take more than that to shake them off.

Wellington. Despite Wainuiomata's exploits in the national knockout competition, Upper Hutt are the Wellington champions. The early challenge, however, came from Randwick, who moved level with Wainui at the top of the table thanks to a surprising 18–6 win.

Christchurch. Surprise packets of the early season Supporters' Trophy competition were Sydenham. Bottom of the table last year, they only avoided relegation by winning a play-off against Kaiapoi, but their form this time suggested much better things to come. Halswell were unable to field their old boy, Brendan Tuuta, the insurance cover required by Featherstone being again the sticking point, but Papanui came up with a rare British import by fielding Rob Ackerman.

THE SEASON IN PAPUA NEW GUINEA

A busy twelve months of international competition will go a long way towards showing how much progress the game is making in the country where it stirs more passion than it does anywhere else in the world.

With Australia and France still due to visit at the time of writing, the Kumuls have every prospect of coming to Britain in the autumn with one Test win behind them. Financial considerations mean that the British leg of the tour will be a short one; just five games, beginning with an intriguing match against Wales in Swansea and ending with the only Test at Wigan, and with Great Britain Under-21s, a Humberside combined side and Cumbria in between. That will be followed by four games in France, including an interesting diversion from the normal route with a game in Strasbourg.

Established internationals such as Bal Numapo – restored to the captaincy this year – and Arnold Krewanty – who has already said that he intends to impress sufficiently on the tour to become only the second Papuan, after Phillip Ralda at Bradford Northern in 1983, to play for a British club – will continue to be leading figures. Others who did well against Great Britain on their 1990 tour, and who are in line to visit Europe for the first time, include the centre, Philip Boge, the half-backs, Stanley Haru and Gigmai Ongugo, and the loose forward, Matthew Elara. A creditable 10–18 home defeat by New Zealand in their last Test of 1990 saw the emergence of such new Kumuls as Goie Waine and Opoe Soga in the backs and the second-rower Kes Paglipari.

Britain's own visit to PNG next summer has been down-graded to a one-Test, three-match stay, which seems scant reward for the Kumuls historic Test victory in Goroka in 1990. Perhaps it should be regarded as punishment for that win and the circumstances in which it was achieved. At least the insulting notion of basing the tourists in Cairns and flying them in for matches was scrapped at an early stage in the discussions.

Domestically, Rugby League continues to dominate the sporting scene in PNG in a way which is unparalleled in any other country. The style of play can be summed up by a typical week-end of results in the Port Moresby competition: a 32–32 draw, a 24–24 draw, a 16–16 draw, and other results of 27–26, 26–24 and 38–14. The days of defence becoming dominant are still some time away in PNG.

In the main leagues, the leaders as the season moved into its second half were: Port Moresby – Tarangau, hotly pursued by Wests and Paga; Goroka – Hawks; Kainantu – Panthers; Kundiawa – Hawks; Lae – Royals; Mendi – Bulldogs; Mount Hagen – Tigers; Rabaul – North Raiders; Wahgi – Tigers.

TWENTY

First Steps in the Soviet Union

David Hadfield

The first stages in the development of Rugby League in the Soviet Union represent the most exciting prospect for the game since the Australians started to play under Northern Union rules in the early years of this century. Since then, of course, two other Test-playing nations – France and Papua New Guinea – have joined Britain, New Zealand and Australia in the fold. But this is bigger – potentially much bigger – provided we do not make the mistake of expecting it all to happen at once.

Influential and powerful figures within the British game – and, to an extent, within the Australian game as well – have been swept along on a wave of boyish enthusiasm over the possibilities of this expansion into the biggest country in the world. That is fine as far as it goes, and certainly preferable to some of the parochial thinking that demands querulously 'what about our own backyard?' the whole time, to the exclusion of all broader visions. It is to be hoped, however, that the glowing expectations are not going to be replaced rapidly by disillusionment and acrimony when the work that is being done in the USSR fails to yield instant, sensational results. Perhaps because the scene is Russia, there is a tendency to expect a swift and decisive revolution, while the reality is that Rugby League must develop there by steady and consistent evolution. Having said that, the extent of the progress in little more than a year since three Soviet clubs, from Moscow, Tiraspol and Leningrad, came to Britain for a coaching camp and their first taste of competition against seasoned players, has been remarkable. In October 1990, timed to coincide with the best shop window British Rugby League has had for many years – the Wembley Test against Australia – Moscow Spartak arrived on a short tour. Beaten by a Welsh Select side and in a nine-a-side Wembley curtain-raiser against a London Select, they ended their visit on an upbeat note by grabbing a last-gasp 23–20 win over Fulham's Alliance team at Crystal Palace. The toast that night was Smirnov – the Moscow full-back of that name who leapt high to take the ball for the winning try. In view of the high hopes being invested in the Soviet adventure, it was disappointing to see the event so poorly supported on an official level by both the British and the Australian camps.

Spartak had emerged from that visit with some credit, but it was already clear that they were a long way from being the best side in the Soviet Union. Two autumn tournaments there had shown conclusively that Moscow Magicians and Tiraspol were out in a class of their own: the Wigan and Widnes of Soviet Rugby League perhaps? The Magicians beat Tiraspol in the final of their Moscow competition, in front of a crowd of 5,000. Phil Larder, Soviet RL's adoptive coach, was sufficiently impressed to declare that: 'The quality of the game was superb ... Moscow Magicians and Tiraspol played Rugby

League of the highest calibre. Their ball control was excellent, and they were able to think six plays ahead.'

The gap between those two sides and the rest was also underlined in the other autumn competition held in Tiraspol. The local side beat Moscow Spartak 56–17, while the Magicians needed to resort to a little sleight of hand to shoot down Kazan Arrows by 86–12, Valeriy Savikin scoring five tries and Igor Nichaev three. The final saw Tiraspol beat the side which seems destined to be their great rivals by 24–10.

The reward for the two clubs' early dominance of the Soviet scene was a trip to France in November 1990. Tiraspol went to Paris, where they beat a local club side and a hastily assembled Dutch side with ease and only lost to a crack French Army team – including the full international David Fraisse – by a narrow margin. The Muscovites travelled on to Toulouse and not only held their own against teams representing French Universities and France Under-20s, but beat a Tarn Selection handsomely in Albi. Three Magicians, including the powerful and prolific centre Nichaev, impressed their hosts so favourably that they were invited to stay on and play with Toulouse Olympique.

By the start of 1991, the Soviets were able to announce the shape of their first fully-fledged professional league championship, consisting of eight teams: three – Magicians, Spartak and Red Arrows – from Moscow; Alma Ata and Baikanor-Leninsk from Kazakhstan; Tiraspol, Kazan and, opting for their city's original name, St Petersburg Lions from Leningrad.

First on the agenda, though, was a pre-season competition that really did emphasise that Rugby League was venturing into a very different world, played as it was entirely on packed snow. But on snow, ice or dry land, Tiraspol and the Magicians showed again that they are the teams to beat. In the first pool in Moscow, the men from Moldavia accounted for Leningrad, Moscow Red Arrows and Noginsk. Magicians had a tougher time of it in their group in Kazan, only drawing with Spartak before finishing on top of their table on points difference. In the final against Tiraspol, they drew again, leaving the balance of power between the two clubs on an even keel.

Some of the scores in that competition (Tiraspol 52 Moscow Red Arrows 0, Tiraspol 70 Noginsk 0, Moscow Red Arrows 72 Noginsk 9, Moscow Magicians 52 Kazan 0, Moscow Magicians 98 Alma Ata 0, for example) point to some alarming disparities of performance, an impression that was borne out in the early weeks of the season proper, in which the 'big two' again swept all before them. That competition was only two rounds old, however, when the Soviet Union hosted its first visit from overseas.

The original plan had been for two English second-division clubs, Leigh and Ryedale-York, to tour in October 1990. Sensibly, it was eventually decided that a visit at the end of the British season, just as the first Soviet league was getting into its stride, would have more impact. By that time, Leigh's financial problems had ruled them out of the venture, and Fulham – despite gathering cash problems of their own – stepped into the gap. Their players, like those of their opponents, made the whole project possible by agreeing to play for nothing, calculating that the experience would be reward in itself.

They would, I sense, now feel vindicated in that belief, because the first

Rugby League tour of the Soviet Union was, in all sorts of ways, a memorable episode in their careers. The first meeting between the two sides, in Alma Ata, was arguably the highlight of the tour. Reliable crowd figures are about as difficult to obtain as fresh vegetables in the Soviet Union, and estimates of the attendance in Alma Ata vary between 6,500 and 15,000. Even at its worst, that was still a healthy turn-out, and the enthusiasm of the crowd prompted Fulham players to say that the atmosphere was more like Wembley than the sparsely inhabited stadium at Crystal Palace to which they have become accustomed. Both sides rose to the occasion by playing out an exciting 20–20 draw. That was followed by two mini-games, in which first Fulham and then Ryedale-York took on a team drawn from Alma Ata and clubs from even deeper into the Soviet east, rejoicing in the title of the All-Stars of Asia, the Londoners squeezing home 6–4 and Ryedale winning by a more comfortable 22–0.

Alma Ata, and Soviet Asia in general, might be well down the pecking order so far as playing standards are concerned, but many in the British party came away greatly impressed by the administration, public interest and potential in this unlikely part of the world. However, Leningrad was a different story altogether. The Soviet Union's second city does not appear to have taken the game to its heart in the same way. There was little advance publicity, and a crowd of only 1,000 or so was at the Lenin Stadium to see a rather dour game, won 18–12 by Fulham, largely on the strength of the goal-kicking and all-round ability of their Australian loose forward, Greg Pearce.

So to Moscow and the real test of how Rugby League was faring in the Soviet Union. The two touring coaches, Ross Strudwick and Gary Stephens, put their heads together to come up with a combined side, while Phil Larder – not unexpectedly – relied heavily on players from Moscow Magicians and Tiraspol. As those two clubs had suggested by their early performances that they were already of English second-division standard, it promised to be an evenly balanced contest.

It did not turn out that way. The Soviets got off to a terrible start by conceding 8 early and unnecessary points through mistakes by their full-back, Belaev. There were signs of resistance in the way the excellent Russian loose forward, Sokolov, made a couple of breaks and the way Kartsev linked with the substitute Sycophsky to allow Nichaev to power his way over. But the tourists – playing rugby well beyond the standard that might be expected from second-division players – took total control with three tries in fifteen minutes before half-time.

The Soviets did not help themselves with some naive defence and a tendency to lose the ball in the tackle, and it was greatly to their credit that they stamped out both those traits – at least temporarily – in the third quarter. They got the reward for that improvement when Pisconov – the winger timed in training as faster than Martin Offiah – latched on to Parshow's cross-kick for the second Soviet try. The respectability that brought to the scoreline was shortlived. Suitably provoked, the combined side lifted their game again and carved through for another three tries and a final scoreline of 42–10.

The Soviet Union launch an attack during their epoch-making match against a Great Britain select team in Moscow in May 1991. A combination of Fulham and Ryedale-York players, the British team won by 42–10.

Soviet Union: Belaev (Moscow Magicians); Pisconov (Tiraspol), Dyatlov (Moscow Magicians), Nichaev (Moscow Magicians), Olar (Tiraspol); Parshow (Moscow Magicians), Kartsev (Moscow Magicians); Zarnba (Tiraspol), Ossachie (Tiraspol), Strach (Tiraspol), Lysov (Moscow Magicians), Senin (Moscow Magicians), Sokolov (Moscow Magicians)

Substitutes: Sycophsky (Tiraspol) for Belaev after 13 minutes, Sharcoff (Moscow Red Arrows) for Lysov after 40 minutes, Tarran (Tiraspol) for Senin after 60 minutes, Gloticov (Moscow Spartak) for Zarnba after 66 minutes

Scorers: tries – Nichaev, Pisconov; goal – Parshow

Great Britain Select: Sullivan (Ryedale–York); Kettlestring (R–Y), Taylor (Fulham), Pitt (F), Smith (R–Y); Browning (F), Dobson (R–Y); Hayes (R–Y), Horton (R–Y), Rotheram (F), Lee (F), Pryce (R–Y), Pearce (F)

Substitutes: Dwyer (F) for Rotheram after 40 minutes, Pinkney (R–Y) for Pryce after 51 minutes, Workman (F) for Browning after 55 minutes, Render (R–Y) for Dobson after 68 minutes, Maxwell (R–Y) for Hayes after 72 minutes

Scorers: tries – Sullivan, Dobson, Horton, Kettlestring, Pinkney, Pearce, Dwyer; goals – Sullivan (3), Pearce (4)

Referee: F. Lindop (Great Britain)

Attendance: 3,200.

Half-time in Moscow and the players leave the field against a backdrop of an historic scoreboard and a disappointing crowd.

On the face of it, the Dynamo Stadium produced two disappointing figures: the 42 points which the first Soviet side conceded and the 3,200 who were there to watch.

The main problem on the playing front was that the forwards, with the shining exception of Sokolov, were too ponderous and too easy to break down with a quick change of direction. Larder, however, had a fair point when he argued that any Rugby League pack composed entirely of recent converts from Union would suffer from the same failings. The addition of two forwards, Sapiga and Georgiev, who were away in the United States playing American Football would make a considerable difference, he believes. In the backs, there was plenty of obvious potential. Gary Stephens moved quickly to offer terms to the fast and tenacious centre Dyatlov as well as to Sokolov, and Larder was happy to recommend Pisconov and Olar to Oldham. Others, including the inventive (but 29-year-old) Kartsev, made it clear that they too would like to play in Britain, and Larder believes that, subject to the Rugby Football League exempting them from the import quota, as many as twenty could benefit from a season in England.

Nobody in the small, select media contingent in Moscow (*Daily Telegraph*, *Independent*, *York Evening Press* and the BBC) took any pleasure in recording the meagre attendance. That 3,200 was a generous rather than a conservative estimate, and it included a fair proportion of spectators who, for one reason or another, did not pay to get in. To be positive, everybody who was there – many of them children – enjoyed the spectacle, despite their side's failure to be truly competitive.

At the moment, the task of playing France, in Corbeil on October 23, looks a formidable one for the Soviets. But Edvard Tatourian, the Soviet league's president and driving force, expects more defections from Rugby Union by then, and also believes that the players involved at the Dynamo Stadium will have learned a huge amount from the experience. The potential is there, but it will take patience and faith to bring it to fruition.

4

Looking Ahead 1991–92

A Preview of the Season and the 1991–92 Fixtures

TWENTY-ONE

A Preview of the Season

Paul Wilson

Early in 1991, Ellery Hanley, the captain of Great Britain, was involved in the year's cheekiest and most successful publicity stunt. This ought to have been good news for Rugby League, but wasn't, since the sport gaining all the publicity was American Football in the shape of the newly formed London Monarchs.

Hanley, to no one's great surprise, never actually played for the Wembley-based Monarchs, though the episode still caused considerable embarrassment at Rugby League headquarters. For one thing, American Football was in the position of direct rival to Rugby League, both in its attempt to become established in the capital and in the general struggle to gain a wider acceptance throughout the country. But more ironic still, and more hurtful to those who had been working to further Rugby League's cause, was that it should be Hanley touting the virtues of a new code via newspapers, television and radio. Hanley, who famously had nothing to say to the Rugby League press. Hanley, the Great Britain captain, who declined to appear on television in the autumn of 1990 when his own sport had a London event to promote.

His antics probably lost Hanley a few more friends within the game which has made him famous, though words like 'traitor' and 'mercenary' were a little strong for someone at least displaying consistency in his actions. Hanley has always been willing to communicate for reward, in Rugby Union's coy phrase, and presumably the Monarchs saw the possibilities of a mutually advantageous transaction.

Superficially, the lesson for Rugby League is that exposure costs. Attention might often be deserved, occasionally earned, but the most reliable way of obtaining it is to pay. A sharp publicity department is an advantage, too, though the Hanley business was only a small, if typically slick, part of the Monarchs' overall operation.

Nevertheless it was instructive, and the rather shabby incident will have served a useful purpose if it convinces everyone of the merit of the argument many have been advancing for years; namely, that London is crucial to the development and perceived status of any sport in this country. For there was a double edge to Hanley's publicity stunt. By attaching himself to a London outfit he greatly increased his own fame. Suddenly all the attention his exploits in Rugby League over the years have deserved but never quite received began to come his way as editors and chat-show hosts queued to fit him into their schedules. The player who had received only grudging praise for leading Great Britain to victory over Australia in the first Test at Wembley in 1990 was fêted three months later for posing in a crash helmet.

To be fair, the Rugby League had recognised the importance of the capital in staging the first Test at Wembley; indeed, no less than 22,000 'southerners' are known to have bought tickets for the game. The official attandance figure of over 54,000 was a record for a Rugby League Test in Britain but was put into perspective by the 61,000 (admittedly including a sizeable proportion of complimentaries) who watched the Monarchs' final match of the season at the same venue.

So obviously the time has come to stop toying with London. The decision to

Chris O'Sullivan's guile and experience played no small part in Warrington's Regal Trophy success in 1991, and he helped Welshman Kevin Ellis settle into Rugby League far quicker than expected.

stage the first Test at Wembley was a bold one made for the right reasons, but one international occasion every four years is hardly going to change anything. Not on its own, however well supported. Public disaffection in the north is likely to grow faster than appreciation in the south if the most eagerly awaited fixture on the international calendar continues to be used as an exhibition game, not least because it is such a wasteful way to fly the Rugby League flag. Anglo-Australian Test matches belong to the people whose culture they share and whose enthusiasm and understanding helped shape them into such distinctive sporting encounters. That culture does not yet include London, and there is no point wishing or pretending otherwise. At the time of the first Test against Australia amateur Rugby League in the capital was in a chaotic state with several promising teams having folded and the position of development officer vacant (it still is), and Fulham once again on the brink of crisis (they still are). Just two years ago the League committed itself to a programme of 'vigorous expansion' in London, fine words which seem to sit unhappily with the sad facts at professional and amateur level.

The game ought now to conclude that its long-standing 'hands-off' policy towards expansion has failed, not only in London but also in most other areas where teams have struggled against the odds to get professional rugby off the ground. If significant gains are to be made, the chances are they will come through a 'hands-on' approach as exemplified by the World League of American Football, the parent body behind the London Monarchs.

The WLAF started with some natural advantages, not least a budget of £30 million raised from American TV and the fashionable allure of all things transatlantic. In direct contrast to Rugby League, American Football in this country had its way paved by television and consequently did not have a hick status to live down. The Monarchs were always pitching to a receptive audience, whereas Rugby League, the game from the northern end of the same country, had always been a cold sell in the south.

Even so the WLAF took few chances and made few mistakes. If London was the only place for the British franchise to base itself, Wembley was the obvious choice of home. It was a home too. The Monarchs played six matches at Wembley in their short spring season which helped them build a rapport with their audience and establish a place for themselves in the city's sporting calendar. They averaged over 40,000 a game, which suggests that a large proportion of their crowds returned for more. Almost every player in every team, whether notionally belonging to London, New York, Barcelona or Frankfurt, was American, yet fans in each new country flocked to the games.

No one is suggesting that Rugby League could mount anything on such a scale – the WLAF was trying to take over the world after all – but in contemplating how best to make the giant leap from Thatto Heath to Hampstead Heath, the British game could do worse than note some general principles. European businessmen were offered franchises at a vastly cheaper price than their American counterparts, in recognition of the uncertainty of the investment in development areas. Only three European bids were accepted, a fourth was considered unlikely to reach minimum standards. All players and their considerable travelling expenses were paid from central funds, leaving franchise holders responsible only for accommodation, food, day-to-day transport and publicity. In return they received the entire gate proceeds from their home matches, the WLAF reimbursing itself through television fees.

As this is a Rugby League yearbook, I had better refrain from examining the activities of another sport too closely, but the point to be made is that not all governing bodies leave teams in new areas to stand on their own feet. Not that the WLAF got everything right. Poor TV ratings in America threaten to undermine the whole enterprise, which just goes to show that there's more to

Bradford Northern's Karl Fairbank drives the ball in against Leeds. Ruthlessly uncompromising, Fairbank remained part of Mal Reilly's Great Britain plans throughout 1990–91.

Paul Lyman on the run for Hull KR against Leeds. Rovers suffered an unhappy 1990–91, avoiding relegation by only 1 point and parting company with long-serving coach Roger Millward, their star winger Tony Sullivan, New Zealander Dave Watson and the Australian star Greg Austin.

development than making friends in different places.

In any case, this is possibly not the ideal time to discuss the funding and viability of clubs in new areas, since Rugby League at the moment has plenty of clubs in established areas looking equally fragile. However, the RFL has now split the league into three divisions for the coming season – something they have wanted to do for quite a while, they say. The third division is likely to continue what the contract payment system started and accentuate the divide between Rugby League's haves and have-nots. There will be casualties, unless some of the game's most notorious under-achievers respond to the challenge in a positive manner. The contract system has tended to catch out the mid-rated clubs, who felt they needed to attract quality players in order to compete at a higher level but really needed to budget more realistically for lack of success and loss of support, but three divisions will be a death sentence for any side unable or unwilling to mount a credible push for promotion from the third in the first few seasons. Opinion about the restructuring of the thirty-six clubs divides on whether this is viewed as a good or a bad thing. Some of the most famous names in Rugby League might not be around by the time of the centenary in 1995, but there seems little point in being famous for events contemporaneous with the Boer War. It is true that Halifax managed to lift themselves from the foot of the second division to champions of the first in under a decade, but there has to be some kind of time limit on sleeping giants, not to mention sleeping dwarves.

As long as clubs are served a reasonable notice of eviction, and are given every chance to climb back into the top flight, the overdue reorganisation cannot be questioned. A system of three divisions seems to fill these criteria, as well as being quite a kind way to cull some of the league's less dazzling lights. The difference, apart from the novelty of so many repeat fixtures in the second division, will not be as great as some seem to anticipate. Rugby League will still be seen to consist of two main divisions. The third division, existing as a sort of twilight zone between professional and amateur leagues, will probably not be seen much at all.

This may seem unduly harsh, but Rugby League is plainly in need of major rationalisation. Very few of its clubs can look their bank manager in the eye, and even the most successful sides seem constantly to be nagged by financial instability. One doesn't need an 'O' level in economics to see why, just a map. Instead of being distributed evenly around the population centres of the nation, as they would be in a perfect world or a business geographer's model, Rugby League teams are crammed into a narrow corridor across the neck of the country. Plus factors, which probably help to explain how such a haphazard scheme survived for so long, include excellent communications via the M62 and a population to draw on roughly equivalent in size to that of Australia, but in the grip of a recession market forces may at last be catching up with Rugby League's crowded market place.

Leigh's difficulties, for example, are frequently stated to be rooted in some unwise overseas purchases and some over-optimistic contract payments. An accountant looking for where the money went might concur with the above assessment, but may only have identified the symptoms of a malaise, not the cause. In a broader context, it is quite easy to see that most of Leigh's money ended up seven miles away at Central Park, Wigan. While the same borough might have supported two professional teams twenty or thirty years ago, before ancient loyalties were tested by television exposure and greater mobility, the present climate sends the weakest to the wall. It was probably no accident that Leigh's last major achievement, the Championship in 1982, came during Wigan's first season back from the second division, just as it cannot be entirely coincidental that the Hilton Park club's present plight came about when Wigan were to be seen on television almost every week and at Wembley almost every season. However, in early August Leigh's former player, Tony Cottrell,

Wally Lewis waves goodbye to the Queensland fans after announcing his retirement from State of Origin football in 1991.

was able to satisfy the Administrator and the RFL that he could revive the club and he is now in charge.

Whether or not Leigh manage to survive, the indications are that other clubs will suffer a similar fate. Hull Kingston Rovers could not afford to keep the players they wanted last season or to pay the wages of an overseas coach, and while it is only a few years since both Humberside clubs were prospering side by side in the same city, a gulf in standards and expectations is beginning to appear which could easily widen rather than close. There have already been calls for Cumbrian teams to pool their resources and form one viable unit. This goes against the grain for traditional supporters but, provided initial hostility can be overcome, would make economic sense. So would merging Salford and Swinton to form a Manchester side, or Warrington and Widnes to play as North Cheshire.

Surely what is important, as 1995 approaches, is to reach the centenary in good health with an appetite for the next 100 years, not to appear as a sprightly centurion who still looks in the mirror and sees an image of the way things looked fifty years ago. Rugby League can be rightly proud of its heritage, and has a duty to protect it, an obligation to make sure that the game is still being played in ten, fifty or 100 years time. It really doesn't matter by whom.

There will be those, there always are, who say that if the game has muddled along for the past ninety-six years it will probably continue to do so. But nowadays, with television setting the sporting agenda and usurping the role of schools, parents and local traditions in firing youthful enthusiasms, no sport can afford to muddle along. The London Monarchs should have convinced us all of that, though even more esoteric sports are getting organised. When something as alien and parochial as Australian Rules makes a serious attempt to gain a foothold in our schools, nothing can be taken for granted. When cricket in the Caribbean is undermined by youngsters who prefer satellite broadcasts of baseball from the American mainland, clearly nowhere is safe.

But Rugby League, everyone says, is enjoying a boom. If only it were true. If only one could really make the world take notice just by purchasing Jonathan Davies or beating Australia on a couple of (separate) occasions. Wigan might be going through a boom period, and to a lesser extent Widnes, Leeds and a few others, and Great Britain under Mal Reilly are clearly enjoying a resurgence. Playing standards throughout the professional game have probably never been higher and the slump of the 1970s is just a bad memory, but while this gives a base to build upon, what has so far been built?

Has the game got a home, like Rugby Union has at Twickenham? No. Any stadium capable of accommodating 40,000? No. Two years ago Rugby League could not boast a single stadium which came up to minimum standards for football's Vauxhall Opel League.

What about less tangible achievements? Has the rift with the amateurs been patched up? Not exactly. Has the vexatious Colts issue been resolved? No. Many within BARLA fear the professional clubs' plan to form a a new Colts league and though the District Development Associations have been granted another season, the future for youth rugby is far from clear.

Perhaps it is not surprising to hear voices in both professional and amateur Rugby League express concern about the impact the Rugby Union World Cup may make later in the year. The unpalatable truth might be that Rugby League only appears so robust because its competitors have taken so long to get their act together. To be ninety-six years old and still frightened of your parents suggests self-doubt, whatever the outward signals may convey.

But rather than end the chapter on so despondent a note, let us look forward to another season of high-octane entertainment, hopefully capped by a successful tour of Australasia in 1992. In the struggle for the Ashes Reilly's Lions will be handicapped by the loss of Andy Gregory and perhaps the perennial uncertainty surrounding Hanley, but will be in no doubt after the events of 1990 that a series win is attainable. A series win in Australia was, in fact, attainable in 1988; it was the doubt which proved the insurmountable problem. Returning with the Ashes will not make everything right with British Rugby League; any more than returning empty-handed would make everything wrong, but life is always that bit more bearable when the Aussies' faces are in the dirt. Isn't that why Test matches were invented?

The Rugby Football League Principal Dates 1991–92

1991	August 25	CIS Insurance Charity Shield: Hull v Wigan (at Gateshead)
	September 1	Stones Bitter League Championship begins
	September 15	County Cup Competitions (1st round)
	September 18	Rodstock War of the Roses (at Headingley)
	September 25	County Cup Competitions (2nd round)
	October 2	Foster's World Club Challenge: Wigan v Australian Grand Final Winner (at Old Trafford, Manchester)
	October 9	County Cup Competitions (semi-finals)
	October 19	Greenalls Lancashire Cup (final)
	October 20	John Smith's Yorkshire Cup (final)
	October 27	Wales v Papua New Guinea (at Vetch Field, Swansea)
	October 30	Great Britain Under-21s v Papua New Guinea (at Headingley)
	November 3	Humberside v Papua New Guinea (at the Boulevard, Hull)
	November 5	Cumbria v Papua New Guinea (at Workington)
	November 9	British Coal Test: Great Britain v Papua New Guinea (at Wigan)
	November 16/17	Regal Trophy (1st round)
	November 23/24	Regal Trophy (2nd round)
	November 30/ December 1	Regal Trophy (3rd round)
	December 7	Regal Trophy (semi-final 1)
	December 21	Regal Trophy (semi-final 2)
1992	January 11	Regal Trophy final
	January 25/26	Silk Cut Challenge Cup (1st round)
	February 8/9	Silk Cut Challenge Cup (2nd round)
	February 22/23	Silk Cut Challenge Cup (3rd round)
	March 14	Silk Cut Challenge Cup (semi-final 1)
	March 22	France v Wales (provisional)
	March 28	Silk Cut Challenge Cup (semi-final 2)
	April 21	Stones Bitter Divisional Premiership (1st round)
	April 26	Stones Bitter Premiership (1st round)
		Stones Bitter Divisional Premiership (2nd round)
	May 2	Silk Cut Challenge Cup final (at Wembley Stadium)
	May 10	Stones Bitter Premiership (semi-finals)
		Stones Bitter Divisional Premiership (semi-finals)
	May 17	Stones Bitter Premiership final (at Old Trafford)
		Stones Bitter Divisional Premiership final (at Old Trafford)

The dates of the Great Britain v France Tests will probably be February 16 (in France) and March 7 (at Headingley) with the Under-21 internationals taking place on the preceding days.

The Rugby Football League
Stones Bitter Championship 1991–1992

First Division Fixtures

1991 Sunday September 1	Bradford N.	v.	Hull KR
	Castleford	v.	Wigan
	Halifax	v.	Featherstone R.
	Hull	v.	St Helens
	Swinton	v.	Wakefield T.
	Warrington	v.	Salford
	Widnes	v.	Leeds
Sunday September 8	Featherstone R.	v.	Swinton
	Hull KR	v.	Halifax
	Leeds	v.	Hull
	St Helens	v.	Warrington
	Salford	v.	Castleford
	Wakefield T.	v.	Bradford N.
	Wigan	v.	Widnes
Sunday September 22	Bradford N.	v.	Salford
	Castleford	v.	Leeds
	Halifax	v.	Wakefield T.
	Hull	v.	Wigan
	Swinton	v.	St Helens
	Warrington	v.	Featherstone R.
	Widnes	v.	Hull KR
Sunday September 29	Featherstone R.	v.	Bradford N.
	Hull KR	v.	Warrington
	Leeds	v.	Swinton
	St Helens	v.	Castleford
	Salford	v.	Widnes
	Wakefield T.	v.	Hull
Sunday October 6	Bradford N.	v.	Leeds
	Castleford	v.	Widnes
	Halifax	v.	St Helens
	Hull	v.	Salford
	Swinton	v.	Hull KR
	Warrington	v.	Wakefield T.
	Wigan	v.	Featherstone R.
Sunday October 13	Featherstone R.	v.	Hull
	Hull KR	v.	Castleford
	Leeds	v.	Warrington
	St Helens	v.	Bradford N.
	Salford	v.	Halifax
	Wakefield T.	v.	Wigan
	Widnes	v.	Swinton
Sunday October 20	Halifax	v.	Hull KR
	Hull	v.	Bradford N.
	St Helens	v.	Salford
	Swinton	v.	Wigan
	Wakefield T.	v.	Leeds
	Warrington	v.	Castleford
	Widnes	v.	Featherstone R.
Sunday October 27	Castleford	v.	Featherstone R.
	Hull KR	v.	Wakefield T.
	Leeds	v.	St Helens
	Salford	v.	Hull
	Wigan	v.	Halifax
Sunday November 3	Bradford N.	v.	Castleford
	Featherstone R.	v.	Salford
	Halifax	v.	Widnes
	Swinton	v.	Warrington
	Wakefield T.	v.	St Helens
	Wigan	v.	Leeds
Sunday November 10	Castleford	v.	Halifax
	Hull	v.	Swinton
	Leeds	v.	Featherstone R.
	St Helens	v.	Hull KR
	Salford	v.	Wigan
	Warrington	v.	Bradford N.
	Widnes	v.	Wakefield T.
Sunday December 1	Bradford N.	v.	Widnes
	Featherstone R.	v.	St Helens
	Halifax	v.	Hull
	Hull KR	v.	Salford
	Swinton	v.	Leeds
	Wakefield T.	v.	Warrington
	Wigan	v.	Castleford
Sunday December 8	Castleford	v.	Hull KR
	Hull	v.	Featherstone R.
	Leeds	v.	Bradford N.
	St Helens	v.	Swinton
	Salford	v.	Wakefield T.
	Warrington	v.	Halifax
	Widnes	v.	Wigan
Sunday December 15	Bradford N.	v.	Warrington
	Featherstone R.	v.	Leeds
	Halifax	v.	Salford
	Hull KR	v.	St Helens
	Swinton	v.	Castleford
	Wakefield T.	v.	Widnes
	Wigan	v.	Hull

Boxing Day Thursday December 26	Bradford N.	v.	Halifax
	Castleford	v.	Hull
	Featherstone R.	v.	Wakefield T.
	Salford	v.	Swinton
	Widnes	v.	Warrington
	Wigan	v.	St Helens
Sunday December 29	Leeds	v.	Hull KR
1992 New Year's Day Wednesday January 1	Halifax	v.	Bradford N.
	Hull	v.	Hull KR
	Leeds	v.	Salford
	St Helens	v.	Widnes
	Wakefield T.	v.	Castleford
	Warrington	v.	Wigan
Sunday January 5	Bradford N.	v.	Hull
	Featherstone R.	v.	Halifax
	Hull KR	v.	Swinton
	Salford	v.	St Helens
	Warrington	v.	Leeds
	Widnes	v.	Castleford
	Wigan	v.	Wakefield T.
Sunday January 12	Bradford N.	v.	Wigan
	Castleford	v.	Salford
	Hull	v.	Warrington
	Leeds	v.	Widnes
	St Helens	v.	Featherstone R.
	Swinton	v.	Halifax
	Wakefield T.	v.	Hull KR
Sunday January 19	Castleford	v.	Bradford N.
	Halifax	v.	Wigan
	Hull KR	v.	Featherstone R.
	St Helens	v.	Wakefield T.
	Salford	v.	Leeds
	Warrington	v.	Swinton
	Widnes	v.	Hull
Sunday February 2	Bradford N.	v.	St Helens
	Featherstone R.	v.	Warrington
	Hull	v.	Halifax
	Leeds	v.	Castleford
	Swinton	v.	Widnes
	Wakefield T.	v.	Salford
	Wigan	v.	Hull KR
Sunday February 16	Halifax	v.	Swinton
	Hull KR	v.	Leeds
	Salford	v.	Featherstone R.
	Warrington	v.	Hull
Friday February 28	Salford	v.	Bradford N.
Sunday March 1	Castleford	v.	Warrington
	Featherstone R.	v.	Hull KR
	Hull	v.	Wakefield T.
	St Helens	v.	Leeds
	Widnes	v.	Halifax
	Wigan	v.	Swinton
Sunday March 8	Bradford N.	v.	Featherstone R.
	Castleford	v.	St Helens
	Wakefield T.	v.	Halifax
	Warrington	v.	Hull KR
Sunday March 15	Featherstone R.	v.	Castleford
	Halifax	v.	Warrington
	Hull KR	v.	Widnes
	Leeds	v.	Wigan
	Swinton	v.	Bradford N.
Sunday March 22	Hull	v.	Leeds
	St Helens	v.	Halifax
	Swinton	v.	Featherstone R.
	Widnes	v.	Bradford N.
	Wigan	v.	Salford
Sunday March 29	Castleford	v.	Swinton
	Featherstone R.	v.	Widnes
	Hull KR	v.	Wigan
	Leeds	v.	Wakefield T.
	St Helens	v.	Hull
	Salford	v.	Warrington
Sunday April 5	Bradford N.	v.	Wakefield T.
	Featherstone R.	v.	Wigan
	Swinton	v.	Hull
	Warrington	v.	St Helens
	Widnes	v.	Salford
Sunday April 12	Halifax	v.	Castleford
	Hull	v.	Widnes
	Salford	v.	Hull KR
	Wakefield T.	v.	Swinton
	Wigan	v.	Bradford N.
Good Friday April 17	Bradford N.	v.	Swinton
	Castleford	v.	Wakefield T.
	Hull KR	v.	Hull
	Leeds	v.	Halifax
	St Helens	v.	Wigan
	Warrington	v.	Widnes
Easter Monday* April 20	Halifax	v.	Leeds
	Hull	v.	Castleford
	Hull KR	v.	Bradford N.
	Swinton	v.	Salford
	Wakefield T.	v.	Featherstone R.
	Widnes	v.	St Helens
	Wigan	v.	Warrington

* Provided Easter Monday is declared a league match day by the RFL.

Second Division Fixtures

1991 Sunday September 1	Leigh	v.	Ryedale-York
	Rochdale H.	v.	Carlisle
	Sheffield E.	v.	Oldham
	Workington T.	v.	Fulham
Sunday September 8	Carlisle	v.	Sheffield E.
	Oldham	v.	Leigh
	Rochdale H.	v.	Fulham
	Ryedale-York	v.	Workington T.
Sunday September 22	Fulham	v.	Sheffield E.
	Leigh	v.	Carlisle
	Rochdale H.	v.	Ryedale-York
	Workington T.	v.	Oldham
Sunday September 29	Carlisle	v.	Workington T.
	Fulham	v.	Leigh
	Oldham	v.	Rochdale H.
	Ryedale-York	v.	Sheffield E.
Sunday October 6	Fulham	v.	Oldham
	Rochdale H.	v.	Leigh
	Ryedale-York	v.	Carlisle
	Sheffield E.	v.	Workington T.
Sunday October 13	Carlisle	v.	Fulham
	Leigh	v.	Sheffield E.
	Oldham	v.	Ryedale-York
	Workington T.	v.	Rochdale H.
Sunday October 20	Carlisle	v.	Oldham
	Fulham	v.	Ryedale-York
	Leigh	v.	Workington T.
	Sheffield E.	v.	Rochdale H.
Sunday October 27	Oldham	v.	Sheffield E.
	Ryedale-York	v.	Leigh
	Workington T.	v.	Fulham
Sunday November 3	Fulham	v.	Rochdale H.
	Leigh	v.	Oldham
	Sheffield E.	v.	Carlisle
	Workington T.	v.	Ryedale-York
Sunday November 10	Carlisle	v.	Leigh
	Fulham	v.	Sheffield E.
	Oldham	v.	Workington T.
	Ryedale-York	v.	Rochdale H.
Sunday December 1	Fulham	v.	Leigh
	Rochdale H.	v.	Oldham
	Workington T.	v.	Carlisle
Sunday December 8	Carlisle	v.	Ryedale-York
	Leigh	v.	Rochdale H.
	Oldham	v.	Fulham
	Workington T.	v.	Sheffield E.
Sunday December 15	Fulham	v.	Carlisle
	Rochdale H.	v.	Workington T.
	Ryedale-York	v.	Oldham
	Sheffield E.	v.	Leigh
Boxing Day Thursday December 26	Carlisle	v.	Workington T.
	Leigh	v.	Fulham
	Oldham	v.	Rochdale H.
	Ryedale-York	v.	Sheffield E.
Sunday December 29	Sheffield E.	v.	Ryedale-York
1992 New Year's Day Wednesday January 1	Leigh	v.	Oldham
Sunday January 5	Fulham	v.	Ryedale-York
	Oldham	v.	Carlisle
	Rochdale H.	v.	Sheffield E.
	Workington T.	v.	Leigh
Sunday January 12	Carlisle	v.	Rochdale H.
	Fulham	v.	Workington T.
	Leigh	v.	Ryedale-York
	Oldham	v.	Sheffield E.
Sunday January 19	Carlisle	v.	Sheffield E.
	Fulham	v.	Rochdale H.
	Ryedale-York	v.	Workington T.
Sunday February 2	Leigh	v.	Carlisle
	Rochdale H.	v.	Ryedale-York
	Sheffield E.	v.	Fulham
	Workington T.	v.	Oldham
Sunday February 16	Fulham	v.	Oldham
	Rochdale H.	v.	Leigh
	Ryedale-York	v.	Carlisle
	Sheffield E.	v.	Workington T.
Sunday February 23	Carlisle	v.	Fulham
	Leigh	v.	Sheffield E.
	Oldham	v.	Ryedale-York
	Workington T.	v.	Rochdale H.
Sunday March 1	Fulham	v.	Workington T.
	Rochdale H.	v.	Carlisle
	Ryedale-York	v.	Leigh
	Sheffield E.	v.	Oldham
Sunday March 8	Leigh	v.	Workington T.
	Oldham	v.	Carlisle
	Ryedale-York	v.	Fulham
	Sheffield E.	v.	Rochdale H.
Sunday March 15	Carlisle	v.	Leigh
	Oldham	v.	Fulham
	Ryedale-York	v.	Rochdale H.
	Workington T.	v.	Sheffield E.

Sunday March 22	Fulham	v.	Carlisle
	Rochdale H.	v.	Workington T.
	Sheffield E.	v.	Leigh
Sunday March 29	Carlisle	v.	Oldham
	Leigh	v.	Fulham
	Rochdale H.	v.	Sheffield E.
	Workington T.	v.	Ryedale-York
Sunday April 5	Leigh	v.	Rochdale H.
	Oldham	v.	Workington T.
	Ryedale-York	v.	Fulham
	Sheffield E.	v.	Carlisle
Sunday April 12	Carlisle	v.	Rochdale H.
	Ryedale-York	v.	Oldham
	Sheffield E.	v.	Fulham
	Workington T.	v.	Leigh
Good Friday April 17	Carlisle	v.	Ryedale-York
	Rochdale H.	v.	Oldham
Sunday April 19	Sheffield E.	v.	Ryedale-York
Easter Monday* April 20	Oldham	v.	Leigh
	Rochdale H.	v.	Fulham
	Workington T.	v.	Carlisle

Third Division Fixtures

1991 Sunday September 1	Batley	v.	Whitehaven
	Bramley	v.	Keighley C.
	Chorley	v.	Dewsbury
	Doncaster	v.	Nottingham C.
	Highfield	v.	Trafford B.
	Hunslet	v.	Barrow
	Scarborough P.	v.	Huddersfield
Sunday September 8	Barrow	v.	Doncaster
	Dewsbury	v.	Hunslet
	Huddersfield	v.	Batley
	Keighley C.	v.	Chorley
	Nottingham C.	v.	Scarborough P.
	Trafford B.	v.	Bramley
	Whitehaven	v.	Highfield
Sunday September 22	Batley	v.	Nottingham C.
	Bramley	v.	Huddersfield
	Chorley	v.	Barrow
	Doncaster	v.	Dewsbury
	Highfield	v.	Keighley C.
	Hunslet	v.	Trafford B.
	Scarborough P.	v.	Whitehaven
Sunday September 29	Barrow	v.	Highfield
	Dewsbury	v.	Bramley
	Huddersfield	v.	Doncaster
	Keighley C.	v.	Batley
	Nottingham C.	v.	Hunslet
	Trafford B.	v.	Scarborough P.
	Whitehaven	v.	Chorley
Sunday October 6	Batley	v.	Barrow
	Bramley	v.	Nottingham C.
	Doncaster	v.	Trafford B.
	Highfield	v.	Dewsbury
	Hunslet	v.	Keighley C.
	Scarborough P.	v.	Chorley
	Whitehaven	v.	Huddersfield
Sunday October 13	Barrow	v.	Bramley
	Chorley	v.	Batley
	Dewsbury	v.	Scarborough P.
	Huddersfield	v.	Highfield
	Keighley C.	v.	Doncaster
	Nottingham C.	v.	Whitehaven
	Trafford B.	v.	Hunslet
Sunday October 20	Batley	v.	Huddersfield
	Bramley	v.	Chorley
	Hunslet	v.	Highfield
	Keighley C.	v.	Barrow
	Scarborough P.	v.	Nottingham C.
	Trafford B.	v.	Dewsbury
	Whitehaven	v.	Doncaster
Sunday October 27	Barrow	v.	Scarborough P.
	Chorley	v.	Hunslet
	Dewsbury	v.	Whitehaven
	Doncaster	v.	Bramley
	Highfield	v.	Batley
	Huddersfield	v.	Trafford B.
	Nottingham C.	v.	Keighley C.
Sunday November 3	Batley	v.	Chorley
	Bramley	v.	Dewsbury
	Doncaster	v.	Huddersfield
	Highfield	v.	Nottingham C.
	Hunslet	v.	Whitehaven
	Scarborough P.	v.	Keighley C.
	Trafford B.	v.	Barrow
Sunday November 10	Barrow	v.	Hunslet
	Chorley	v.	Scarborough P.
	Dewsbury	v.	Doncaster
	Huddersfield	v.	Bramley
	Keighley C.	v.	Highfield
	Nottingham C.	v.	Batley
	Whitehaven	v.	Trafford B.
Sunday December 1	Batley	v.	Keighley C.
	Bramley	v.	Whitehaven
	Doncaster	v.	Chorley
	Hunslet	v.	Nottingham C.
	Highfield	v.	Barrow
	Scarborough	v.	Dewsbury
	Trafford B.	v.	Huddersfield
Sunday December 8	Barrow	v.	Trafford B.
	Batley	v.	Doncaster
	Chorley	v.	Bramley
	Huddersfield	v.	Dewsbury
	Hunslet	v.	Scarborough
	Nottingham C.	v.	Highfield
	Whitehaven	v.	Keighley C.

* Provided Easter Monday is declared a league match day by the RFL.

The 1990–91 Season

Sunday December 15	Bramley	v.	Barrow
	Dewsbury	v.	Chorley
	Doncaster	v.	Whitehaven
	Keighley C.	v.	Hunslet
	Highfield	v.	Huddersfield
	Scarborough P.	v.	Batley
	Trafford B.	v.	Nottingham C.
Sunday December 22	Scarborough P.	v.	Doncaster
Boxing Day Thursday December 26	Barrow	v.	Whitehaven
	Batley	v.	Dewsbury
	Chorley	v.	Trafford B.
	Hunslet	v.	Bramley
Sunday December 29	Huddersfield	v.	Scarborough P.
	Nottingham C.	v.	Doncaster
1992 New Year's Day Wednesday January 1	Bramley	v.	Hunslet
	Dewsbury	v.	Batley
	Trafford B.	v.	Chorley
Sunday January 5	Chorley	v.	Huddersfield
	Bramley	v.	Trafford B.
	Dewsbury	v.	Barrow
	Doncaster	v.	Keighley C.
	Highfield	v.	Scarborough P.
	Whitehaven	v.	Nottingham C.
Sunday January 12	Barrow	v.	Chorley
	Batley	v.	Highfield
	Huddersfield	v.	Whitehaven
	Keighley C.	v.	Bramley
	Nottingham C.	v.	Dewsbury
	Scarborough P.	v.	Hunslet
	Trafford B.	v.	Doncaster
Sunday January 19	Barrow	v.	Nottingham C.
	Bramley	v.	Scarborough P.
	Chorley	v.	Keighley C.
	Dewsbury	v.	Trafford B.
	Doncaster	v.	Highfield
	Hunslet	v.	Huddersfield
	Whitehaven	v.	Batley
Sunday February 2	Dewsbury	v.	Keighley C.
	Doncaster	v.	Batley
	Highfield	v.	Whitehaven
	Huddersfield	v.	Chorley
	Nottingham C.	v.	Bramley
	Scarborough P.	v.	Barrow
Sunday February 16	Barrow	v.	Huddersfield
	Batley	v.	Bramley
	Chorley	v.	Nottingham C.
	Hunslet	v.	Doncaster
	Keighley C.	v.	Scarborough P.
	Trafford B.	v.	Highfield
	Whitehaven	v.	Dewsbury

Sunday February 23	Highfield	v.	Chorley
	Keighley C.	v.	Nottingham C.
	Whitehaven	v.	Hunslet
Sunday March 1	Bramley	v.	Doncaster
	Chorley	v.	Whitehaven
	Dewsbury	v.	Highfield
	Huddersfield	v.	Keighley C.
	Hunslet	v.	Batley
	Nottingham C.	v.	Barrow
	Scarborough P.	v.	Trafford B.
Sunday March 8	Barrow	v.	Dewsbury
	Batley	v.	Scarborough P.
	Highfield	v.	Bramley
	Huddersfield	v.	Nottingham C.
	Trafford B.	v.	Whitehaven
Sunday March 15	Doncaster	v.	Barrow
	Highfield	v.	Hunslet
	Keighley C	v.	Trafford B.
	Nottingham C.	v.	Chorley
	Scarborough P.	v.	Bramley
Sunday March 22	Barrow	v.	Batley
	Bramley	v.	Highfield
	Chorley	v.	Doncaster
	Dewsbury	v.	Nottingham C.
	Trafford B.	v.	Keighley C.
	Whitehaven	v.	Scarborough P.
Sunday March 29	Batley	v.	Hunslet
	Chorley	v.	Highfield
	Doncaster	v.	Scarborough P.
	Keighley C.	v.	Dewsbury
	Nottingham C.	v.	Huddersfield
	Whitehaven	v.	Bramley
Sunday April 5	Bramley	v.	Batley
	Highfield	v.	Doncaster
	Huddersfield	v.	Barrow
	Hunslet	v.	Chorley
	Keighley C.	v.	Whitehaven
Sunday April 12	Barrow	v.	Keighley C.
	Dewsbury	v.	Huddersfield
	Doncaster	v.	Hunslet
	Nottingham C.	v.	Trafford B.
	Scarborough P.	v.	Highfield
Good Friday April 17	Huddersfield	v.	Hunslet
	Trafford B.	v.	Batley
	Whitehaven	v.	Barrow
Easter Monday* April 20	Batley	v.	Trafford B.
	Hunslet	v.	Dewsbury
	Keighley C.	v.	Huddersfield

* Provided Easter Monday is declared a league match day by the RFL.